The Politics of
American Discontent

The Politics of American Discontent

How a New Party Can Make Democracy Work Again

Gordon S. Black
Benjamin D. Black

John Wiley & Sons, Inc.
New York • Chichester • Brisbane • Toronto • Singapore

This text is printed on acid-free paper.

Library of Congress Cataloging-in-Publication Data

Black, Gordon S.
    The politics of American discontent : how a new party can make democracy work again / Gordon S. Black, Benjamin D. Black.
        p.   cm.
    Includes bibliographical references and index.
    ISBN 0-471-59853-4 (cloth)
    1. Third parties (United States politics) 2. Democracy—United
States. 3. Perot, Ross, 1930–   . 4. United States—Politics and
government—1989–   5. Public opinion—United States. I. Black,
Benjamin. II. Title.
JK2261.B616   1994
320.473—dc20   93-48659

Printed in the United States of America

10 9 8 7 6 5 4 3 2 1

Acknowledgments

This book is the product of contributions from a number of people, without whose support it would not exist. The original study, which provides much of the data on American discontent and was an impetus for the book, was sponsored by B. Thomas Golisano, the CEO and founder of Paychex, Inc., one of the leading entrepreneurial firms in the United States. In April of 1992, we believed that the national media and most of the opinion polling was missing the size, depth, and significance of the revolt that was occurring in national politics. We posed the possibility of conducting a major national study to Golisano on a Friday; two days later he agreed to sponsor the study. The results, released in early June 1992, became known under the same title as this book. Golisano is one of those entrepreneurs who constantly give back to the community. He shares the conviction of many of America's leading entrepreneurs that this country is in big trouble, but he is one that will try to do something about it.

When we released the study in June, we were joined by one of America's leading political scientists, Theodore (Ted) J. Lowi, the John Senior Professor of Government at Cornell University, and the past president of the American Political Science Association. Lowi is, and has long been, the leading academic advocate both of the creation of a new political party and the breakup of the hegemony of the two national parties. His encouragement and support led to the contract for this book with John Wiley & Sons, and his reading of the first draft of a major portion of the book dramatically aided us in more accurately refocusing the book on our primary target.

The book also benefited substantially from support of the Gordon S. Black Corporation and the members of its Operating Committee, particularly David Clemm, president and COO. The firm supported followup studies between June 1992 and June 1993. In addition, it supported hiring Benjamin Black in November 1992 as co-author of the book, and it patiently watched while the two amateur authors took twice as long to complete the book as originally envisioned. This book would not exist without the corporation's support, which amounted to many thousands of dollars and lots of encouragement.

We are also grateful to Warren Mitofsky and Murray Edelman at Voter Research and Surveys (VRS), both for allowing us access to data and for hiring Benjamin Black to work on the exit polls of the 1992 election. They, along with Humphrey Taylor, president of Lou Harris & Associates, contributed both data and insights to the book, and we appreciate the contributions. In addition, Everett Ladd, the director of the Roper Center, encouraged publication of some of our data in the *Public Perspective*, which is the journal produced by the Roper Center.

Another very unexpected source of support arose in March 1993. We were called by Clay Mulford, one of Ross Perot's principal advisors, and asked to conduct a survey for Perot and United We Stand, America. This led to three national surveys, each following one of his national television presentations. With Mr. Perot's permission, we have used some of the released and unreleased results in this book. During the period the studies were conducted, we worked extensively with Perot, Mulford, and Sharon Holman, United We Stand, America's media relations manager. They were exceptionally enjoyable people to work with, and we came to appreciate many aspects of what they are attempting to accomplish with United We Stand, America. Some of these insights are contained in the book.

Ross Perot is a public figure who excites strong emotions, both positive and negative. Whatever he chooses to do eventually, we are mindful of the fact that he is the agent that made the mobilization of the discontent possible, and he has the responsibility for directing where much of this discontent will go in the future. That is a tremendous responsibility, and for all of our sakes we hope that he makes the best possible decisions.

In addition, two other organizers of discontent need to be included in our acknowledgments. The first is Jack Gargan, the retired investment advisor in Florida who took more than $45,000 of his own retirement funds and placed six newspaper ads advocating that we Throw the Hypocritical Rascals Out (T.H.R.O.). The second is Lionel Kunst, who organized the Coalition to End the Permanent Congress. Both men have put immense effort, their own money, and their tranquility on the line to alert the American people to the theft of their democracy by the incumbents. They are every bit the patriots that Thomas Paine or Samuel Adams were. If we could find a thousand of each of them, we could easily remove America's intransigent and irresponsible institutional leaders from their perches of arrogant power. At the time of this publication, Jack Gargan is running for governor of Florida as a member of the Independence Party.

Closer to home, we need to acknowledge the huge role played by our editor, Emily Loose, in the writing of this book. We are amateur writers. She is not. Through careful and thoughtful editing, she reduced the size of the original manuscript by a third and reorganized much of the presentation. In the end, if the reader thinks the book reads easily, that is her contribution. We could not have completed the book without her. She was aided by Associate Managing Editor Nana Prior. Our thanks also to Laura Van Toll at Impressions, who did the typesetting, and to Mary Ray Worley, also at Impressions, who provided superb assistance with the detailed final editing of the book. In addition, Gordon Black's administrative assistant, Bobbi Stackman, read every word of the manuscript, proofed much of it a second time, and made many corrections. She was encouraging all the way and could not have been more helpful.

As most authors realize, family members and friends always play a role in books and that is the case here. Gordon Black, the father of the team, wishes to thank his wife Lonny, who listened endlessly to the arguments and contributed substantially with her own numerous insights from the political battlefields; and his other children and stepchildren, Aaron, Lindsay, Nathaniel, and Brooke. Benjamin Black, the son, wishes to thank his mother Judy Brandzel, Emil Gottwald, Aaron Black, Anne Kilpatrick, and Kyle Karnes, who listened patiently to his complaints and provided many needed diversions.

Father and son books are unusual, we understand. This book was a collaboration in every sense of the word, and one that we will both remember with pleasure. Each of us drafted some of the chapters, to be redrafted by the other. Both of us gathered data for the various chapters. The book benefited from the original polling the firm contributed, the various data that were available through VRS, and the Roper Center Poll Database. We will both take equal credit for its virtues and flaws. We differed consistently on only one point throughout the writing. Gordon Black is optimistic that Ross Perot will eventually direct United We Stand, America toward the construction of a full-scale national political party like the Gaullists in France who supported Charles DeGaulle in the rebuilding of the French political system. Benjamin Black has a decidedly more pessimistic view of the Perot movement, seeing little evidence that Perot will convert UWSA into a movement that attracts the breadth of active leadership necessary to sustain a broad-based political movement. We will both find out later who is right. In the meantime, we have both learned a lot from each other, and we hope the reader finds the argument valuable.

Contents

The Seductive Illusion
of Change

Deep down in our hearts we know that we have bankrupted
America and that we have given our children a legacy of bankruptcy.[1]

—Senator John Danforth (R-Mo.)

The election of 1992 was allegedly about change. Bill Clinton talked
about change at every stop along the campaign trail. Ross Perot led the
most successful independent candidacy since Teddy Roosevelt, and
large-scale retirements from the House of Representatives promised
that, at long last, even Congress would get a shot of fresh thinking and
insight. The voters clearly voiced their discontent through the polls
and, suddenly, in the spring of 1992, many poured into the political
arena to create the Perot candidacy. For the first time in decades,
American voters seemed ready to exact revenge for years of increasing
frustration with their leadership.

On the surface, the results of the 1992 campaign appeared sufficiently different to warrant expectations that real change would come.
Debate had at last focused on the major issues facing the country: the
budget deficit, the economy, health care, and trade. An incumbent
president was sent to early retirement. One hundred twenty-four members of the massively unpopular 102nd Congress (14 in the Senate and
110 in the House) would not be back for the 103rd, and term limit initiatives passed with landslide victories in fourteen states. Clinton's
"New Covenant" was proposed to solve the deficit problem without a
tax increase on the middle class, and "managed competition" was
promised as a way to provide universal health care. Finally, Washington would be free from gridlock caused by divided government.
Unfortunately, the reality of modern politics quickly intervened and the

1

voters were faced with the truth in the tired, old cliché, "The more things change, the more they stay the same."

The old ways of Washington quietly reappeared even before Clinton took the oath of office. The vast majority of the new members of Congress had, after all, hitched a ride to Washington the old-fashioned way—on the wings of special interest money. Of the 110 incoming freshmen congressmen, 99 accepted a total of $15 million from Political Action Committees (PACs) for their campaigns. Gene Green (D-Tex.) raised the most from PACs, $409,700, while 55 other first-term congressmen raised over $100,000 each. To make matters worse, the PACs, after they knew who won, quickly funneled an additional $1.2 million in contributions to the freshmen. Many of the faces had changed, but the federal money game had not.[2]

In fact the little known truth is that the 1992 general election returned 93 percent of House incumbents who decided to run despite a check-bouncing scandal, the recession, and a 16 percent approval rating for Congress in the general public.[3] Why? Because the election was in many ways the same old story: the supposedly beleaguered incumbents overwhelmed their opponents with a tidal wave of campaign money. To be specific, the median Democratic incumbent spent $517,594, while the corresponding Republican challenger spent a mere $83,201. Likewise, the median Republican incumbent spent $485,778, while the Democratic challenger spent $68,324.[4] And in this "government of the money, by the money," PAC contributions accounted for 47.4 percent of all funding given to House incumbents. As in the past, the political and economic state of the country and even the general disgust of the voters had very little impact on the congressional races in which incumbents ran. Of course, many incumbents chose not to run, which resulted in the promise of the large new freshman class.

By April 1993, however, the once-vaunted freshmen, those 124 new members who were supposed to shake things up, started to sound either like disillusioned idealists or hardened career politicians. They surely could not have missed the hint when the congressional leadership denied Eric Fingerhut (D-Ohio) a seat on the Public Works and Transportation Committee after he had the audacity to deliver a demand on behalf of the freshmen for 90 days to formulate a far-reaching reform package.[5] Some freshmen seemed never to have intended to rock the boat. One representative, John McHugh (D-N.Y.), went so far to maintain the status quo that he hired the congressman he had defeated to work on his staff for $75,000-a-year.[6] Others started to sound remarkably like the pork-obsessed congressmen they had replaced. Representative Corrine Brown (D-Fla.) explained her choice for committee assignments bluntly: "I come from 14 counties that have a lot of needs. I have four airports, a seaport, buses, roads . . . . This seems to be the most important priority. . . ."[7] So much for the broad national interest. Even Representative Ernest Istook (R-Okla.), who was elected on an anti–government waste platform by using the campaign slogan "A pig is a pig no matter whose pigpen it's in," took a seat on the Appropriations Committee and later admitted that he hadn't "killed any pigs yet."[8] When the freshman reform package was released, it was dramatically scaled back and was largely scoffed at by the leadership. One thing this reform package did do was offer a depressingly accurate commentary on the state of congressional politics. The freshmen lamented, "In election campaigns and in the halls of Congress, special interest money consistently undermines representative government. Well-financed special interests use their considerable clout to distort the message or drown out the voices of the people."[9]

The underlying reality about the new Congress is that Tom Foley (D-Wash.), who was first elected to Congress in 1964, is still the Speaker of the House; Senator Robert Byrd (D-W.Va.), first elected to Congress in 1953, is still Chairman of the Senate Appropriations Committee; and Senator Bob Dole (R-Kans.), first elected in 1960, is still the Senate Minority leader. The entire Democratic leadership in the House was returned. Clinton, behaving similarly, started naming key Washington insiders to the major posts—Senator Lloyd Bentsen to the Department of the Treasury, Congressman Les Aspin to Defense, one-time lobbyist and Democratic National Committee Chairman Ron Brown to head Commerce, and a host of lobbyists and political consultants to lesser posts. It was the same old story that has been played out every four years for decades.

What is the result? Take the case of the budget bill. During the campaign, Bill Clinton held out a vision of the budget process that portrayed unified Democrats dancing together like a well-choreographed chorus toward a balanced budget. Instead, it took every ounce of political capital the president could muster to pass his deficit reduction plan, and then by only a single vote in the House and by the tiebreaking vote of Vice President Albert Gore in the Senate. So much for the end of government gridlock. On this crucial issue Congress failed to provide even a semblance of the change so eagerly anticipated.

In order to understand why the president couldn't muster more support, we must understand the role of the special interests. As the budget spectacle neared its showdown, the process was shaped by the same major special interests that had never stopped playing business-as-usual politics. The *Wall Street Journal* documented a few obvious examples: The oil industry, upset over the proposed energy tax, had given $4.7 million in unregulated "soft-money" donations to both the

Republican and Democratic parties in the last election cycle and donated $7.1 million directly to candidates. Predictably, the original broad-based BTU tax did not survive. PACs representing health professionals, foreseeing a battle over health care reform, primed their own pump with $17.6 million in contributions. The air transport industry, interested in gasoline tax exemptions, funneled another $9.5 million to candidates.[10] Overall, PACs representing thousands of special interest groups contributed exactly $180,468,505 to congressional candidates in 1992—a 21 percent increase over 1990.

The power of special interests was particularly vivid in the manner in which the most often-cited example of wasteful, archaic programs—the federal farm subsidies—escaped serious damage during the budget debate. In a little-noticed move, the House Agriculture Committee inserted a three-year extension of the commodity price support programs into the House-passed reconciliation bill, meaning that these programs, which pay farmers *not* to grow crops, are protected from the budget ax until 1998.

The disparity between the rhetoric and promise of the 1992 presidential campaign and the early actions of the Clinton administration was even more striking than usual. Yet even a cursory glance at recent American history reveals an all-too-consistent pattern in this regard—the huge dissonance between what is promised by a new President and what is delivered. In 1964, for example, Americans elected Lyndon Johnson because he promised peace in Vietnam. Instead, within months, he manufactured an incident in the Gulf of Tonkin and began bombing the North Vietnamese. Richard Nixon was elected in 1968 because he promised a plan for ending the war, combined with a new sense of honesty and candor. Instead, we got four more years of war, and Watergate. Jimmy Carter promised to reduce the "misery index" (inflation plus unemployment) from 12 percent. Instead, the misery index soared to nearly 30 percent. Ronald Reagan promised smaller government, balanced budgets, and fiscal integrity. Instead, the government grew dramatically, and Reagan helped produce the worst deficits in history, doing nothing to contain a budgetary process that is out of control. George Bush won in part because he asked us to read his lips when he promised "no new taxes." Instead, we received the enormous tax increase of 1990 combined with a budget that in the end failed to include the spending cuts promised by Congress. Is it any wonder that 71 percent of the public agrees that "there is practically no connection between what a politician says and what he will do once he is elected," according to a CBS News/*New York Times* Poll taken in late April 1992? The sad truth is that we have come to expect lies, distortion, and deception as everyday occurrences in politics.

America periodically invests its hope for the future in a new presidency.[11] Each time for nearly three decades the result has been profoundly disappointing because the promises of the election are subverted by a political process that warps policy into something decidedly different from what the majority of Americans want. Every four years, the national media focuses nearly all of our attention on the presidential contest, largely ignoring Congress. Each time, *the Congress remains largely unchanged* and the process of politics as usual goes on unabated.

America—the national media, the pundits, the voters—is in love with the idea of the omnipotent presidency, and we are chasing a seductive but false prophet. The manipulated mirages of the modern campaign, promulgated by public relations advisors, advertising executives, and pollsters, turn a handful of relatively impressive governors and senators into glorified presidential contenders—magicians who promise with impunity to fix all the nation's ills. And even as our expectations are so unrealistically inflated by the presidential campaign, after the election we gradually become aware that things are only continuing to get worse.

A better avenue for change, the one most often cited by political scientists, is to change members of Congress. One academic, Morris Fiorina, states why he believes this is true:

> Academic studies suggest that incumbent congressmen maintain a marked stability in their positions over time. If you wish to know how a congressman is voting in 1970, the chances are very good that his 1960 voting record will tell you. *As a consequence, the only reliable way to achieve policy change is to change congressmen.*[12]

A healthy democracy requires at least the fighting chance that changes in public sentiment will be reflected in the composition and control of Congress. Unless power in Congress shifts periodically with the changing views of Americans, policy will not change. However, turnover, by itself, is not enough. Indeed, as we have suggested, early indications are that even with such high turnover as in 1992, Congress will change the views and behavior of its freshmen, and not the other way around.

Unless something dramatic takes place, we must accept that the House of Representatives will continue to run its business very much as usual. For many reasons—incumbency advantage, redistricting, and money—the electoral system at the congressional level is profoundly unresponsive to changing public sentiment. We will expand on this later, but the key point is that as long as there is little competition against candidates who are heavily funded by special interests, we cannot expect legislators to change their behavior by fiat and focus on the broader concerns of the country.

Hope, Renewal, or Despair

The failure of the 1992 election to produce significant movement in a new direction highlights several important things about our political system. As we have said, *changing presidents is not the answer to the problems we face.* These problems are more deeply rooted. The failure of the American political system is a problem more than three decades in the making. Public attention focuses so much on the immediate that we often ignore historical processes. The 1992 election comes at the end of a thirty year period of similar institutional failures. Bill Clinton may disappoint us, but he is far less responsible for the current conditions of American politics than a host of problems in the political system that have progressively worsened over this thirty year period. Future elections will prove just as disappointing as 1992 if we continue to focus on the present with no understanding of these deeper, structural problems emanating from the past.

We will argue that the key to understanding the failures in the system is the crucial role of the absence of competition in the election of members of Congress and the individual state legislatures. Americans can get as angry as they like, but that anger is completely irrelevant politically in the absence of genuine electoral choice. Just as we are enamoured with the vision of the omnipotent presidency, we are overly impressed with the notion that all we have to do to shape up Congress is throw the bums out. Doing so might have some validity if it were possible, but Chapter 2 presents persuasive evidence that it is virtually impossible to replace large numbers of legislators through the electoral process either at the state or national level (unless large numbers of incumbents decide not to run). No single element has more impact on the condition of our society and its policies than the systematic destruction of political and electoral choice by the entrenched incumbents of both parties. *Electoral competition is the linchpin of all democratic theory and practice, and the virtual elimination of electoral competition by the incumbents is the single most important underlying cause of most of what troubles Americans today about politics.*

Our feelings about our country and about our role as citizens are largely products of our opportunity to have some influence over our destiny as a people. If our right to choose is destroyed, our faith in our power as citizens will also be destroyed, along with our faith in the democratic process itself. Carry the frustration of our expectations of our democracy far enough, and we will begin to lose our affection for the country as a whole, not to mention for our leadership and for our fellow citizens. In this book, we will show just how far down that road we have gone.

The Pyramid of Gain

Right now, voters in the United States are deprived of electoral choice in approximately 90 percent of the seats in the House of Representatives and the state legislatures.[13] In most races a challenger's name is listed on the ballot, but most of these challengers are token candidates who have no chance of winning because they lack funding or other visible support. They cannot muster adequate support because their own political party has conceded the seats they are seeking to the party in power on the assumption that their challengers cannot defeat the incumbents. That concession, which may be realistic under the current system, guarantees a near permanent monopoly by the incumbents, and this invulnerability is the corollary of the loss of real choice for the public.

Incumbent invulnerability is created by a combination of factors designed to destroy political competition and to guarantee long-term monopoly over seats by incumbents. These factors, which will be explored in more depth later, include:

1. Successful gerrymandering of legislative districts.
2. Erecting barriers to prevent new parties and new candidates from getting on the ballot.
3. The incumbent's ability to provide services to specific interests within the district.
4. Professionalization of legislative service such that "politics" and office-holding become full-time activities at all levels.
5. Flagrant and rampant abuse of the privilege of mailing free letters and reports to constituents (the franking privilege).
6. Growth and use of professional legislative staff for election duties.
7. Greatly disproportionate access of incumbents to PAC funding from special interest groups.
8. Failure of both political parties to mount serious campaigns in most districts.
9. Willingness of incumbents to disassociate themselves both from their own political parties and from the legislature of which they are a part.

We call this combination of factors the "Pyramid of Gain" in Chart 1, and we emphasize *gain* because it is important to understand that

Chart 1 **The Pyramid of Gain**

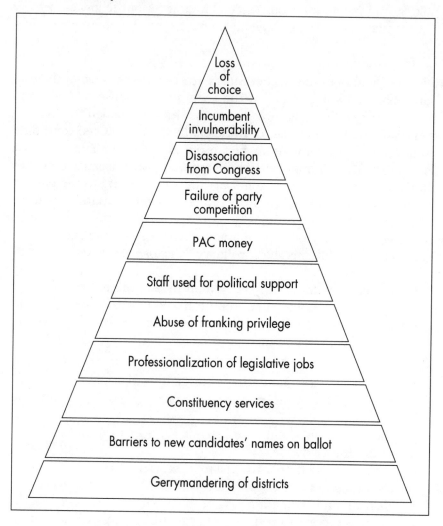

the loss of choice is the direct result of collusion between the two major parties, who manipulate these means to protect their incumbents. We assert that the pursuit of reelection, and the financial gains and power that go along with it, are far more important to both parties than the pursuit of principle or good government.

Legislators of both parties, in Congress and in the separate states, have worked together over a long period of time to monopolize the resources required to win elections, and the result is that the electoral process has been skewed to the distinct advantage of incumbents. One can make a strong case that they seek to limit democracy itself by refusing to face challengers on an even playing field. *By implication, if we wish to restore the quality of American democracy, a primary objective must be the restoration of electoral competitiveness.*

The Pyramid of Democratic Shame

One profoundly adverse effect of the destruction of choice in our elections has been the intense alienation of Americans from their political leadership, from the political parties, and from their role as democratic citizens. In Chapter 4, we trace the growth in that alienation from the early 1960s to the present, showing a pattern of increasing disaffection that almost perfectly parallels the decline of competitiveness in legislative races. The most disturbing implication of the data presented is the remarkable extent to which Americans are adopting attitudes of alienation, cynicism, fatalism, and even despair about the government. In Chart 2 we describe this process as a "Pyramid of Democratic Shame" because we are describing the processes by which the failures of our government and politics have led to voter nonparticipation and the failure of the voters to voice their demands.

Many voters today believe, accurately enough, that they can do little to affect the outcomes of elections, and that their votes are worth-

Chart 2   **The Pyramid of Democratic Shame**

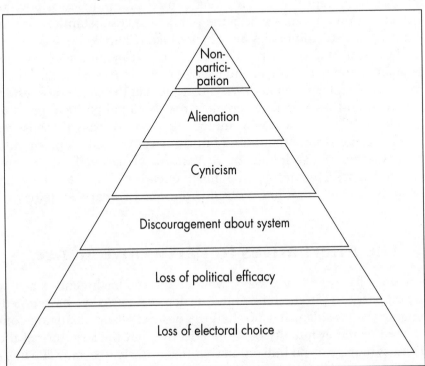

less compared to the influence of money and organizational power. They are also convinced that officeholders largely ignore their most profound concerns. If we want more Americans to become engaged in our government again, which is a crucial component of a well-functioning democracy, we must restore the ability, not just the abstract right, of Americans to exercise their influence through choice.

The Pyramid of Fiscal Pain

The loss of electoral choice also plays an insidious part in the country's fiscal problems. The lack of competitiveness in elections has virtually severed Congress from accountability to the American people, and the price to the country of this security for incumbents is a massive payoff system to the organized interest groups that fund incumbent reelections. Certain large-scale interests receive massive gains through this system—public employees, the elderly, farmers, arms manufacturers, large industry, the welfare bureaucracy, and others—because they fund the elections of incumbents. On issues such as welfare, education, and gun control, overwhelming majorities in the public want reforms that are thwarted by legislatures that cater to organized minorities.

Thus, much of our public policy falls into two unpleasant categories: policies that lead to excessive spending, far beyond what the public would accept if it had a direct choice, and policies of governmental inaction on issues where the public wants substantial change, but powerful issue minorities are opposed (see Chart 3).

The restoration of electoral choice is, therefore, a crucial component in affecting real change, and we will argue in this book that there is a means of restoring choice. We will argue that the single most effective way to do so would be to create a new national political party to support candidates who would run for office on precisely those issues of public responsibility that both political parties ignore. A new political party, running candidates on a platform of national reform and political fairness, would be the most effective threat to the cozy monopoly of power that has evolved within the two-party system.

The Alternatives to Party Governance

There are of course many ways, besides the establishment of a new political party, to pursue reform in our democracy. As we have noted, changing the president has not had the desired effect. Changing congressmen would eventually be more effective, but the structure of the current system gives no indication that this is likely to occur. The literature on reform debates the merits of a number of other ideas for effec-

Chart 3   **The Pyramid of Fiscal Pain**

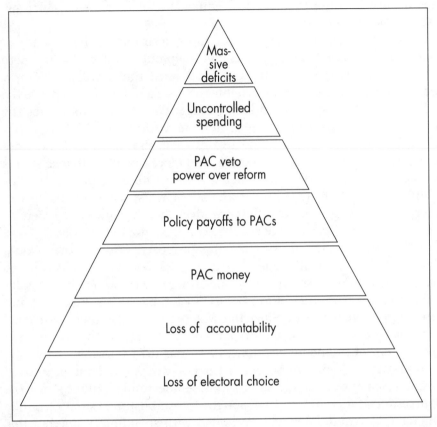

tive reform—term limits, a balanced budget amendment, public financing of campaigns, new congressional rules, reform of the franking privilege, and so on. Aside from the issue of whatever may be the merits of each of these reform proposals, there is the underlying problem that they all rest on a false assumption: *that there exists a political force with both the motivation and the power to institute the reforms that are needed.* In the absence of this force, all those well-intentioned recommendations are of limited value. There are reasons to conclude that most (but not all) of these reforms would end up either being manipulated to serve the interests of those in power or would simply be ineffectual.

Consider term limits, for example. Term limits would be a very useful reform in some respects because they would block the ability of legislators to accumulate excessive power through the domination of committees. Here we mean the kind of domination wielded by Robert Byrd (D-W.Va.), who uses his influence on the Senate Appropriations Committee to funnel enormous amounts of federal revenue to his state.

Term limits would see to it that chairmanships of the major commit-tees do not become the practical equivalent of judgeships—lifelong, irrevocable appointments.

Although forced turnover is probably desirable in the absence of more fundamental reforms, one cannot help but wonder whether there are excessive expectations for the good term limits will do. Simply replacing faces in the current structure of costs and benefits that rule the political system may result in little change. Would legislators react any differently if they were limited to six terms? We don't know. Frankly, they might become even more protective of their shortened and therefore more precious tenures, making them even more unwilling to take stands on the tough issues. Or, with their eyes on future employment, they might be even more receptive to the sweet whisperings of the special interests. We accept that it is the incentives that structure the system in which legislators operate that must be changed, not just the nameplates.

Also, in the current system, any proposed reforms that would change the fundamental power structure of Congress are certain to prompt shrewd partisan maneuvering either to gain some kind of polit-ical advantage from the reforms or to block the reforms. Case in point: campaign finance reform. Since the Watergate scandal, there have been many attempts at crafting a more equitable, cleaner, and more compet-itive system of financing elections. First, the 1974 reforms created the current PAC system, which acts as a massive incumbent protection machine, leaving challengers notoriously underfunded. In response, the Democratic leadership in 1977 sought to establish a system of public financing for candidates who complied with spending limits, but this attempt was blocked by a Republican filibuster. This exact scenario was repeated in 1979 and again in 1988.[14] The Republicans, in their defense, had good reason to be particularly fearful of these reforms. For exam-ple, the bills introduced by the Democrats contained tight restrictions on the amount a political party could contribute to each of its candi-dates—the Republican candidates' lifeline—but allowed unions unlim-ited contributions which would invariably go to Democratic candi-dates.[15] These reform proposals were designed to favor the narrow interests of the reformers, and partisan differences in their likely conse-quences killed any chance of true reform.

So we are left with a basic and fundamental question: how do we make fundamental changes in a system where changing the executive does little good, and where it is unclear that changing congressmen in itself would do much good or is even possible? Here we come to the central thesis of this book, which is that America needs a new, centrist-based political party, a party of moderates, in order to reform the sys-tem and force through the changes in policy that are needed. A corollary, and crucial, argument that will be developed in this book is that the political condition has evolved to the point where the formation of such a party can succeed.

The Fundamental Role of the Political Parties

Why do we invest so much hope in the promise of a new party? After all, few political commentators have cast a critical eye on the role of the political parties in the decline of American democracy. Debate about problems instead usually centers either on the responsibility of individual voters and their failure to throw the bums out, or on the pernicious role of organized groups. The media plays a good game of documenting partisan bickering but has been virtually silent on the role of the political parties in the debacle of the budget crisis, for example.

If the parties have been neglected, this is probably because they have failed to live up to their potential in almost every respect. An examination of the comparison between the theory of the role of parties in a democracy and the reality of the contemporary American two-party system reveals that the two parties are, in fact, the great underachievers of American politics—so much potential, so little performance. Professor James Sundquist provides a succinct description of the party system as it is supposed to operate:

> Political parties are formed because groups of people, each sharing a philosophy and a set of goals, desire governmental power in order to carry out their programs. In competition with one another, they present their programs to the people in an open and free election. The party or coalition that wins the support of a majority of the people gains control of the government and enacts its program. The minority party or parties form an opposition, with the power to criticize, debate, and delay but not to block. After a few years, the voters in another election render a verdict on the majority's stewardship. If they approve what has been done, they return the ruling party or coalition to office. If they disapprove, they turn the incumbents out and entrust power to an opposition party or combination of parties. At all times, one of the parties, or a combination, is responsible for the government, possesses authority commensurate with its responsibility. . . . The political party is the tie that binds, the glue that fastens, the bridge or the web that unites the disparate institutions that make up the government.[16]

This clearly is not the way our two-party system has been functioning. As 40 years of Democratic domination of the House demonstrates, even if the public at large disapproves of the stewardship of the party in power, changing the leadership is no simple matter. Moreover, we have a minority party that most often offers only rhetoric as opposed to effective alternatives, largely because it has so little expectation of governing Congress, now or in the foreseeable future.

American political parties have never really fulfilled their ideal role, but the trends of the past 30 years have exacerbated their failings.[17] Prior to the late 1950s, the electoral system and the leadership of Congress were responsive to the changing political and economic conditions of the day. After the late 1950s, however, there is little relationship between shifts in public sentiment and the control of Congress. Chart 4 documents the total votes received nationwide by Democratic House candidates and their corresponding seats in the chamber from 1910 to 1992. From 1910 until 1950, the voting behavior in House elections was fairly dynamic, as the percentage of Democratic popular vote started near 50 percent in 1910, dropped to 35.8 percent by 1920, and rose to 55.8 percent by 1936. However, the graph shows that the popular vote in House elections has remained practically flat since the late 1950s—never lower than 50.2 percent in 1968 and never higher than 57.6 percent following Watergate in 1974. The shifts that characterized the earlier era are entirely absent. More importantly, those earlier shifts dramatically impacted the composition of the House. The Democrats went from controlling almost 70 percent of the seats in 1912 to controlling 30 percent only eight years later, before rising above 70 percent in 1932.

Chart 4   **Democratic Popular Vote and Seats in House Elections (1910–1992)**

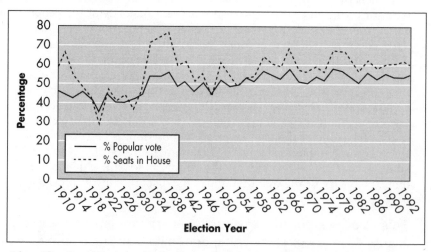

Adapted from Harold Stanley and Richard Neimi, *Vital Statistics on American Politics,* 3rd edition.

The implication is that no matter how badly Congress performs in the current context, the House as an institution will not suffer serious political consequences from its performance. Why is this really so bad? One reason is that according to the theory of parties, the electoral fortunes of the president and his party members in Congress should be intimately connected for a number of reasons. This connection creates an enormous pressure for the president and his party's leadership in Congress to work together toward a common goal. The president becomes the true leader of his party, and policy accomplishments and failures are not easily deflected from the president to Congress, or vice versa. Government then functions as a joint venture.

Today, the electoral fortunes of members of Congress and of the president are not tied closely enough. To see this, reflect on the fact that from 1960 until today, we've had four incumbent presidents removed, and only one of those due to a scandal. By contrast, in House elections we have had numerous scandals to react to—from Abscam to the House Bank—not to mention stagflation, enormous deficits, and economic busts, and yet the House manages to move right along, seemingly impervious to all of these national problems. The consistency in the return of incumbents shows that the composition of Congress is not dependent primarily on national factors, but rather is determined by more local issues. The particular point to make here is that the near invulnerability of members of Congress produces an institutional battle between the executive and the legislative branches where, for example, a single senator from an oil state will be able to kill broad-based energy taxes, and where budget battles will continue to be decided by single votes.

A key to understanding why this problems exists is to understand that House races are decided by very different factors than are presidential elections or, to a lesser extent, Senate races. Presidential races, of course, are decided primarily by national forces. Senate races, while they have a large parochial component, still ebb and flow to some degree with the changing tide of American sentiment—the most recent example being in 1980, when Reagan's electoral success translated into 12 new Republican senators and an incumbent reelection rate of only 55 percent. Elections for the House are determined much more by narrow constituency factors.

As the system now stands, congressional legislators of both parties protect their reelection both by providing service functions between constituency interests and the bureaucracy, and by satisfying the needs of the interests that fund their campaigns—largely PACs and corporations. Both have powerful "issue minorities" that greatly complicate their ability to advocate reforms. At the 1992 National Republican

Convention, a poll we conducted for *USA Today* and NBC News disclosed that 47 percent of the delegates were "born-again Christians," and 79 percent considered themselves conservative or very conservative.[18] The Republican delegates were much more conservative than the public at large, and even more conservative than the Republican voters at large. A similar poll we conducted of the 1992 Democratic delegation showed that nearly half were employed by the government in some fashion.[19] Right now, what we have in American politics is one political party dominated by the "moral majority" of the new right and the other political party dominated by the public employee organizations and members that live off the existing domestic program revenue stream.

As long as the major factor in campaigns is the ability of the incumbent to dominate the opposition with a flood of money, with national issues playing little or no role, special interests will predominate in determining policies supported by representatives over the broader views of a majority of the public. As long as this dynamic is paramount, it is very difficult to cut unneeded programs, and it is very difficult to change the status quo in policy arenas that are dominated by organizations that oppose such changes.

We believe that the only way to ensure that the broader interests of the public are given priority over the narrow special interests is to create a new party to represent these broader interests and introduce real competition into Congressional races. The only democratic institution capable of fundamentally altering the cost/benefit structure of politics is the political party. The reason is simple: political parties define the political marketplace; they offer the candidates that voters can choose and they can thereby define the political agenda. The current condition of the Democrats and Republicans is similar to that of General Motors, Ford, and Chrysler in the mid-1970s. The automobile manufacturers had grown lazy. For half a century, with relatively little foreign competition, they had controlled the domestic market, vastly limiting the choices of the American people. What happened? The Japanese started to export a better product, and each year, a larger and larger percentage of Americans were buying the better product, despite their loyalty to the American manufacturers.

At the beginning, the American automobile manufacturers ignored the new products streaming in from Japan. They said that the American people wanted big cars—Buicks, Oldsmobiles, and Cadillacs—and the American people didn't care about safety or gas mileage. They were wrong. After awhile, they could no longer ignore the imports, which were eating up more market share every day. The Japanese were producing a strikingly better product at a lower price. Next, the automobile companies cried: "Foul!" They said that they were poor, misbegotten victims of unfair trade practices and cheap foreign labor. They wanted higher tariffs in order to artificially and institutionally limit the choices of the American people. However, that plan didn't work either.

In the end, there was no one to blame but themselves. When this realization occurred, a remarkable thing happened—the American automobile manufacturers decided to make better cars. To do so, they completely redesigned their enormous, fat, slow bureaucracies into new, leaner organizations that served the wishes of their customers. And although the story is not over, they are making better cars today and are successfully competing with the Japanese on their own terms. While they haven't stemmed the tide, they have certainly made strides in the right direction. In the process, the winner has been the consumer, who has better choices and better prices from all the manufacturers.

What the research in this analysis proposes is that we unleash the same type of competitive forces that caused the revolution in the automobile industry into the political arena. If a new political party can provide a set of proposals more in line with the needs of the voters, the other parties will be forced either to adapt or die. The failures of the two-party system have created a chasm in the electorate: a large group of voters distinctly different from partisan Democrats and Republicans. These voters are liberal or moderate on social issues, profoundly conservative on fiscal issues, and disturbed by the loss of their democratic influence. They are committed to the novel idea that the government should be open, fair, honest, accountable, and balance its books. Ideologically, they are the center of American politics. They don't fit in anywhere, and their voting mobility makes them a crucial factor in any statewide or nationwide coalition. Every four years, the two major parties scheme and plan how to convince these voters to temporarily enter the party fold. But, once in power, the party officeholders are free to serve the interests of the partisan core that is their political base. The result: the socially moderate, fiscally conservative political reformers are always the bridesmaids and never the brides. They are treated with respect, only to be given a mere taste of what they want. The choice is simple. This group of voters can continue begging for scraps at the existing partisan plate, or they can pursue the option of serving themselves by creating a party that will represent their interests.

Changing the operation of government is no easy task, but it has been done before through the creation of a new political party. In modern democracies, fundamental change—without resorting to force—occurs through the planned application of power by a broad-based political organization. For example, in response to the endemic weakness of both the French political parties and constitutional structure, General Charles DeGaulle returned from retirement to lead a centrist movement of political reform that restructured the political system of France. Prior to this intervention, the French government had suffered a near-complete breakdown of political authority. Beset by a weak institutional structure and fractured political parties, the French people suffered through one failed government after another. The role of the political parties in France during this period is frighteningly similar to our own. Professors Roy Macridis and Bernard Brown explain:

> The political parties themselves progressively lost the bulk of their membership in the years after the liberation. The public was becoming disaffected from a system in which party pledges had no relevance to government policy. The alienation of the public from the parties and the political system led eventually to the *alienation of the parties from the public*. . . .[20]

It was the French version of "gridlock," called in French the "immobilisme." DeGaulle, a national hero, led a centrist revolt that formed a new political party and captured control of the Assembly. Although the Gaullists eventually lost power, they exerted effective control in France long enough to rewrite the French constitution and to leave institutions and reforms that permitted France to be governed in a far more reasonable manner. According to Macridis and Brown, De Gaulle and the Gaullist Party

> succeeded in directing the strong wave of nationalism into a Republican channel. He played the role of Rousseau's legislator in attempting to launch a system embodying the national interest. . . . above the welter of interests and ideological conflicts.[21]

Historical examples of the rise of centrist party power can also be seen in more diverse situations. As India emerged from colonial rule under the British, it was beset by a numbing array of ideologies and regional and class-based movements, all fighting for power in the independent India. Out of this morass grew a centrist, nonideological political movement that unified the disparate groups under the banner of nationalism and created the Congress Party, which provided stability in a time of great need and ruled as the dominant power for 20 years. It did so by subverting ideology to broader concerns. As K. L. Kamal of the University of Rajasthan explains, at the outset of the movement, "Publicly, the leaders generally stressed the importance of being concerned with and loyal to the nation, rather than to more parochial, regional, linguistic, racial, caste and class groups."[22] By doing so, the Congress Party created an organized party government despite the numbingly chaotic political diversity of the country. Both the Congress Party and the Gaullists are examples of successful centrist movements that won political power in complex political conditions.

Right now, there exists a market for a very different type of political party, with a very different message for the American people. If an organization can be created that will provide the right set of proposals and will be free from the demands of special interests, the research we will present demonstrates consistently that the voters are ready to buy the new political product. If this occurs, the other parties will be forced to improve their own product in order to compete. In the process, voters will get real choice and our democracy will be strengthened.

The Competitive Advantages of a New Party

A new political party should have certain attributes that distinguish it from its competitors. First, the new political party must be value-centered as opposed to the candidate-centered character of the existing parties. Currently, each individual candidate who utilizes a party label need not pay much heed to any commonly held ideals aside from reelection. As Professor Kay Lawson notes:

> It is now popular, as well as accurate, to describe our parties as electoral machines, instruments to get out the vote for largely self-selected candidates who campaign on programs they and their advisers have created independent of the party.[23]

In order to alter this state of affairs, the political party we would create must be, from the outset, based on a core of beliefs and commitments that serve as organizing principles for party activists and candidates. The most fundamental commitment should be to the development of a style of political party process that emphasizes a commonly held core set of values about democracy, political process, and responsible government. The goal is to create a political party based heavily on common principle and values, instead of relying excessively on personal ambition and individual power. We must take the concept of political organization beyond platforms and policies and into the realm of reshaping political discourse—reshaping the means of politics as well as the ends.

By establishing a clear position on the subject from the beginning, the politics would be in consonance with the organizational structure. The concept of a party based primarily on values rather than on ambition is a powerful one, and later we will show the implications of creating a new, centrist political party on issues ranging from the budget deficit to welfare reform. In the process, we will explain how a new party can bridge the enormous gap between the people and the government and create a unique opportunity to enact a platform of reforms that will serve to rebalance the relationship between the needs of the country as a whole and the special interests that currently dominate the political debate.

The values we are talking about here are those that have to do with the political process. We need to rebuild the political process itself by establishing standards of behavior, in and out of office, that will force the other two major parties to change themselves fundamentally, as the only way they can successfully compete. The party itself should promote an internal party process that is fundamentally democratic. Candidate selection processes should be designed to promote widespread participation in the context of the values of the party.

Yet, invariably, a strong party organization would be required to enforce the ideals on which the party would be founded. Even more important, the political party would have to create a membership basis that would fund its candidates. Without internal funding by party members, the candidates would either have inadequate financing or would be forced to rely exclusively on the contributions of affluent Americans. We will show evidence later that internal funding within the party is possible and would be a huge competitive advantage against the current PAC system of funding.

Can It Happen?

Political cynics and the Washington establishment will scoff at the idea of a powerful new centrist party. Impossible! they say. Yet, a two-party system depends, in the end, on having others who believe in its primacy. Voters who have positive feelings about the two-party system will not vote for a new party. Voters who like or are satisfied with the potential of the current leadership will not look outside that system for new leaders. Voters who have affection for the current political parties will not create ties to a new one. Although these conditions might have existed in the 1950s, the success of Ross Perot's candidacy and an analysis of the current state of public opinion shows that the majority of voters today are no longer tied to the current party system. If voters no longer believe in the two parties, then the system itself becomes a house of cards, dependent for its sustenance on institutional barriers like ballot access laws, and campaign finance restrictions.

The number of people who call themselves politically "independent" has been consistently rising for the past 30 years. This trend is one powerful piece of empirical evidence that the relevance of the two parties in the electorate has seriously declined. As individual voters started to identify less with a political party, they also started to believe less strongly in the two-party system. The growing sentiment against the two-party system counters very deeply held beliefs by generations of American voters. Steven Rosenstone et al. describe the roots of this belief:

> To the American voter, the two parties are as legitimate as any institution formally prescribed in the U.S. Constitution. Children grow up learning about the president, the Congress, and the Democrats and Republicans. Most have never even heard about Libertymen, Greenbacks, or Prohibitionists. Voters are socialized into a two-party system by the common portrayal of elections as contests between Democrats and Republicans.[24]

During the 100-year period from 1864 to 1964, only the Populist James B. Weaver (8.5 percent of the popular vote), Theodore Roosevelt (27.4 percent), and the Progressive Robert Lafollette (16.6 percent) polled more than 6 percent of the popular vote as a presidential candidate. *Yet, in the mere 24 years from 1968 to 1992, we have already witnessed three candidates who were able to poll more than 6 percent on election day:* George Wallace (13.5 percent), John Anderson (who received 6.6 percent election day, but reached as high as 25 percent in the polls,) and Ross Perot (19 percent).[25] Is this trend a mere coincidence?

It is quite possible that the appearance of three major candidates in such a short time is more evidence of the changing nature of the two-party system. Revolutions do not happen overnight. Conditions evolve which allow revolutions to take place and we have been witnessing that very evolution in regard to the two-party system. The recent electoral success of third-party candidates indicates a dual trend: an increased willingness on the part of voters to look outside the major parties, and an increased willingness on the part of national political figures to challenge the efficacy of the major parties.

To some, the American two-party system dominated by the Republicans and Democrats is as durable and fundamental as the Constitution itself. And, indeed, many theories have been created to "prove" with twenty-twenty hindsight why the two-party system is inevitable. The most common theory claims that the existence of single member "winner take all" districts create pressure for groups with varied interests to combine their efforts in pursuit of office, thereby maximizing the probability of electing a candidate sympathetic to their cause. This need to receive 50 percent of the vote in order to elect a representative supposedly leads to an aggregation of political interests. Other theories concentrate on cultural homogeneity, conflict between regional commercial interests, and social consensus. None of these theories seems to be fully explanatory and the relationship between cause and effect seems very unclear. For example, Great Britain has the same single member districts and cultural homogeneity, but has had three parties—the Conservatives, the Liberals, and the Labourites—who have competed in some fashion for many decades. And, if single member districts and plurality elections are the key, why was France a bastion of fractured multipartyism under the Third Republic?

Although these theories are useful in explaining some cases of two-partyism, they are of little help in explaining why the Democrats and Republicans have dominated American politics for 150 years. Some observers claim that their long existence is proof of their inevitability. But this longevity is rare in comparison to the histories of other democracies, and therefore, should be seen as *unusual* rather than *inevitable*—an important distinction. At some level, one cannot escape that there must be an attitudinal basis in the electorate which perpetuates the dominance and stability of both the two major parties and the two-party system. As Professor Frank Sarouf of the University of Minnesota explains:

> Once the two-party system was launched, its very existence then fostered the values of moderation, compromise, and political pragmatism which ensure its perpetuation. The system created deep loyalties within the American public to one party or another and deep loyalties to the genius of the two party system itself.[26]

It is precisely these loyalties that have been eroding. Public opinion researchers have been asking questions regarding the willingness of voters to look outside the two-party system since before World War II. Table 1 tracks the responses to questions asked between 1938 and 1984 about potential support for a third party. The data reveal a consistent increase in the support for alternatives outside the two parties over the last 50 years. The questions deal directly with the need for a third party or whether the respondent would support a third party over the current ones. The consistently increasing trend indicates that as partisanship and electoral competition decreased, the voters started to concurrently search for new political choices. The two-party system exists, partly because people once believed in it and partly because of institutional barriers. The table shows that during the 1930s, in the midst of the Great Depression, the support for a new party, in addition to the Democrats and Republicans, was 13 percent. The problems in the county were severe, but the people still had confidence in the system. That percentage rose slowly to the mid-20s during the 1960s, to the 30s and 40s during the 1970s and 1980s. Table 2 shows that by 1992, as many as 63 percent of Americans believed there was a need for change.

The attitudes began changing in the mid-1960s. The political parties, already weak by European standards, started to lose their hold on

Table 1 **Support for a Third Party (1938–1984)**

Year	Question	Source	% Support
1938	What parties would you like to see competing in the next presidential race? Response (3): Republicans and Democrats and a new strong third party.	Roper	13
1944	On the whole, how do you feel about the present setup of the political parties in the United States—do you find that you are usually satisfied with the stands taken by one or the other of the present big parties, or would you like to see a strong new party entirely different from either of the present parties?	Roper	14
1964	Suppose a new party were organized which would represent a middle-of-the road viewpoint. Do you think that you would vote for it?	Gallup	22
1967	Would you like to see a new political party established whose principles were more in line with your point of view or are you generally happy with the parties we have	Gallup	27
1978	It has been suggested that the nation needs a new party—one that appeals to people who are middle of the road in their political views . . . Do you think that there is or is not a place for such a center party today?	Gallup	41
1979	It has been suggested that the nation needs a new party—one that appeals to people who are middle of the road in their political views . . . Do you think that there is or is not a place for such a center party today?	Gallup	37
1980	Suppose there were three major parties—the Republican party, the Democratic party, and a new center party that would appeal to people whose political views are middle of the road, in between those of the Republicans and Democrats. If there were three such parties, which party would you favor—the Republican party, the Democratic Party, or the new Center Party?	Gallup	34
1981	Suppose there were three major parties—the Republican party, the Democratic party, and a new center party that would appeal to people whose political views are middle of the road, in between those of the Republicans and Democrats. If there were three such parties, which party would you favor—the Republican party, the Democratic Party, or the new Center Party?	Gallup	34
1982	Suppose there were three major parties—the Republican party, the Democratic party, and a new center party that would appeal to people whose political views are middle of the road, in between those of the Republicans and Democrats. If there were three such parties, which party would you favor—the Republican party, the Democratic Party, or the new Center Party?	Gallup	25

Table 1   *Continued*

Year	Question	Source	% Support
1983	Agree/Disagree: We should have a third major party in this country in addition to the Democrats and Republicans.	ABC/ WPost	44
	Agree/Disagree: Neither Republicans or the Democrats stand for things I can go along with, and it is time to have a reasonable mainstream alternative in a new third party.	Harris Survey	39
	Agree/Disagree: Since so often it doesn't seem to make any difference whether Republicans or Democrats win, the country needs a third party that will offer really new ideas for a change.	Harris Survey	44
1984	Agree/Disagree: We should have a third major party in this country in addition to the Democrats and Republicans.	ABC/ WPost	41

Adapted from data collected by The Roper Center Poll Database. All samples are national.

the American voters and were transformed into enormous, centralized, electoral machines. Neither party had a clear identity because there was a hodgepodge of positions taken by the parties' candidates. The political parties simply became less relevant to the political process. A. James Reichley, author of *The Life of the Parties*, describes the result:

> By moving the direction of parties further and further from grass-roots party organization, and by emphasizing process over substance, they weakened the bonds of emotion and self-interest that formerly attracted most voters to one major party or another.[27]

The deterioration of political attitudes, which we will present in detail, has created a market for a new type of political party—a party designed to represent a group of citizens appropriately. At the base of that market are 19 million Americans who rejected the products of the major parties and voted for the independent candidacy of Ross Perot. This numerical figure is an underestimation of the true size of his support. At one point in late May 1992, Perot's support neared 40 percent in the horse race question asked by the major polling organizations—leading both Clinton and Bush. The symbolic implications of a third-party candidate leading both major party candidates should be seen as another indicator of the state of our two-party system. It simply could not have happened in an earlier era.

Even though Perot received only 19 percent of the vote, his support was unprecedented in the modern era. Voter Research and Surveys, the consortium of the major news organizations that conducts election night projections and analysis, asked about 4,000 voters leav-

Table 2 **Support for a Third Party (1992)**

Date	Question	Source	% Support
June 4, 1992	Would you favor or oppose the formation of a third political party that would run candidates for president, Congress, and state offices against the Republican and Democratic candidates?	Yankelovich, Clancy, Schulman (likely voters)	58
July 7, 1992	Agree/Disagree: We need a third major political party, because it would make the government do a better job of addressing the problems our country faces.	Peter Hart and Breglio Research (registered voters)	55
July 9, 1992	Would you favor or oppose the formation of a third political party that would run candidates for president, Congress, and state offices against the Republican and Democratic candidates?	Yankelovich, Clancy, Schulman (likely voters)	59
July 16, 1992	Would you favor or oppose the formation of a third political party that would run candidates for president, Congress, and state offices against the Republican and Democratic candidates?	Yankelovich, Clancy, Schulman (likely voters)	58
Oct 22, 1992	Would you favor or oppose the formation of a third political party that would run candidates for president, Congress, and state offices against the Republican and Democratic candidates?	Yankelovich, Clancy, Schulman (likely voters)	63

Adapted from data collected by The Roper Center Poll Database. All samples are national.

ing the polls a very simple question: "Would you have voted for Ross Perot if you thought he had a chance to win?" A surprisingly large number, 36 percent, indicated that they would have.[28] Therefore, Perot's vote and his level of support are not congruent quantities. We will present survey research findings that demonstrate that these voters are ready to look outside the current paradigm for political leadership and solutions to the nation's problems.

It is not only the quantity of Perot's support, but the quality that is important. An analysis of his voters reveals that the most disconnected and frustrated in the United States are basically political moderates. Our political system has succeeded in alienating the segment of society that should never be alienated—the political center. They are, as Professor Theodore Lowi has accurately dubbed them, "the radicalized moderates."[29]

As this third political force now exists, it is more like a mob squad than a political sniper. A discontented centrist party is vulnerable to the same misguided hope that one charismatic leader can solve all of this country's ills through executive action. But the executive branch does not possess the power, on its own, to provide that which is promised during the election campaign.[30] It is possible that the political moderate can be swayed by the symbolic appeals and promises of either major party. There is little doubt that Perot's success has made the political elite very nervous and that they will offer tidbits of reform to keep the public from feeling so isolated. But based on the available data, it seems likely that the public is too frustrated to accept that kind of appeasement.

The time has come to consider a broader form of political action. The advent of a new party presents a unique opportunity to enact fundamental changes in the electoral and policy process. It is not an understatement to say that a new, centrist political party would have the opportunity to turn our eighteenth-century system of government into a twenty-first-century system of government, capable of meeting the needs of future generations and fluid enough to reflect the ever-changing tide of public sentiment.

≈ 2 ≈

Democracy Dying: Not with a Bang, but a Whimper[1]

And you shall take no bribe, for a bribe blinds the officials, and subverts the cause of those who are in the right.

—*Exodus 23:6*

When 99.2 percent of all incumbents get reelected, many of them without opposition, there is more than the PAC issue at stake. Democracy is at stake.[2]

—*House Minority Leader Robert Michel (R-Ill.), 1988*

The Pyramid of Incumbent Gain

What really is a democracy? What exactly does it mean to say a political system or process is democratic? A common mistake is to define democracy in terms of the right to vote, but while the right to vote and to participate is very important, the most essential element of a democracy involves choice. A democracy is a political system in which citizens have *both the right and the opportunity to choose between candidates*. Take away choice and you have taken away the essence of what it means to be democratic. After all, elections are regularly held in countries with dictatorships, but there is no choice except to vote for the party in power.

If we want to preserve *our* democracy, we must protect the right and opportunity to choose; among candidates, if we are talking about representative democracy; or on ballot initiatives, if we are talking about direct democracy as practiced in many states such as California. A real choice among viable candidates is the key guaranteeing that officeholders will pay serious attention to the people who elected them, *and this right to choose must be considered seriously abrogated if the outcomes of elections can be dictated in advance. Unfortunately, that is precisely what has been happening for some time now in American democracy.*

Protecting Choice in the Constitution

When the original rules of the game of our American democracy were established, the framers of those rules were very much concerned with the preservation of the right to choose, and they expressed this concern in two ways. First, they created the First Amendment, which protected many of the preconditions of free and fair choice, such as the freedom of expression, the freedom of the press, the right of peaceful assembly, and the right to petition the government. In addition, they set up the "separation of powers," a set of rules designed to reduce the possibility that a coalition of forces could be brought together to subvert the constitutional rules themselves.

The constitutional founders were realists about the abuses of power that officeholders were prone to exploit.[3] They had experienced abusive power through both the British Crown and the arbitrary and capricious rules under which some of the states were governed until the American Revolution, when they earnestly sought to craft institutional arrangements that would protect against such abuses. Their emphasis was on providing for healthy competition, reducing the potential either for abusive minorities or abusive majorities to dominate the process unfairly.

On the whole, the original constitutional arrangements proved remarkably successful in preventing abusive concentrations of power. There are, however, three striking historical exceptions. The first is the deprivation of the political rights of African-Americans. Up until the Voting Rights Act of 1964, whites in the South, the Border States, and parts of the North conspired to use every means at their disposal to deny blacks their rightful access to the polls, political choice, and political power. After Reconstruction ended with the election in 1872, the 13th, 14th, and 15th Amendments were essentially ignored by the state and federal courts, and the "separate but equal" doctrine elucidated in *Plessy v. Ferguson* was used to sanctify official segregation. It took over one hundred years and an immense civil rights struggle to ensure African-Americans the basic right to full participation in the political process.

The second example is the denial of women's right to vote until the passage of the 19th Amendment in 1919. Again, this right was not granted without a struggle of great intensity and long duration, and the female organizers of the earliest feminist movement became experts at agitation.

The final example of the failure of the American political process to protect democratic choice is the existence of political machines that controlled politics in nearly every major urban center in the United States during the latter half of the nineteenth and the first half of the twentieth centuries. Americans today have little memory of how powerful and pervasive these machines were. Mayor Richard Daley, of Chicago, was the leader of the last traditional political machine Americans have had direct experience with, and his machine collapsed with his death in the 1970s. We have lost our first-hand knowledge of the tyranny that such machines can exercise.

The machines used a familiar set of tools to ensure their power—gerrymandering, patronage, control over nominations, government contracts, preference to businesses, advancement of workers in the system, control over law enforcement and the judiciary. Machine domination's real currency of power was, however, the combination of public money and political patronage, with patronage aimed specifically at the delivery of votes during primary contests. The humorous motto of the "graveyard" vote in Chicago was: "Vote early, vote often, and vote forever!" The joke was that these votes were taken from the names on tombstones on the south side of the city. Indeed, at its high point, the Democratic-controlled Chicago Board of Elections could provide a guarantee of nearly 90,000 "unlively" voters.

Political machines finally lost control both because they eroded from within and because Americans killed them off with a whole set of political reforms launched as part of the Urban Reform Movement and the Progressive Movements. These reforms included the initiative, the referendum, the recall at the state level, the establishment of civil service, new state banking and contract regulations, and the professionalization of city management.

We raise these three examples to illustrate a fundamental argument of this book: *Entrenched political power can be removed only by equal political power, and the only power for reform of consequence in the United States must be exercised through the mechanism of fair elections, driven by grassroots forces.* Each of these historical struggles was against unilateral and unrestrained political power, power employed by a set of officeholders who retained their position by denying choice, suppressing dissent, and rewarding loyalty.

Today, in a similar fashion, the flow of money from special interests to congressmen and state legislators has effectively shielded them from the democratic process in a manner no less threatening than the destruction of political choice under the great machines. By providing enormous incumbency advantages, officeholders are inoculated from public outcry by the inability of anyone to challenge them in fair elections, and they have become, in the words of the *Wall Street Journal,* the "elected aristocracy."[4]

Why Is Competition So Important?

Americans understand that the United States is a *representative democracy,* meaning that the people rule through legislators and executives who are directly responsible for the creation of public policy. Our legislators and executives are elected as representatives of our interests, but there is no simple way they can translate the will of their constituents directly into public policy. This is partly because it is often difficult to know exactly what their constituents want on any given issue. Even if they do know, there are often conflicting elements within their constituency who want different things, and legislators are faced with a choice of which part of their constituency to represent. In addition, some of these interests are national in character, although they may have groups attached to them that are located in the legislator's district.

Under the best of circumstances, then, we have to expect that legislators are representing only some of the interests of most constituents only some of the time. But beyond this, there is a troubling question that needs answering. In a district where there is little or no electoral competition, what exactly is the motivation of the legislator for paying much attention to what most constituents want? In the ideal case, the representative must represent the interests of the broadest possible portion of his constituency in order to stay in office. But without effective electoral competition, what is the motivation for representing the broad interests of a constituency, even if that constituency is a vocal one?

Electoral competition is the force that produces pressure on legislators to be responsive to their districts. The only reason legislators will react to the broader needs of their constituencies is if they must do so in order to be reelected. Otherwise, it is far easier to satisfy the needs of organized, politically active groups, often at the direct expense of the broader interest, if that's all that is needed for reelection. Therefore, electoral competition is one of the key factors that can encourage legislators to represent voters, rather than groups or financial contributors.

Additionally, when an incumbent faces a relatively equal challenger on relatively equal grounds for the loyalties of voters in a district, certain other positive natural consequences follow. The incumbent's record will be portrayed extensively using paid media by his or her opponent, improving the information voters have available. The incumbent will be forced to pay attention directly to voting blocs in the district and make clear choices among competing local interests. With the outcome of the race in doubt, voter interest is stimulated and participation increases. And finally, increased voter interest encourages the media to provide the public with better information than is the case when incumbents run unopposed or with only token opposition.

A single congressional district in western New York State very nicely illustrates the absence of political choice. A local Democratic congresswoman, Louise Slaughter, defeated a single-term conservative Republican incumbent in 1986. The district she represented in 1990 was Republican in registration by a wide margin. In 1988, her district supported Bush over Dukakis by nine percentage points and was once the district of the long-time Republican leader, Barber Conable. Setting aside issues of her competence and personal appeal, the congresswoman's voting record and activities in Congress are markedly at variance with the dominant views of the residents of her district. She has, for example, one of the strongest records in Congress in favor of organized labor in a community where organized labor has been traditionally weak, and is dominated by a largely white-collar workforce from Kodak, Xerox, and Bausch & Lomb.

The fact is, however, that Congresswoman Louise Slaughter is nearly invulnerable, so much so that it is difficult for the Republican party to recruit a decent candidate to run against her. The results of the last two congressional elections clearly illustrate her electoral strength. In 1988, in her first reelection bid, she ran against a young local lawyer who had virtually no political experience, John Bouchard. To his credit, he was able to raise $310,000, a very impressive amount for a political novice. Indeed, this amount of money places him in an elite group of congressional challengers of incumbents who are able to jump the huge hurdle of finding adequate financing. For the congressional Democrats, the money was a warning shot across Slaughter's bow. In response, she was able to raise a staggering sum, $802,704; enough in the geographically dense media markets of upstate New York to literally drown her opponent in advertising. About half of this money came from PACs representing their own narrow interests. The result was that Slaughter received 57 percent of the vote: a comfortable win. As congressional seats go, however, this is considered a competitive race for an incumbent.[5]

The effect was chilling for any other candidates who would consider running against Slaughter in the future. In 1990, the only candidate willing to run against her was able to raise a paltry $24,712. This is not enough to pay for a single professionally produced commercial. In response to this minimal threat, Slaughter spent $322,216 and the result was predictable. She won by 18 percentage points, this time against what Monica Bauer and Herbert Alexander have accurately called a "token challenger:"

> A token challenger is just a name on a ballot; he or she does not raise enough money to go on television or engage in a visible campaign. In 1988, 230 challengers in House races had a median spending figure of less than $50,000. That means that 83 percent of all challengers were unable to raise enough money to achieve even the most minimal visibility to the electorate.[6]

How can Slaughter, a liberal Democrat living in a traditionally Republican district, be invulnerable? By the last official count in 1992, Congresswoman Slaughter had received $473,871 in campaign contributions, of which 62 percent came from various sources of PAC money. Since 1985, she has received a total of $1.3 million in PAC money, with over $200,000 coming directly from unions or organizations connected with public employees.[7] It seems fairly obvious to potential Republican challengers that she can have virtually all the money she wants, if she needs it. Local Republicans cannot possibly raise half- to three-quarter of a million dollars to run against her. As a result, the opposing candidate in 1992, who lost by a margin of under ten points, was a little-known county legislator who was outspent by a margin of two to one, and ended his campaign $130,254 in debt. This debt is the cost of challenging an incumbent.[8]

Yet this local example is hardly unique. Similar situations are repeated all over the United States, for Republicans and Democrats alike, and Congresswoman Louise Slaughter is by no means the worst offender. Let's take a look at the 1992 elections to see how widespread the lack of electoral competition is. In June of 1992, a paltry 16 percent of the public approved of the way Congress was doing its job, yet the public sent back 93 percent of the incumbents who decided to run in the general election.[9] The voter discontent, which caused such a stir in the media and seemed so threatening to even the most respected incumbents, turned into a whimper. Only 24 incumbents were defeated in the general election, and most of these because of the effects of redistricting, or ethically questionable behavior in the House banking scandal. In comparison, the number of defeated legislators was far less than following Watergate, when 40 legislators were removed in the general election.

Overall there was, however, an extremely large turnover in 1992, with 110 new members coming into the House. The size of the entering class has been cited by some observers as a sign that the electoral system is becoming more responsive, but the turnover was not due to increased competitiveness in House elections. With a couple of exceptions, the electoral system has returned over nine out of ten congressional legislators each election cycle for the past 30 years, and the 1992 results do not indicate a change in this trend (see Table 1). Instead, the large turnover in 1992 was the result of a combination of other factors only marginally related to two-party competition.

There was an unusually high number of retirements in 1992—53 in total—and it is important to point out that these retirements were encouraged by campaign finance regulations which allowed members to take with them accrued campaign contributions as personal income. All told, 33 members pocketed campaign contributions totaling $8.6 million. Most legislators were able to pocket, individually, hundreds of thousands of dollars, with the largest amount going to Congressman Larry Hopkins (R-Ky.), who pocketed $660,688, with which he is free to do whatever he wants.[10]

In addition, the retirements were also encouraged by the lavish congressional pensions, paid for by the taxpayers. Of the candidates who left office in 1993, fully 65 House members, and 5 senators will receive over a million dollars in taxpayer money over the course of their lifetimes, if life spans conform to the actuarial tables. For example, this year retiring Representatives Charles Bennett (D-Fla.), William S. Bloomfield (R-Mich.) and Dante Fascell (D-Fla.), will draw a hefty $93,500 each in 1993. Rep. Les AuCoin (D-Oreg.), who lost a Senate challenge to Bob Packwood (R-Oreg.), stands to make nearly $3,000,000 on his federal pension. To make matters worse for the taxpayer, when Congress increased its pay from $89,500 to $125,100, the legislation included a clause that automatically provided a cost-of-living (COLA) raise if the economy worsens. These COLAs also apply to the pension program, protecting the politician against inflation in the future. Pension plans with COLAs are all but *nonexistent* in the private sector. Ironically, some politicians end up making more retired than they did when they served. Former House Speaker, Carl Albert (D-Tex.), who retired making $44,600, will make $114,213 in 1993.[11] In addition to those who retired, 13 candidates decided to seek other offices; so a total of 66 of the 110 vacancies were not even the result of elections, let alone competitive elections.

A total of 19 incumbents were defeated in party primaries. Of these, 8 incumbents bounced more than 100 checks in the House banking scandal, and another 4 were forced to run in primaries against another incumbent because their states lost seats following redistricting, forcing some districts to be combined. Some of the others, like the once-powerful Steven Solarz (D-N.Y.), had to run in drastically redesigned districts that contained only a few of their original constituents.

Of the 24 incumbents defeated in the general election, 11 incumbents bounced more than 30 checks at the House bank; all but 5 had at least 1 bounced check; and one was indicted for racketeering, bribery, and tax evasion (notably, he still received 45 percent of the vote). Five incumbents were forced to run against other incumbents as a result of redistricting, and three Democratic incumbents were narrow losers in districts redrawn to be Republican by a wide margin.[12] Therefore, even the seven percent incumbent loss rate in the 1992 general election is basically attributable to major electoral gaffes and the effects of redistricting, not an increase in electoral competitiveness.

This result is even more discouraging considering the increased ability of congressional challengers to attract money and the improvement of the quality of the challenging candidates in this election. Given all the media attention, many potential candidates thought that this was the year to fight entrenched incumbents, and the perception of opportunity attracted opposition candidates of unusual experience in government and campaigning. Unfortunately, once again the raw power of incumbency reigned supreme, proving the point that the electoral system is no longer a mechanism for change. Competition and true political choice, the very bedrock of a democracy, is currently more the product of voluntary retirements than of a competitive two-party system.

The History of Declining Electoral Competition

It is important to understand that 1992 was hardly an anomalous year as far as the reelection of incumbents goes. In 1990, there were only 50 congressional races out of 435 where the winner won by less than ten percentage points. Ten percentage points is normally considered a landslide. In fact, over 160 seats were won with more than seventy percent of the vote. As in 1992, what little turnover there was could be attributed almost exclusively to either retirement or scandal. Overall, of the 406 House incumbents seeking reelection, 79 were unopposed and the vast majority held enormous fund-raising advantages over their competition.

Table 1 shows that, in fact, the right to choose has been compromised all across America for many years. The ability of voters to express their views on the direction of governmental policy is clearly a function of whether or not voters can determine the outcomes of elections.[13] Given the well documented dissatisfaction with Congress as an institu-

Table 1 **Incumbency Success in House Elections**

Year	Incumbents Seeking Reelection	Defeated in Primaries	Defeated in General Election	Percentage Reelected
1972	390	12	13	94
1974	391	8	40	88
1976	384	3	13	96
1978	382	5	19	94
1980	398	6	31	91
1982	393	10	29	90
1984	411	3	16	95
1986	393	3	6	98
1988	409	1	6	98
1990	407	1	15	96
1992	349	19	24	93

Adapted from Maisel in *Money, Elections, and Democracy*, p.121.

tion that has mounted over the years, an electoral result where only 5 to 10 percent of incumbents lose each election is clearly not a true expression of public sentiment. For example, just before the 1990 elections, fully 73 percent of the public disapproved of Congress's record. Yet, the electorate sent 96 percent of the incumbents back to Washington.[14] And in 1992, Congress's approval rating dropped to 16 percent, the lowest figure in the history of modern polling.[15]

Another interesting trend is displayed in Chart 1, which shows that elections in the House have been becoming increasingly one-sided for many years. Beginning in the early 1960s, the percentage of seats won by incumbents with more than 60 percent of the popular vote has been rising. In addition, the number of candidates who have essentially won landslide races has been pathetically high for the last 20 years. The number of House incumbents who have received more than 60 percent of the vote in their district has increased from the high 50s and low 60s in the early part of the 1960s, to the present rate of between 78 percent to 84 percent. In 1992, the widespread voter discontent and redistricting decreased the margins slightly, as 64 percent of incumbents won with over 60 percent of the vote, a figure almost identical to the 1974 elections following Watergate. This decrease simply proves that voter discontent can influence margins, but not elections. If a presidential candidate wins with over 60 percent of the vote, the pundits call it a landslide. Yet, in House races, landslides are business as usual.

Chart 1   **Percentage of House Incumbents Reelected with Greater Than 60% of Vote (1960–1992)**

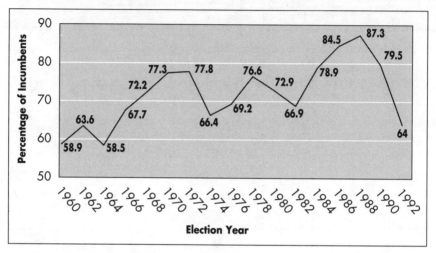

Adapted from Harold Stanley and Richard Neimi, *Vital Statistics on American Politics*, 1992, and *Congressional Quarterly*, April 19, 1993.

Disturbingly, a similar pattern seems to be developing in Senate races, which have historically been more competitive. In 1984, 35 percent of the Senate incumbents received more than 60 percent of the vote. By 1988, this figure had risen to 58 percent.[16] The 1990 midterm elections were as bad for Senate challengers as for House challengers, with 27 of 28 incumbents reelected for an incumbency success rate of 96 percent, and this figure declined only slightly in 1992, as 85 percent of the Senate incumbents were returned to Washington.[17] All the voter anger didn't impact the Senate one bit. The 102nd Congress contained 57 Democrats and 43 Republicans, and the composition of the 103rd Congress is identical. Among the winners was the perennially unpopular Senator Alfonse D'Amato (R-N.Y.), who at election time had only a 35 percent approval rating in New York State.[18]

Even in the first half of the century, the system was much more responsive to changing public sentiment. Although incumbents have always had significant electoral advantages, there was once enough competition to displace the power structure in Congress. In 1948, for example, the Democrats managed to gain 75 seats in the House after Harry Truman went on a tirade against the "do-nothing" 80th Congress, giving him a decisive majority to pursue the controversial Marshall Plan to rebuild Europe.[19] Such a swing today is all but unthinkable.

The result of this situation is clear. The voters are uniformly denied a reasonable political choice in congressional elections. Without choice, there is no real debate. Without debate, there is no way for public opinion to have any impact on the Congress or the state legislatures through district representatives. *When choice is gone, democracy is destroyed as surely as Boss Tweed and the Tweed Ring destroyed it while robbing New York City of $500 million in the middle of the nineteenth century.* As we stated before, democracy, after all, is not defined by the right to *vote*. It is the right to *choose* that really matters. As Professor L. Sandy Maisel states, "A minimal criterion for an effectively functioning election system is that officeholders are held accountable for their actions. . . ."[20] The only way to hold them accountable is through elections wherein they stand a reasonable chance of facing defeat.

Why? The Basis for Incumbent Indestructibility

Incumbent indestructibility in American politics is the result of a series of easily identifiable and understandable causes. Foremost, of course, is the institutionalized access to the vast funding of Political Action Committees (PACs), which goes almost exclusively to incumbents. We will cover the role of money in considerable detail, but before we do, there are a number of other key elements that are not as obvious or widely understood.

The creation of new district lines following the census has always been a primary tool of incumbency protection. New lines are commonly drawn in order to maximize the electoral base of the party in control, a process referred to as gerrymandering. Gerrymandering was a relatively inexact science in the days before computers, but it has grown increasingly sophisticated with their use. The state legislatures control the process and invariably create districts that leave the current incumbents protected. The courts must approve of the lines, but are disinclined to disturb the deals as long as the racial minorities are guaranteed seats.

The irony of gerrymandering is the surprising degree of cooperation that occurs between the two parties. In general, the Republicans and the Democrats collude in each state to decide which incumbents in both political parties will be protected and which will be sacrificed, and this is particularly true in any state where there is divided control of the legislature and governor. With computers, however, this process became even more efficient and precise.

The electoral consequences of gerrymandering can be quite severe, as Barry Keene (D) of the California State Senate explains:

In the 1960s, '70s, and '80s, sophisticated, computerized redistricting maximized the number of safe seats in Congress and the legislature. For all practical purposes, occupants became unaccountable if they failed to solve problems; they won reelection almost automatically. They could hold policy hostage to their ideological wishes. Extremists on each side became more stubborn, leaving the center too lean to act.[21]

In 1992, for example, the Democrats in the Texas State Legislature were able to draw new districts that undoubtedly hurt the Republican candidates. The Republicans won 48 percent of the House vote in the state, yet they received only 9 seats out of 30, a disparity that can be explained only by gerrymandering. Even worse, in 1984 a majority of Californians voted for Republican congressmen; however, the congressional delegation included nine more Democrats than Republicans.[22]

Another key factor in incumbent advantage is the ability and willingness of incumbents to run against the institutions of which they are a part, blaming all of the problems on others in the legislatures while absolving themselves from responsibility. With ineffective competition, it is all too easy for a legislator to claim that he is the good guy struggling against all those other bad guys voted in by all those other voters.[23]

This, in combination with the delivery of "pork," creates the paradox commonly found in public opinion research where individuals *approve* of their congressman, but *disapprove* of the institution. The ability of legislators to attract federal revenue to their district in the form of construction projects, economic development programs, or even direct subsidies in the case of agriculture, enables them to pay off key constituencies who reciprocate by supporting the legislator politically and financially. It is not that the voters simply absolve their legislator of blame for the condition of the country, but without effective competition, it is too difficult for the average voter to make a connection between specific actions in the legislature and their representative. Local projects are an easy way to help the district, and with no one to pressure the legislators, they are effective tools of incumbent protection.

Yet another key factor is a game of "you scratch my back, I'll scratch yours" between the Congress and the federal bureaucracy, which permits the incumbents to perform all kinds of "constituency service" based on access to that bureaucracy. The federal bureaucracy dispenses billions of dollars across the United States in the form of services, contracts, grants, building projects, and special economic development programs, all of which can be used to assist legislators electorally. Routinely, the bureaucrats perform such services for the legislators as finding a lost Social Security check, and they earn the support of the legislators on matters of importance to the agencies, such as funding decisions and program evaluations.[24] The more the government does, of course, the greater the number of favors a member of Congress can do for his or her home district. The staggering growth of federal spending since 1960 is, therefore, one of the key factors aiding the ability of incumbents to ensure their own reelection.

A final advantage enjoyed by incumbents is their access to increasingly excessive staff and office resources, especially mailing programs, which make it possible for the incumbents to spend virtually all of their time running for reelection, using public funds and other resources in the process. Chart 2 traces the growth in personal legislative staff between 1967 and 1987. The degree to which the Congress was able to increase its own appropriations in the face of increasing deficits and other financial pressures is staggering. From 1946 to 1986, the consumer price index rose 450.8 percent, *but the legislative branch appropriations rose a staggering 2,859 percent.*

These staffers are often lawyers, who will move in and out of government over the course of their careers. More than the officeholders, staff members develop long-term ties to the special interest groups that support the members of the House and Senate. Staff positions are prized as stepping stones in careers that include service in the Congress, the administration, and in the interest groups that lobby both branches of government.

Chart 2   **Growth of Congressional Staff (1967–1987)**

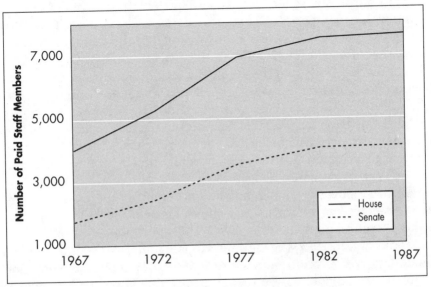

Adapted from data collected by the Congressional Research Service, 1992.

The original justification for expanding congressional staff was to enable members to deal with the emerging complexities of modern public policy and decrease the dependence on the executive branch for information. The justification and the reality, however, are quite different. When many of these staffers are in government, they spend much of their time working on the reelection of their employer, all at the public expense. They are performing constituent services and writing political newsletters and press releases. The congressional staff looks more like a taxpayer-funded reelection machine than a legislative office.[25]

The abuse of staffing is exceeded, however, by the abuse of free postage, called the frank. Remarkably, in 1988, members of Congress used their franking privileges to send out roughly 804,997,000 pieces of mail to constituents.[26] This amount is enough to send every voter in the country eight pieces of what amounts to nothing more than political campaign literature, all at taxpayer expense. The value of this mail is best understood by asking how much it would cost for potential challengers to incumbents to send out over 800 million pieces of mail if they had to pay for the full cost of a mailing. It would cost between $250 million and $400 million, depending upon the number of pages in the mailing, for congressional challengers to match this effort. By implication, this means that members of Congress are providing themselves with a campaign subsidy whose market value is worth between $547,000 and $920,000 per incumbent, all paid for by the taxpayer.

The extent to which the leadership of Congress is willing to cross our ethical boundaries when using public resources is vividly demonstrated by a franking scheme cooked up in 1992. In that year, Congress permitted its members to engage in a taxpayer-funded preelection mailing to voters in new areas to be included in the members' district boundaries after the 1992 redistricting was complete. Of course, it didn't bother anybody that these voters were not the legislators' current constituents. This practice was stopped only when the Court of Appeals upheld a suit brought by the Coalition to End The Permanent Congress enjoining Congress from further mailings to the newly acquired voters of the new district.[27] According to some political scientists, "the frank is now a government license to bury voters under mounds of propaganda designed to ensure reelection."[28]

All these advantages are not as important as the overwhelming ability of incumbents to raise large sums of money for their campaigns. Electoral competition requires large outlays of money on the part of the candidates. In 1992, the winning House candidates spent $239 million dollars, a 35 percent increase over 1990.[29] Without large amounts of money, a candidate has no way to ensure that voters will know who the candidate is or what he or she stands for.

The single most powerful weapon in the incumbent's financial arsenal is the PAC system. The total contributions to congressional campaigns by PACs have risen from $55.2 million in 1980 to $149.7 million in 1990, and $180.4 million in 1992.[30] These contributions are notoriously one-sided. Overall, in 1992, $126.7 million of this PAC money went to incumbents, while only $21.3 million went to challengers.[31]

Even if quality candidates run, they cannot succeed in today's electoral environment without adequate funding. Past academic research has shown that the key to competitive congressional campaigns is the amount of money a challenger is able to raise. If a challenger is adequately funded, the amount of money spent by an incumbent becomes much less important. As political scientist Alan Abramowitz notes:

> The main reason why incumbents have been winning more often and by larger margins during the 1980s is not because they have been doing more for their constituents, but because the cost of House campaigns has increased dramatically while the ability of House challengers to raise campaign funds has declined. Unless these trends are reversed, we can expect to see more extremely high rates of reelection for House incumbents in future elections.[32]

The data from the 1992 campaign support this conclusion. The elections became competitive only when the challenger had reasonably sufficient funds to run a competitive campaign. Table 2 illustrates the relationship between a challenger's funds and competitive races. The median spending figure for congressional challengers who won was eight times higher than the figure for those candidates who lost by greater than ten points. Any attempts to reform the system must address the inability of challengers to raise money. Predictably, current reform efforts in Congress concentrate only on spending limits and fail to address this fundamental dynamic.

Table 2 **House Challenger Spending by Electoral Margin (1992)**

Election Outcome—Vote Received	Number of Candidates	Median Total Spending
Lost—40% or less	182	$ 50,458
Lost—41%–45%	58	206,560
Lost—Greater than 45%	33	248,152
Won—Less than 55%	19	397,841
Won—55%–60%	6	468,487
Won—60% or more	10	293,744

Adapted from data collected by the Federal Election Commission.

The relationship between money and votes does not always work as one might expect. The magnitude of the money is dependent on the nature of the race. If the challenger is going to win easily, there is less demand for money, just like a "shoo-in" incumbent needs less money than a competitive one. Therefore, the amount of money spent decreases if the challenger wins by over 20 percentage points. These few one-sided challenger victories are usually due to redistricting, scandal, or minority dominated one-party districts.

In contrast, for incumbents the relationship between money and competitiveness is reversed (see Table 3). In this situation, the important factor is the weak incumbent, not the money that is spent in the campaign. The irony is that weak incumbents are likely to be fund-raising powerhouses. The weaker an incumbent is electorally, the more money he needs to raise in order to mitigate his weaknesses, and he typically enjoys easy access to vast funding sources. In addition, this type of incumbent will establish and utilize money networks far in advance of his campaign. Also, for contributors interested in access, it is politically more beneficial to help a member of Congress who is in trouble than one who is safe. A PAC that contributes to a legislator in need will have little trouble gaining access to that legislator in the future. Lastly, there are many politically and ideologically motivated groups who contribute to candidates based on policy positions. These ideologically motivated groups tend to concentrate their resources where they perceive they can influence the outcome of the race. The same tendency is true for the campaign committees of both the Democratic and Republican parties.[33] As a result, in close races, incumbents can muster enormous financial resources to their cause.

Table 3   **House Incumbent Spending by Electoral Margin (1992)**

Election Outcome—Vote Received	Number of Candidates	Median Total Spending
Lost—40% or less	3	$792,318
Lost—41%–45%	5	716,401
Lost—Greater than 45%	16	859,805
Won—Less than 55%	47	746,611
Won—55%–60%	55	619,914
Won—60% or more	224	405,592

Adapted from data collected by the Federal Election Commission.

Chart 3 documents the flow of PAC money in House races where an incumbent is running, and dramatically displays the gross inequities in the flow of funds to incumbents. The data illustrates that the money cannot possibly be for reasons relating to political beliefs or causes, but simply serves as a mechanism to pay off the congressmen that contributors know will be returning to Washington in January. In fact, in 1992, 37 percent of all House campaign funds for the incumbents were provided by PACs.[34] For incumbent Democrats, the reliance on PAC money is far more severe. From 1986 to 1992, Democratic incumbents received between 49 percent and 52 percent of their campaign contributions from PACs, while Republican incumbents received between 37 percent and 41 percent.[35] The share of money donated to incumbents by PACs was greater than any other single source of financing, including individual contributions.

The same trends in campaign funding evident in House races are becoming evident in Senate races as well. The PAC money involved in Senate races is not of the same magnitude, because Senators enjoy a much wider base of support from which to pursue individual contributions, lessening their dependence on the PACs. Yet Chart 4 shows that the funding from PACs is following the identical pattern in Senate races as in the House.

Chart 3   **Distribution of PAC Money in House Incumbent Races (1979–1992)**

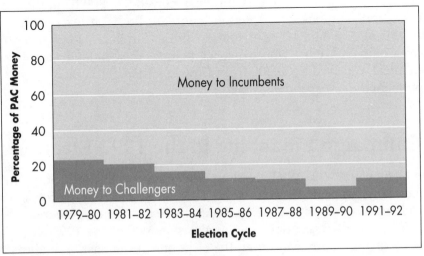

Adapted from *United States Statistical Abstract: 1992* and Federal Election Commission.

Chart 4   **Distribution of PAC Money in Senate Incumbent Races (1979–1992)**

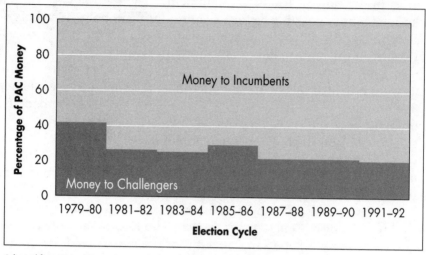

Adapted from *United States Statistical Abstract: 1992* and Federal Election Commission.

To make matters worse, interest groups are able to magnify their fund-raising capabilities by "bundling" donations. Specific industries, groups, or corporations may supplement their PAC donations by accumulating individual donations. There were some notable examples of bundling in the 1990 elections. For example, the various official organizations representing lawyers gave $4.6 million in PAC contributions to congressional candidates, but lawyers contributed a total of $14 million in individual contributions. Senator Bill Bradley (D-N.J.), a member of the Senate Finance Committee, received $71,800 from the executives and families of Shearson Lehman Inc., far exceeding the theoretical $5,000 PAC contribution limit. Similarly, Representative Dave Camp (R-Mich.), whose district includes the headquarters of Dow Chemical, received $100,200 from Dow executives in a race where his opponent *did not spend one dollar.*[36]

Campaign Financing in the 1992 Elections

On the surface, the 1992 elections appeared to be more competitive financially than previous elections. The increase in funding for nonincumbents was largely an artifact of an increase in the number of open seats. The early indications and analysis show that the 1992 elections were worse in many ways than the elections of the past. A analysis by Common Cause found that:

- 83 percent of incumbents in the general election were unopposed or in races where the challenger failed to raise *half* the incumbent's campaign treasury.
- Two-thirds of all challengers were not able to raise even a paltry $100,000. In most cases, this figure would be the minimum amount necessary to manage a marginally competitive campaign.
- In the 48 close races in which incumbents received less than 55 percent of the vote, the incumbents had an average of $708,000 versus $208,000 for the challengers.[37] More importantly, in the vital last two weeks of the campaign, the incumbents enjoyed a *six to one* advantage in available money.[38]

As we have noted, the giving practices of PACs contribute to the unfair advantages incumbents enjoy. According to data released by the Federal Election Commission, in the 1992 general election the average Democratic incumbent received $288,937 in PAC money, while the average Republican challenger received $19,918. The average Republican incumbent received $214,397 in PAC money, while the average Democratic challenger received $46,748.[39] This one-sided pattern of PAC contributions greatly eases the already enhanced ability of incumbents to raise money. In addition, for a challenger, campaign fund-raising is a vicious circle—*you can't raise money unless you're competitive and you can't be competitive unless you raise money.* Chart 5 shows the median spending figure for incumbents as compared to the candidates that challenged them from the opposing party.

Chart 5   **Median Spending of House Incumbents and Challengers (1992)**

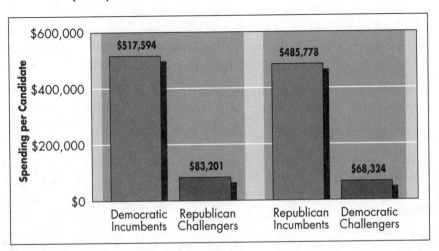

Adapted from data collected by Federal Election Commission.

Obviously, these figures are so preposterously one-sided that they make a mockery of the concept of fair and open elections. Regardless of the reason, this system of funding is a travesty, making real democracy all but impossible. In races where the financial resources are distributed so unfairly, whose message will be heard, who will answer attacks, and who can afford slick campaign commercials?

This is a system of intentionally created electoral monopoly. If this were an economic marketplace, the Federal Trade Commission would throw it out on the grounds that it violates antitrust regulations. In addition to creating one-sided races, *the present campaign financing system discourages potential candidates from running for office.* A would-be challenger faces a fiscal mountain solidly possessed by an entrenched incumbent. The daunting task of trying to scale that mountain discourages most serious people from making the attempt.

Moreover, the process of soliciting campaign contributions on this scale makes political prostitutes of most candidates, causing them to sell their influence for money, and this discourages many people with ethical sensitivities from seeking office at all. The check-kiting incidents and the campaign fund retirement bonuses in 1992 demonstrate that far too many of those elected to Congress have exactly the kind of ethical insensitivity that we need to avoid. As a consequence, most U.S. voters today have no real choice for state and federal legislative offices. We will never have a strong electoral system without being able to attract quality candidates, and we cannot attract quality candidates with this system of financing in place.

To most Americans, as we shall see later in this book, these campaign contributions are simply legalized bribery. In contrast, the contributors claim that they are buying access, not votes. But the public is not deceived when members of Congress fervently maintain they aren't influenced by the campaign money they receive. The public simply calls that lying. Senator Bob Dole (R-Kans.), who received $1.6 million from PACs for his 1992 campaign, explains the practical result of PAC funding:[40]

> When these political action committees give money, they expect something in return other than good government. It is making it difficult to legislate. We may reach a point where everybody is buying something with PAC money. We cannot get anything done.[41]

In short, we have created a system of campaign finance in which all incumbents are able to raise enormous amounts of money at will. Yet, at the same time, the PAC funding process systematically underfinances all but a select few challengers. As a direct result, our two-party system is essentially a system of two parties that control one-party districts to the virtual exclusion of the other party.[42] If we are going to do anything to reinvigorate our political system, addressing this disparity must be a primary concern. The issue comes down to whether or not we can realistically expect the parties in power to do anything about it beyond making symbolic gestures.

Will the New Members Change Anything? No!

Many commentators have predicted that the new class of House members will be a revitalizing force for reform in the legislature. As far as campaign finance goes, however, the Class of 1992 has already shown that they are savvy politicians who know how to use special interest money to their advantage. The PACs quickly funneled $1.2 million in contributions to the freshmen in the months following the election. Says Frank Sorauf, a political scientist at the University of Minnesota, "They [PACs] rush to establish contact, access, whatever, as soon as the election is over.[43]

The current federal campaign finance laws actually facilitate the ability of PACs and special interest groups to influence freshmen congressmen. Under the current rules, the money that is given to freshmen is not counted against the legal contribution limits for the current election cycle if the money is used to retire debt left over from the previous campaign. What this means is a PAC can contribute $5,000 in the summer of 1993, which is counted against the 1992 campaign spending limits, and then write another $5,000 check for the 1994 campaign. This certainly would seem to violate the spirit of the $5,000 PAC contribution limit. Freshmen legislators who win, therefore, can raise a fortune to retire debt acquired during the past campaign, and the PACs are happy to provide the bailout to a winner who now is a sure bet to have influence. In addition, this rule enabling PACs to contribute to a campaign that is already over is one of the great disincentives for a PAC to support challengers and long-shot candidates. After all, it makes it in the PAC's best interest to wait and see how the election turns out before giving a challenging candidate money.[44]

The States: Atrophied Democracy

As bad as the federal congressional election system is, it looks like a thriving democracy when compared to the pathetic condition of our state politics. The two-party system at the state level should be declared dead and taken off to the morgue. Although the problem of declining competition and the influence of money in elections has been dealt with, documented, and discussed at the national level, the state electoral systems have received relatively little scrutiny. We were interested to see the extent to which the electoral system had failed at the state level. We decided to focus on three states and compare levels of electoral competition and the sources of money in state elections. What we found was that it was exceedingly difficult to find anything out.[45] We were shunted from bureaucrat to bureaucrat, sent on wild goose chases, and told that they didn't keep track of things like election results! The worst was New York, which could spend $60 billion in taxpayer money on who knows what, but could not be bothered to computerize their election board's file system. We got practically nothing from them on the influence of money in state elections.

We purposely chose large, demographically diverse states—Illinois, California, and New York. After all, if any real, living two-party systems are to be found, they should be in states large enough to contain enough natural political enemies to foster some healthy competition. Unfortunately, this was not to be the case.

Illinois

On the surface, Illinois would appear to be a prime example of a healthy two-party system. In 1990, in the statewide election for governor, the winner carried the state by only three points. Statewide, the two parties spent roughly the same amount, with the Republicans spending a total of $30.3 million and the Democrats spending $27.6 million.[46] However, once the analysis delves into the state legislative races, a familiar scene appears—complete domination by the incumbents (see Table 4).

One result of the financial inequities is the creation of a political system that is invulnerable to electoral challenge. Rather than being a series of districts where two parties compete to choose a representative and people have at least a semblance of choice, the state is simply a series of districts where one candidate dominates to the exclusion of any challenge. In 1990, in only nine races out of 138 separate elections did the winner win by less than ten percentage points. In total, 93 per-

Table 4 **Total Expenditures in Illinois Incumbent Legislative Races**

Institution	Incumbents	Challengers
General Assembly	$8,109,958	$2,026,757
Senate	1,089,602	306,456
Representatives	5,145,732	959,810

Adapted from data collected by the Illinois State Board of Elections.

cent of the state legislative races were landslides, and 56 of them were unopposed. Most of the money challengers did receive was concentrated in a few select races.

The following histogram, Chart 6, displays the distribution of the Democratic vote. If a two-party system is competitive, the majority of the races should be clustered around the center of the graph in the "competitive range." A race is considered competitive if the Democrats received between 45 and 55 percent of the vote, meaning that the distance between the winner and loser in a two-person race was within ten percentage points. The bimodal distributions, used originally in David Mayhew's work to display the "vanishing marginals" at the national level, indicate that few seats at the state level are even slightly competitive.[47] As academics like Morris Fiorina and David Mayhew have noted, a democracy can only express shifting public sentiment through the existence of marginal districts where legislators face a reasonable chance of defeat. In 1990, these "marginal districts" were completely absent and legislators were immune to shifts in opinion.

The chart also demonstrates the static level of party competition. The distribution of safe seats after the redistricting in 1992 is almost identical to what it was in 1982. The percentage of safe Republican seats had barely shifted in a decade. The Democrats seem to see a small percentage of their seats shift from safe to competitive, just after redistricting. The problem with redistricting is that a district drawn with a 65/35 split in two-party registration creates the statism that the graph demonstrates. Opposing party candidates are encouraged by the uncertainty of redistricting to challenge the majority party. However, once the minority party receives only 35 percent of the vote, there is little motivation to challenge that party until the next census redistricting. This is democracy at the margins and voter choice is the loser.

In 1992, like 1982, the combination of serious redistricting and voter discontent led to a general increase in the competitiveness of state legislative races. The truth is that having over 20 percent of the races at least somewhat competitive is, in all fairness, pretty good by today's standards. Yet this is an illusion of a redistricting year. Although the number of unopposed Republicans dropped considerably, the two-party system in Illinois is essentially dominated by Republican candidates who win in landslides and Democratic candidates who win with little opposition. As time goes on, the bimodal distribution so evident in the 1990 elections will reappear and the system will atrophy again.

California

California can practically be considered a country in itself. With the largest population in the country and an extremely diverse population,

Chart 6   **Two-Party Competition in Illinois (1982–1992)**

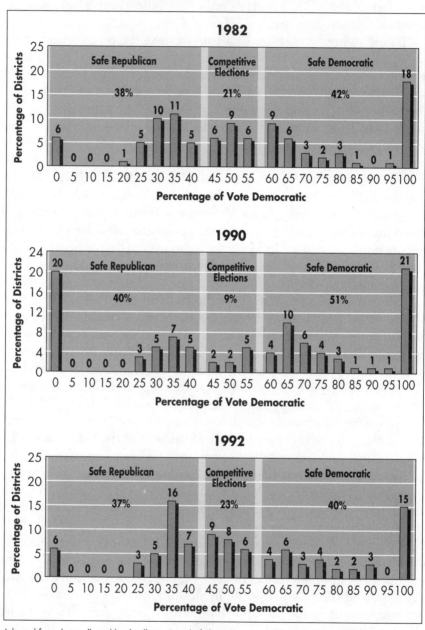

Adapted from data collected by the Illinois Board of Elections.

a two-party system should be thriving there. In California, politics means money—and lots of it. Like its real estate, California politics is extremely expensive. Races for mere state assembly seats can cost in the millions of dollars. The nature of the two-party system in California, however, is quite different from Illinois. In California, democracy exists largely at the margins—but at the margins, the parties put up one heck of a fight.

Table 5 summarizes the contributions during the last three weeks of the 1992 campaign in all races involving incumbents. The contributions during the last three weeks are key because they can make or break a campaign. Overall, the balance between incumbents and challengers is unusually fair. The challengers received about 31 percent of all the money contributed in races where there was an incumbent. But this analysis masks the reality that the overwhelming majority of this money was concentrated in seven select races. In the remaining races, the national pattern of meaningless challengers reemerges. In these 67 races, the incumbents received $6.50 for each dollar received by a challenger. *In 45 of these 77 races, the challenger did not receive one dollar in contributions during the final three weeks.* How do voters have an authentic electoral choice if the challengers have little or no ability to make themselves and their views known in the community? Political communication is not free.[48]

The two political parties poured money into the open seats and the few monetarily competitive incumbent races. During the last three weeks of the campaign, the two parties contributed almost $4.4 million to their candidates. In the midst of this wealth, why did 45 races either have no challenger or have a challenger who went without receiving even one dollar during the final three weeks of the campaign? The political parties and the PACs engage in strategic campaigning, concentrating their resources on the few seats in which they assume they have a chance. With the majority of less-competitive seats, they make the strategic decision to ignore the possibility of choice for the voters of these districts. Thus, the districts are made "safe" by the collective decision that they cannot easily be won. Again, it is democracy at the margins. And in 1992, a year in which Californians were angry at the depressed economy, encouraged by major redistricting, and outraged at the prolonged dead-

Table 5   **Total Contributions in California Incumbent Legislative Races (October 18–November 3, 1992)**

	Incumbents	Challengers
All races	$4,967,026	$2,274,876
Top 7 challengers	1,801,784	1,787,909
Remaining 67 races	3,165,242	486,967

Adapted from data collected by the California Secretary of State.

lock in the budgetary process that lasted until nearly August, the 1992 election remained almost completely without serious political choice for the voters. Despite the money that flowed to some challengers, incumbents are all but unbeatable in California:

- In 1992, only 1 out of 77 state legislative incumbents was defeated for a reelection rate of 98.7 percent.
- In 1990, only 5 out of 91 incumbents were defeated for a reelection rate of 94.7 percent.

The campaign of the majority leader, the powerful Willie Brown, Jr. (D) is a case study of what is wrong with the Californian system in particular, and party systems in general. Here an incumbent Speaker of the Assembly runs the state assembly like a herder over his flock. With the tremendous influence he wields, it is no surprise that every imaginable special interest wants to give him money, and that the amounts are staggering. Running against a Republican who raised a paltry $1,197 in the first half of 1992, Brown raised $1,874,297 and spent $924,546 before the general election even got underway. There was no chance that Brown was going to lose, and in the end his token challenger received 19 percent of the vote. Yet in the last three weeks of the campaign, despite the fact that he had no real competition, Brown received $314,100. With no legitimate political need for these funds, this is bribery—pure and simple. If it was not so offensive politically, it would be funny. Yet those who are in power at every level of government contend that the money doesn't matter; they are above being influenced by such unimportant sums of money. With both parties taking part in the charade, there is nobody to dissent and tell the real story to the voters. Again, the voter is the loser. Table 6 represents just a sample of the contributions that poured in to Brown during the final days of his campaign.

The past two California statewide elections display trends similar to that of Illinois—a political party system consisting of two parties competing in one-party districts. One difference, however, was the redistricting in 1992, which did not cause the margin of victory for the candidates of either party to decrease. Out of the 99 elections in which there was at least one major party candidate, only 15 races were decided by less than ten points in 1990 and only 12 were decided by less than ten points in 1992. This lack of competition is not much of a surprise given what we know about the ability of incumbents to protect themselves. What is disturbing, however, is the fact that in 1992 there were 33 open seats out of 100 races, compared to only 9 open seats in

Table 6   **Late Contributions Over $10,000 to Willie Brown, Jr. (October 18–November 3, 1992)**

Contributor	Amount
RJR Reynolds Tobacco Co.	$25,000
CA Society of Certified Public Accountants	13,000
Atlantic Richfield Company	12,000
CA Manufacturers Association	12,000
Food 4 Less Supermarkets Inc.	12,000
Southern Pacific Transportation Co.	12,000
CA Teachers Association	10,000
Continental Medical Systems	10,000
Healthsouth Rehabilitation Corp.	10,000
Integrated Health Services	10,000
Girardi and Keese	10,000
International Union of Operating Engineers Local	10,000

Adapted from data collected by the California Secretary of State, January 1993.

1990. Usually, open seats are the battlegrounds of two-party politics because no candidate enjoys the natural incumbency advantage, thereby increasing the uncertainty of the outcome. Yet despite the large increase in open seats between 1990 and 1992, there was little increase in competitiveness. The fact that an increase of 27 open seats did not increase the overall two-party competition indicates that the culprit must lie beyond just incumbent advantage. There was no state in the nation with more discontented voters than California, but the system is set up to create one-sided victories.

Chart 7 presents the distribution of the winning margins in elections for the California Senate and Assembly. For California, we had to use a slightly different method for calculating the distributions than we used for Illinois. There are a large number of fringe- or single-issue third-party candidacies in California, usually Libertarian or Peace and Freedom candidates. These candidates can garner anywhere from 5 to 15 percent of the vote. In Illinois, almost all the races are two-party races and there are no official statewide third parties. Therefore, simply charting the distributions of the Democratic vote in California, as we did for Illinois, is not always indicative of the margin of victory. For example, in a three-person race, a Democratic candidate could win with 50 percent

Chart 7   **Two-Party Competition in California Senate and Assembly (1990 and 1992)**

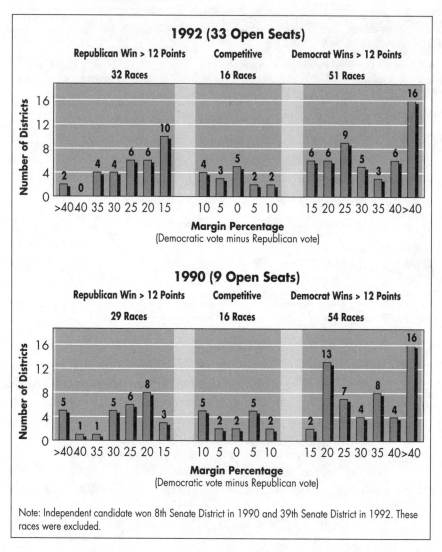

Note: Independent candidate won 8th Senate District in 1990 and 39th Senate District in 1992. These races were excluded.

of the vote, but still win by 10 percentage points if there was a third candidate in the race who received 10 percent of the vote, leaving 40 percent for the Republican candidate. Therefore, if the analysis concentrates only on the Democratic vote, this winning margin would be misrepresented. In order to account for this, we have calculated the percentage of the vote that was Republican and subtracted from the Democratic vote to find the margin. As a result, regardless of third-party voting, the competitiveness of the race is still measured equally in all races.

In both years, only 16 seats were competitive within 12.5 points, by the generous standard we have chosen to use, with incumbent reelection rates of 94 percent or greater in each of the years. If incumbents cannot be defeated in California, despite the worst public opinion ratings for governor and legislature in the history of the Field Poll, then a democratic mechanism for allowing public sentiment to effect public policy no longer exists.

New York State

In New York, state-level incumbents are almost never defeated, and it is considered a major event when just two seats change hands in either the Senate or the assembly. According to the *New York Times Magazine*, in September of 1992, 147 of the 190 incumbents running for reelection were uncontested in their primaries.[49] In many cases, there would have been challenges, but the incumbents are extremely adept at using the arcane New York campaign laws to force opponents off the ballot. As a result, the entire legislature is absolutely immune to electoral challenges. In New York, the state legislature has been hopelessly gridlocked, as for more than 20 years the Republicans have held the state Senate while the Democrats have held the assembly.

In the 1990 census redistricting of legislative boundaries, the Republicans drew the electoral map for Senate districts and the Democrats controlled the shape of assembly districts, perpetuating a system that is all but written in stone. *The result: Despite the strong anti-incumbency sentiment that existed in 1992, just one incumbent lost his bid for reelection out of the state's 190 incumbent lawmakers (excluding two incumbents who were forced to run against other incumbents).* This represents a reelection rate of 99 percent. The following tables capture the hopelessness of New York State politics.

Table 7 shows that in a state where only 32 percent of the voters are registered Republicans, the party has somehow drawn 27 ironclad, unbeatable Republican districts in the state Senate, meaning that they must win only 4 of the remaining 33 to maintain a majority. Additionally, because the state is strongly Democratic by registration, the Democrats have exerted even more control over the districts in the assembly. They have crafted 79 seats where, in 1992, they won by greater than 20 points. *These seats alone guarantee the Democratic party a majority* in the 150-seat body no matter what the party does or how much the public wants to throw it out. There is simply no way to overcome districts as one-sided as these. Even the most blatant apologist for one-party domination must admit that this situation is entirely unfair to the principles of democracy and voters' right to competitive choices.

Table 7   **New York State Legislative Races (1992)**

State Senate: Party and Margin of Victory	Number of Races
Republican wins—Greater than 20 points	27
Republican wins—10 to 20 points	6
Competitive—Margin less than 10 points	2
Democrat wins—10 to 20 points	1
Democrat wins—Greater than 20 points	24

State Assembly: Party and Margin of Victory	Number of Races
Republican wins—Greater than 20 points	41
Republican wins—10 to 20 points	3
Competitive—Margin less than 10 points	12
Democrat wins—10 to 20 points	14
Democrat wins—Greater than 20 points	79

Note: Excludes 57th District where there was no major-party candidate.

To make the situation more pathetic, the majority leader of the Senate, Ralph Marino (R), tried to rationalize the outcome as evidence that voters actually prefer divided government.[50] In New York State, the nearly $60-billion budget in 1993 is largely determined by less than five people, including the governor, and the only way these five seem to leave office is through a lucrative retirement or an occasional indictment. As a result of this control by the few, the state budget has grown at more than twice the rate of inflation since 1980, even as the population of the state is shrinking.

Texas

We were going to complete a similar analysis with Texas, but a cursory glance at the data indicated that an in-depth analysis was not needed. The lack of competition in the state elections was almost laughable. In 1992, 111 out of 181 seats for state senator and representative were unopposed by major party candidates. Only the Libertarians seemed to want to challenge the party in power. With this kind of odds, why bother to hold elections at all?

Recapturing a Captured Democracy

As we have shown, money and power now completely rule the political marketplace, real political choice has died, and perhaps democracy has died along with it. We are ruled by a tyranny more dangerous than a dictatorship. It is a tyranny of the velvet glove, of the sweet and meaningless promise, of the corruption of honesty and candor, of the favor delivered to a grateful constituent. It is a tyranny that spends a fortune each year to persuade us that its intent is benign, all the while stealing our future and our children's future in the process. We, all of us, have permitted ourselves to be lulled into complacency while our own officeholders accomplish what communism and fascism failed to achieve. Without a gun being fired, the politicians have almost entirely eliminated democratic choice in American state and national elections. What our ancestors fought and died for, this generation of Americans has given away of its own volition—without visable outrage and without revolt.

All the trends and institutional factors described in this chapter have attributes in common. Primarily, they enhance the ability of incumbents to ensure their own reelection. But perhaps more significantly, these factors have a chilling effect on the motivation of every potential electoral challenger. If a potential challenger knows that an incumbent has enormous fund-raising capability, fundamental communication advantages, and a district that is drawn overwhelmingly in the incumbent's favor, there will be no challenge except under extraordinary circumstances.

If we wish to recapture our democratic institutions, *we must restore the competitiveness of elections*. If we accept this tenet, then the logical question is, how can we restore competitiveness? What will break the political monopoly held by incumbents at both the national and the state level? There are many people who think that the needed competitiveness can be restored by procedural changes that will emerge from the current Congress—a little change in finance laws, restricting PAC money, tinkering with the personal staff expenditures, and others.

At the same time, we must realize that reforms such as these usually have unintended consequences and rarely achieve the goals for which they are designed. These legislative proposals are not really the product of reformers, but they will be designed by people who wish to avoid the full impact of the rules. Moreover, in the present context, they will be designed by Democrats who will work hard to convince us that the laws they might reform are as fair to the Republicans as they are to themselves. This is not to say that procedural reforms cannot have beneficial consequences. They certainly can, and it is worth pursuing the specific reforms we mention. But we must realistically ask ourselves whether we can expect those who benefit from the current hegemony of power to give up that power. That is not a likely scenario, and nothing less would achieve the needed result.

What are we, as voters and citizens, left with? What are the fundamental forces that drive the outcomes of public policy? How does the average citizen fit into this system? If the democratic citizen is no longer a political force of any consequence, how does that voter regain a place in the system? These are the central issues, and ones we will deal with in detail throughout this book.

However, there is a more pressing question. If the vast majority of legislators are funded primarily by special interests that seek narrow policy goals, and if the public can no longer simply throw the bums out, then what drives policy outcomes in America? In other words, what are the practical effects of the loss of political choice?

═ 3 ═

A Process That Can't Say "No"

A government which robs Peter to pay Paul can always depend on the support of Paul.

—George Bernard Shaw

The Pyramid of Fiscal Pain

The most damaging consequence of the erosion of the electoral power of the average citizen is that in policy after policy, the American political system fails to cope with a whole series of critical problems which threaten our future. These problems—the budget deficit, health care costs, education, the trade deficit, urban violence, etc.—are so destructive that they have already measurably reduced future generations' prosperity, opportunities, and standards of living. The great travesty is that this failure occurs even when there is broad public agreement both on the importance of the problem and on the appropriate solutions. If this circumstance continues unabated, our children will inherit a world increasingly dominated by violence, despair, hopelessness, and diminished economic possibilities.

The essence of the problem is that today in America we are faced with a political system where officeholders find it extremely difficult, and most times impossible, to say "no" to the large, highly organized, and well-financed coalitions that pursue their own financial self-interest through the political structure. These infamous organizations, which we will describe as "complexes," depend upon the revenue stream from the government in a particular area of policy. A complex includes those who benefit directly and indirectly from the government revenue, e.g., businesses, unions, bureaucrats, and associations. And while they may occasionally compete on some issue of policy, they are united as a group by the desire to protect and expand the federal revenue stream that sustains them. They have evolved in virtually every area of policy, but they are especially prevalent where the government either provides consistent, long-term revenue or exercises regulatory control that can inflict substantial costs or provide substantial benefits to the organizations and groups that are part of the complex.

Pluralism Gone Wrong

American democratic theory suggests that there should be nothing wrong with this interest-group process. In fact, political theorists in America have long applauded the virtue of organizational interests and diversity. An entire school of thought evolved in political theory around the idea of pluralism, whereby significant benefits are brought to the political system through the theorized tendency of interest groups to compete vigorously with each other. In a perfect pluralistic system, the demands of each group would always be balanced by the demands of every other group. If ten individuals get together, for example, and they each want and need part of $1,000 worth of services or goods held in common by the group, then such a balance would generally have to occur. In this ideal (and highly unrealistic) system, the ten participants could agree to increase the $1,000 to something more, but they could do so only by persuading themselves as contributors (taxpayers) to ante up the money. This kind of system would be in balance, and expenditures by the group would undoubtedly equal the taxes they imposed on themselves.

According to the theory, both Congress and the president are supposed to balance respective demands on the government, trading one interest against another in an effort to reconcile demands in a way that would result in a balanced budget. In practice, of course, as Americans know well, this is simply not the way it works. Instead, we have created a system of government where the vast majority of interests have been able to dominate a small policy area, building political networks to protect their programs against any attempt to control or reduce funding. The agricultural complex, for example, dominates agricultural policy by controlling the agricultural committees in the House and Senate.

The pluralism that seemed so attractive in theory has yielded to a distinctly ineffective reality precisely because the competition among various interests has never materialized. Instead, the current political system seeks to satisfy the maximum number of group claims, while rendering government impotent to undertake effective and coordinated action. The effect of this form of interest-group politics was aptly articulated by Professor Theodore J. Lowi in his book, *The End of Liberalism:*

> Interest-group liberalism possesses the mentality of a world-univer-salized ticket-fixing. Destroy privilege by universalizing it. Reduce conflict by yielding to it. Redistribute power by the maxim of each according to his claim. Purchase support for the regime by reserving an official place for every major structure of power.
>
> In the process, liberalism has promoted concentration of demo-cratic authority but deconcentration of democratic power.[1]

In other words, by attempting to satisfy the maximum number of group claims, power is so decentralized that by giving all groups some power, no one has any real power to do anything. In this system, the democratic authority bestowed on the legislators by the polity is sim-ply parceled out among the various groups who seek to advance their own ends in the system. Is it any wonder that in the 1993 budget nego-tiations, not one single program was completely eliminated? In the end, the elected officials can no longer tame the monsters they have created.

As a result, rather than compete for federal funds, almost every interest becomes insulated from competition, leading inexorably to a budget process where the pressure to spend excessively is overwhelm-ing. The establishment of a priority of claims, which is vital to rational public administration, never occurs. The entire political system is "biased" in favor of greater and greater expenditures. Our system, in fact, has developed what might be described as an "addiction" to over-spending. *By overspending, we don't mean "spending that is simply more than advisable," but rather spending that the public would never authorize if legislators were forced to take the issue to a direct vote of the people.*[2]

This definition of the term "overspending" is intended to be nar-row and to highlight the role of voter consent. Polls on this subject pro-vide conflicting information. On the one hand, they show that the pub-lic would actually *increase* spending in some areas of policy, while significantly restricting spending in others. On the other hand, how-ever, virtually every significant poll indicates that the public would vote for lower levels of spending, as opposed to increased taxes. In a poll we conducted for United We Stand, America, in April 1993, for example, the voters indicated overwhelmingly that they would balance the budget with greater spending cuts as opposed to tax increases. When asked whether to cut spending, increase taxes, or do both, 53 percent choose spending cuts, 38 percent wanted both, and 4 percent chose tax increases only. Overall, 60 percent wanted $2.00 of spending cuts for every $1.00 of tax increases, compared with 27 percent who wanted a $1.00 to $1.00 ratio, and 5 percent who wanted only tax increases. Changing these questions might change the results somewhat, but there is little doubt that the public is increasingly antagonistic toward spending, and would put a tight rein on the officeholders if they could.

The fact is that the American political process has developed a persistent tendency to expand government expenditures despite persistent majorities among the general public who oppose this expansion. This tendency operates at every level of government, not just federal. The budget of New York State, for example, has expanded at more than twice the rate of inflation nearly every year for the past decade, despite a static population and a public angry over excessive taxation and spending. The tendency persists in the face of the most massive peacetime deficits ever faced in American history, and it operates despite repeated attempts in Congress to control it through legal restraints, like Gramm-Rudman-Hollings budget process in the 1980s and the Congressional Budget Act of 1974. Even most of the interest-group leaders who are part of this process agree that the resulting overspending, with massive deficits, is dangerous to our future and must be controlled.

The hope that this tendency will be reversed is voiced with every change of administration in Washington, D.C., and the state capitals. Despite such optimism, the tendency to spend excessively and imprudently continues. The primary difference in Republicans and Democrats is not in how much they spend, but in where the money is allocated. Republicans favor the defense complex while Democrats favor entitlements and public employees.

The problem of deficits is larger than the individual legislators or the specific budgetary processes in which they operate. The failed budget reforms of the 1970s and 1980s are a testament to that. Uncontrollable government expenditures are the outgrowth of the way the political system operates, and therefore demand a political response. We will argue that the only force capable of fundamentally altering the political environment is a political party, but not a party whose candidates depend on PAC financing. *The political party that can change this process is a party whose candidates are financed by their own members.*

At the time of this writing, the Clinton budget, which passed by the narrowest of margins, proposes to deal with *the rate at which the deficit escalates, but not with the fact or cause of the deficit itself.* The plan claims a $496 billion deficit reduction effort, and supposedly balances tax increases and spending reductions at approximately a one-to-one ratio, with about $250 billion of both. Obviously, we cannot say for certain that this program will be a failure. However, 30 years of prior experience has to count for something, and experience leads us to believe that Clinton's program will prove just as unsuccessful in taming the budget as very similar budgets implemented in the past. For example, as with the 1990 Bush deficit reduction plan, the tax increases are imposed immediately—in fact, retroactively to the beginning of 1993, while according to the *Washington Post*, fully 60 percent of the total spending reductions are not scheduled to take effect until 1997 and 1998,[3] allowing future Congresses plenty of time to renege on such promises as they did following reforms in 1986 and 1990. To make matters worse, billions of dollars worth of projected savings depend on the assumption that Congress won't renew popular tax breaks, like those for research and for hiring disadvantaged workers, when they are due to expire over the next few years. Most likely, these tax breaks will be renewed, just as they have been in the past. Most importantly, the Clinton plan lacks the tough controls necessary to stem growth of the entitlement programs, which are the largest and fastest-growing portion of the federal budget.[4] Unless future Congresses are more willing to withstand the political pressure caused by the cuts, the result will be a continuing trend of larger deficits.

What is perhaps more telling is the spending that was left in the budget. Despite the cries of woe from Congress, the "pork"-ladened agricultural subsidies that were cut $13 billion in 1990 were cut just $3 billion in 1993, meaning that the mohair and honey producers will still be paid up to $50,000 apiece in annual direct government subsidies. Other interesting expenditures include:

- $1.2 billion in economic assistance to pay counties in the Pacific Northwest affected by legislation protecting the spotted owl.[5]
- $500,000 to fund exhibits in the Ice Age National Scientific Reserve in Wisconsin.
- $9 million to the National Textile Center.
- $2.5 million for a parking garage in Iowa.
- $192,000 for the Beluga Whale Committee.[6]

In reality, total spending will actually rise by a minimum of 5 percent in 1994, including reductions in defense, and total spending is actually *planned* to increase in every year of the budget at a rate nearly two times greater than inflation, even with continued declines in defense spending. This is Congress's idea of an austerity budget and vigorous self-control. If this program works perfectly, projected deficits will reach a low point of approximately $210 billion in the fourth year of the budget, when they will begin a sharp upward trend again, and the total debt will rise by approximately $1.1 trillion over the course of the plan.[7] Most likely, however, Congress will increase spending in a wide variety of areas outside of the budget and actual deficits will be considerably higher.

In the end, there was evidence that the public was willing to accept more drastic measures to reduce the deficit, especially in spending cuts. In February of 1993, President Clinton had a substantial amount of political capital to expend. The public was ready and willing to accept major tax increases and policy upheavals. Indeed, with 12 years of relative inaction on the domestic side, it was a relief for many Americans just to hear a president talk about the deficit and our domestic problems in a forthright way. Moreover, the polls found that the public was willing to support tax increases, if those increases were matched by two to three dollars of spending cuts for every dollar of tax increase. After the budget's passage, however, the polls found that a majority of Americans were already skeptical, especially about the spending cuts. In an August 1993 *USA Today*/CNN Poll, 56 percent said the budget would not reduce the deficit, 58 percent said that it did not control spending, and 55 percent indicated that it will not improve the economy.

So the question becomes this: *If nearly everyone of importance in American politics, Republicans and Democrats alike, agree that continued deficits are dangerous and unacceptable, why is it that these same people can do nothing to limit or stop the problem?* This is the crux of the issue. The problem is *not* corrupt politicians or some general decline in public morality. As we have stated earlier, American politics is not consumed with evil or immoral people. The problem is also neither the sole product of evil intent on the part of the special interests and their lobbyists, nor the result of having the Republicans or Democrats run the government. The responsibility for excessive spending, and massive deficits, belongs about equally to both parties, despite the fact that each party tries to present itself as the party of fiscal prudence. Overspending has persisted, in various levels of intensity, for more than three decades regardless of who is in power, although the two parties differ on which interests they've supported the most. The problem is that we have created a system that cannot control itself, despite repeated attempts to do so. This simple fact means that the political process is broken. Time and time again, well-intentioned and qualified candidates run for Congress and the state legislatures planning to promote budget reform, only to find their intentions subverted by the needs of election financing and the pressures to conform to the existing way of conducting business in the legislative process.

To be fair, we will in a moment argue that the structural failure to which we refer leads as well to the systematic "undersupply" of certain types of public policy. In other words, the government provides far less of the policy or service than the public would grant, if they were allowed a part of the decision. Overspending (oversupply) and under-supply are both reflections of a system that is failing to reflect the widely held preferences of the public at large.

An Example: The Politics of Federal and State Pensions

One example of how groups can convert political power into govern-mental benefits that are not paid for by current tax revenue can be seen in the growth of federal employee pension programs. By any standard, the federal and state pension programs are far and away more lucrative than anything found in the private sector. As you might expect, public employees are among the most powerfully organized groups in Amer-ica, contributing tens of millions of dollars to fund political campaigns and providing one of the largest and most effective sources of workers for elections. Therefore, it is not surprising that the pension programs for public employees represent one of the most expensive systems for paying off a powerful lobby on record. Private pension systems are required by the tough Employment Retirement Income Security Act to put aside funds to cover the cost of future pensions during the years in which the employee works. Yet the state and federal government fail to practice what they preach by exempting themselves from the require-ments they impose on private employers. All of this is done in as pri-vate a way as possible, and the public is largely ignorant of the full effect of these decisions.

The reason (though they do not say so) that officeholders exempt their own employees is simple; they are thereby able to give overly gen-erous pension and future health benefits to a powerful and very large interest group without the necessity of asking the taxpayers for an immediate tax increase to pay for those benefits. In short, they are able to disperse accountability for their actions by passing the cost onto future generations. To make matters worse, by indexing pensions to inflation, congressmen can pay off federal employees, while giving the appearance that they are saving money. Budget expert Allen Schick explains how this is done:

> The issue facing politicians is quite different when pensions are adjusted by discretionary action than when they are automatically indexed to price changes. If inflation were running at four percent a year, a discretionary adjustment of two percent might be recorded as an increase, but if pensions had been indexed, the same two percent would be scored as a cutback.[8]

If public officials applied the same rules to themselves on pensions that they require of private employers, they would be forced to tell us

Chart 1 **Federal Civil Service Retirement Plan Funding (1970–1990)**

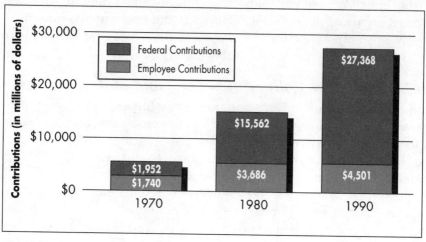

Adapted from data collected by *The Statistical Abstract of the United States, 1992*.

what they are really doing, what it will really cost, and what financing those measures require here and now from the taxpayers. Instead, they prefer to do the unthinkable: create a fiscal catastrophe for future generations rather than behave responsibly themselves today. Neither side, Republican or Democrat, desires an outright confrontation with the most powerful unions in most states.

The pension payoff is not illegal, but it is unethical and anti-democratic. The problem is that no one is watching or thinking about the consequences. Consider the ratio of federal civil service employee contributions to their pension fund compared to the amount the federal government contributes. In 1970, for every $1 the employee put into the fund, the federal government put in about the same amount. By 1990, however, the government was putting in over $6 for every $1 the employees put in the pension fund (see Chart 1). There is no private fund that matches this level of investment.

How We Emptied the Federal Purse

The road to hell is paved with good intentions.

—George Bernard Shaw

The breakdown and failure of our current political structure results from a series of steps along the way, and each step is the product of good intentions. The problem with government, and perhaps life itself, is that we cannot easily know all of the consequences of our actions. Nowhere is this more true than the story of how we permitted interest groups in America to get completely out of hand.

Step One: John Maynard Keynes and the Deficit

John Maynard Keynes is unquestionably one of the greatest of all economists, who did his most important work during the first half of the twentieth century. Until the intellectual revolution ignited by Keynes, Americans of nearly every walk of life and political persuasion generally believed that deficit spending was dangerous, immoral, and downright un-American. James Payne describes the mindset:

> Even as late as the 1940s for example, members of the House Appropriations Committee felt their duty was "constantly and courageously" to protect the Federal Treasury against thousands of appeals and imperative demands for unnecessary, unwise, and excessive expenditures.[9]

Even our politicians in the state capitals shared this belief, and 41 of the 50 state constitutions require balanced budgets because of this.[10]

This form of fiscal conservatism was the dominant American ideology from before the Revolution to the beginning of the Great Depression. Fiscal and monetary conservatism have been debated repeatedly over the course of American history, with the issue reaching a distinct peak in the arguments over the gold standard and the free coinage of silver promoted by the Populists during the last three decades of the nineteenth century. But despite various impassioned pleas for more liberal policies, fiscal conservatism was the basic principle on which the American economy prospered. American money was backed by gold, and the money supply was basically controlled by the growth of the supply of gold, which conveniently grew by about three percent a year for most of our history. This system was enormously successful, promoting increasing standards of living and economic growth, and providing additional support for the twin beliefs that governments were not supposed to spend more than they raised in taxes, and less government was far better than more government in most instances.

The temptation to spend public money was not an invention of the modern Democrats, as many Republicans would have us believe. President Calvin Coolidge stated flatly that "nothing is easier than spending public money. It does not appear to belong to anybody. The temptation is overwhelming to bestow it on somebody."[11] Keynesian economics and the Great Depression are the true sources of the change in our belief systems in regard to government spending and deficits.

Keynes argued persuasively that government spending was a fiscal tool that could be used to promote economic growth and expansion and to avoid the sharp swings in the natural business cycles. Ironically, when Franklin Roosevelt ran for the presidency in 1932, he ran as a fiscal conservative, promising to reduce the deficit and balance the budget, which was most certainly not a Keynesian approach to public policy. The economic collapse in 1932 and 1933 was so severe, however, that Roosevelt became a Keynesian by necessity, promoting greater government spending out of a desperate need to create jobs and the appearance of government action. Roosevelt's programs were somewhat successful, but the real proof of the Keynesian approach to fiscal policy was produced by the enormous economic success of the rearming of Germany, Europe, and the United States for war. The rearming for war ended the worldwide Depression and allowed the government to justify major tax increases, driving government growth. The success of the fiscal stimulus made Keynesians and New Dealers out of nearly everyone and, as Allen Schick points out, this fundamentally changed the dynamics of the budget process:

> The New Deal did more than merely enlarge the federal government. It also changed public attitudes toward public expenditure and paved the way for more active and expansive policies. Government now was expected to be much more than a caretaker and watchman. It would provide vital benefits to the American people. Through public expenditure, homes would be built, land reclaimed, personal income cushioned against economic and other shocks, health care improved.[12]

In addition to addressing needs during serious economic crises, Keynesian theory provided the complementary intellectual justification that government could be used, like a finely tuned instrument, to both stimulate the economy when it wasn't performing to expectations and be a tool of social economic justice. With the acceptance of these two powerful moral and intellectual forces, both of which pushed for increased governmental expenditures, the manner in which we viewed government spending was changed forever.

In the election of 1936, responding to the contrast between an energetic president demanding government action and a fiscally conservative Republican, Alf Landon, the American electorate reinstated Roosevelt in one of the great electoral landslides of all time. In the process, Roosevelt forged the modern Democratic coalition. Young voters turned to the Democratic Party in droves. African-Americans, Jews, and Catholics had begun to shift to the Democratic Party in the late 1920s, but the 1936 election made their move into the Democratic coalition complete. Since then, at the congressional level, the Democratic Party has controlled the

Senate for 48 out of 56 years and the House of Representatives for 52 out of 56 years. This powerful electoral coalition, which had long been converted to the ideological belief that government spending could be used both as a tool of social justice and as a means to stimulate the economy, maintained an iron grip on the newly enlarged and unprotected federal purse. With the moral imperative to control government spending removed, the growth of modern government ensued. Keynesian monetary philosophy converted more than Democrats, however. Even conservative Republican Richard Nixon was eventually converted, proclaiming, "Now I am a Keynesian" in 1971.[13]

Our purpose here is not to argue the virtues of small government versus big government; nor are we interested in a protracted liberal versus conservative debate. Instead, we are simply arguing that several fundamental premises or beliefs in American life have changed over the course of this century, and that these changes played a devastating role in the process of unbalancing the budgets in America and legitimizing interest-group claims for federal revenue.

During the past half-century, we have found nothing comparable to take the place of the control that the prior belief system exerted over our elected officeholders. As the failure of the 1974 budget reforms and the Gramm-Rudman Act in 1985 illustrate, written law designed with the expressed goal of controlling expenditures has certainly not been able to match its effectiveness. In fact, one of the central ironies in our political history is that the federal government produced balanced budgets with little trouble when there was no budget process to speak of, before World War II. Before then, the budget was simply the outcome of dozens of separate uncoordinated actions by congressional committees.[14] In contrast, today we have a highly professional and centralized system, with hundreds of economists in the OMB, CBO, GAO, and EOP, using powerful computers and mathematical models to balance the budget, and even with all this technical expertise, we can't seem to make the numbers add up.

Step 2: Eisenhower and the Growth of Complexes

In one of his last speeches, President Dwight D. Eisenhower offered his famous and remarkably prescient warning of things to come. His concern was that the massive newly created "military-industrial complex" would, through its simple size and breadth, exert an undue and inappropriate influence over public policy in America. Eisenhower, as the former commanding general of the allied forces, understood very well the enormous energies that could be focused politically by the massive peacetime military establishment. Until the Cold War, America had never had a large peacetime military, and although the army has always had some influence politically, that influence has historically played little role in most of the important aspects of American life. Certainly the members of Congress were unimpressed by the influence of the army prior to World War II, and they routinely spurned new military programs even when doing so appears, in hindsight, to have been very shortsighted.

Yet Eisenhower was sophisticated and knowledgeable enough to recognize the confluence of interests in defense spending: between the defense contractors and unions, who were motivated by jobs and profits; the military bureaucracies, who measured professional success in new weapons systems, bases, and personnel; and the congressmen and senators who contrived to use powerful positions in their institutions to obtain defense facilities, industries, and jobs in their home states and districts. As we mentioned earlier, the members of the armed services committees in both houses, not accidentally, are the recipients of billions of dollars in federal expenditures for their constituencies.

What Eisenhower failed to see, however, was that the very same process, although perhaps on a smaller scale, would evolve in virtually every major area of government activity and expenditures as domestic programs grew concurrently with peacetime military spending. In America today, we have any number of such complexes: welfare, health, agriculture, public education, private higher education, real estate, public employees, the space program, social security, Medicare, and many more. Each one of these complexes has, to varying degrees, the same objectives:

- To protect against any reduction in the flow of economic benefits from the government to the interests represented in the complex.
- To promote additional economic resources for those same interests.
- To secure a concentration of those economic benefits for states and districts of senators and members of Congress in strategic positions to help the interests in the complex.
- To promote, where feasible, regulations favorable to the interests in the complex.

Although Democrats and Republicans differ somewhat on which complexes they are most inclined to favor, there is more cross-party agreement on protecting each complex than there is disagreement. Each complex tends to follow the same procedures:

- The organized leaders of each complex claim to represent, usually without any accuracy, the whole population sharing the supposedly common interest.
- Organized coalitions are staffed and financially maintained in the state capitals and Washington, D.C.
- These coalitions include paid lobbyists and well-connected law firms, and these intermediaries provide much of the access to decision makers.
- There is a regular "circulation of elite" from the government to the private groups and back into the government again, and this includes many retired or defeated elected officials.
- The coalitions provide income to key members of Congress and the Senate through their ability to provide PAC funding for campaigns and direct support in the form of soft money for the political parties.
- The coalitions promote frequent and fervent communications between constituents and their representatives on issues of concern to the leaders of the complex.

Academic studies, most notably *Pork Barrel Politics*, by John Ferejohn, have documented how congressional funding for executive agencies and outside interest groups controlled by members of appropriations and oversight committees invariably benefits those same legislators.[15] Therefore, legislators who are directly responsible for governmental benefits have a tendency to receive the benefits of governmental expenditures, creating a vested interest in increasing those benefits. In other words, members of Congress can dole out taxpayer money in the manner that most benefits them electorally. While this may be obvious, there is an unfortunate corollary effect. As the benefits of a particular program are spread to a larger group, more members of Congress have a vested interest in expanding that program, making it increasingly hard to control the growth of the program. Thus, Medicare, Medicaid, and Social Security become politically untouchable.[16]

One visible result of the explosion of interest groups involved in the political process has been the complete domination of the information used to make policy decisions. Any decision-making process requires the best, most complete information if it is to be consistently successful. In his book, *The Culture of Spending*, James L. Payne documents that in the congressional persuasion process, the ratio of people who seek additional federal spending to those who oppose federal programs is "several thousand to one"—a fact that any observer of congressional politics already knows.[17] To illustrate this domination of the process, he analyzes the testimony of over 1,060 witnesses who were called to appear before congressional committees on a diverse number of policies and in many different types of hearings. His results are remarkable. He found that an amazing 95.7 percent of the witnesses called to testify *supported* the program involved, 3.7 percent gave the program neutral or mixed reviews, and a paltry 0.7 percent opposed spending on the program.[18] We must understand, therefore, that members of Congress are constantly subjected to rationales for continuing or increasing spending on each specific program, yet they rarely hear any strong individual arguments *against* the expenditure of public funds. As Payne describes:

> On almost every one of the hundreds of specific spending programs, however, persuasion is strikingly one-sided. Decision-makers in Washington find those favoring governmental programs everywhere, while opponents of specific programs are largely absent.[19]

On the side of increasing federal spending, there is a formidable list of people who are highly motivated to petition Congress vigorously for funds, and to argue just as vigorously against cutting funds:

1. *Program administrators:* The personal egos and careers of bureaucrats depend on their ability to make their organizations thrive and grow. The administrators will commonly pay to produce expensive studies "proving" the effectiveness of their programs, and will produce a litany of very selective statistics illustrating the effectiveness of the public investment. These analyses are rarely, if ever, challenged or even closely examined.
2. *State and local officials:* Any reduction in the federal funds will increase the pressure on the state governments to provide the corresponding reduction of services. It is therefore in their best interest to support actively the expansion of federal programs that provide them relief. To further their ends, they have formed institutions like the National Governors' Association to lobby the federal government and protect their interests.
3. *Lobbyists for private organizations:* These are often, of course, the ex-congressmen and federal administrators who have carved out a living by selling their knowledge of the policy process and their own personal connections within the policy network. They are the hired guns for every interest with a checkbook, from Japanese industry to rural bankers.
4. *Spokesmen for business:* They are obviously interested in seeking special tax breaks and subsidies, while being able to offer congressmen the prospect that supporting their industries will lead to economic expansion and job production.

As more evidence, Payne notes that the number of groups dedicated to reducing spending, nationally, is perhaps in the twenties. By comparison, the number of groups dedicated to increasing spending is in the thousands.[20]

Step 3: The Rise of PACs

One of the key elements in the success of the complexes is the ability of these coalitions to raise and dispense campaign funds through the PAC system. In *All the President's Men,* journalists Bob Woodward and Carl Bernstein tell of the shadowy informant, "Deep Throat," who constantly admonishes them to "follow the money" when seeking to break the story of the cover-up of the Watergate scandal. That admonition applies here as well. The 1972 presidential election of Richard Nixon was a case study in the corruption of the political process. High-placed government and party officials routinely strong-armed business leaders whose firms had a powerful interest in some aspect of government policy. Millions of dollars in campaign funds were raised in this manner, sometimes through very coercive threats and more often with the enthusiastic participation of people who thought their large campaign contributions were purchasing access and political influence.

The public reaction to the description of this process in the news accounts brought demands for reforms to the process of funding presidential and other campaigns, and this outcry led to the Campaign Reforms Acts of 1974 and 1976. One of the intentions behind these acts was to force a higher degree of public exposure of campaign contributions through an elaborate reporting system, ridding the process of the wealthy fat cats. Yet, the practical result of the campaign reforms was simply to replace one set of influence seekers with another—the Political Action Committees.

In politics, there are several different types of financial contributions. First, there is "family" money, contributed either by the candidate or the members of candidate's immediate family. This kind of money, of course, has few strings attached, but most people in America are not rich enough to fund more than a small portion of their own campaigns. The courts, however, have said that the First Amendment under the free speech doctrine prohibits Congress or the states from limiting the amount of money a candidate can spend out of his or her own resources.

The second kind of money is what we will call "issue money." Issue money is contributed to a campaign largely because of the candidate's stand on some issue or another and is given largely out of passion and conviction. Individuals or groups will give this type of money only to politicians who agree with them on issues. The most successful modern candidates at attracting large amounts of issue money include Senator Barry Goldwater (R-Ariz.) in 1964, Senator George McGovern (D-S. Dak.) in 1972, and Governor Ronald Reagan (R-Calif.) in 1980. All three had little difficulty raising millions of dollars from small contributors.

The third type of money is what we will call "interest money." The PAC funding system is organized around this type of money. Interest money is donated for purely practical reasons, and on the whole, it is not concentrated on candidates who are seen as potential losers or even long shots, whatever their convictions. Interest money is concentrated in the campaigns of the most powerful members of the committees of interest to the complex. It goes to Democrats and Republicans alike, but somewhat more overall will go to the dominant party in the legislature. It is particularly concentrated in the campaigns of sympathetic incumbents who are facing a reelection struggle in their districts, but large amounts of money are sometimes distributed fairly widely as a token gesture to incumbents who often don't need it. All in all, very little money goes to those who challenge incumbents, regardless of how sympathetic the challenger is to the interest.

The impact of these strategies that funnel money primarily to incumbents is to make them nearly invulnerable, a point we discussed at length in the previous chapter. In effect, the campaign reforms of the 1970s had the unintended effect of producing the PAC conduits through which the complexes dominate the legislative process. And the interest groups have proved extremely adept at maintaining their cash flow to the politicians, despite the attempts to control it. Campaign finance reform bills have been introduced into the House and Senate on at least ten separate occasions since the passage of the 1974 law, only to fail in the midst of partisan bickering. It is hardly coincidental that the explosion in PAC spending came at the same time government expenditures and deficits were ballooning in the late 1970s and early 1980s. Chart 2, which shows the rate at which these organizations were established, illustrates how quickly interests were able to adapt. The ink was hardly dry on the 1974 act before the number of PACs increased exponentially.

The PAC money assumes its importance because of a fourth step that began with the election of President John F. Kennedy in 1960.

Step 4: The Advent of the Media Candidate

The clincher in the process has been the rise of the importance of PAC money in the modern media campaign. John Kennedy was really the first modern political candidate. With his good looks and quick mind, he excelled on television in a manner never before seen in American

Chart 2   **Total Number of Political Action Committees (1974–1990)**

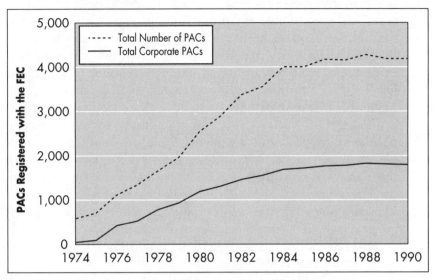

Adapted from Harold Stanley and Richard Neimi, *Vital Statistics on American Politics*, 1992.

politics, and he demonstrated that television is the media by which all modern candidates are defined. He also mastered the "Madison Avenue style" of commercial presentation of his messages, and he was the first presidential candidate to plan and execute his entire campaign based on continuous polling of the American voter.

The problem with this form of campaigning, however, is that it is very expensive. The more successful the use of the media, the greater the need for huge amounts of money to execute the campaign communications program. Campaigns for governor and senator today in the larger states will often exceed $10 million, and congressional campaign budgets in the major markets often exceed $750,000. Where do candidates obtain these exorbitant resources to seek jobs that generally pay less than $125,000 a year?

We answered that in the previous chapter. The facts are simple and not in dispute: incumbents can easily obtain the money from the interest groups and PACs that need something out of the government, while challengers cannot, by and large, obtain needed money unless they are very rich. Although official Washington often acts as if the American voters do not understand what is being purchased through these contributions, nothing could be further from the truth.

Putting all these steps in the process very simply, we can summarize the process:

1. America *lacks any real restraint* today to protect it from the tendency to overspend and run up huge deficits. The entire system is stacked toward overspending. There is no political impetus to force the prioritization of public efforts or to limit the money that can be spent by the government. Because the government can seemingly obtain an unending flow of money to support its habits, there are no adverse consequences to increased spending and considerable consequences to decreased spending.
2. Both the state capitals and Washington are today dominated politically by powerful coalitions, which we have called complexes in deference to Eisenhower, and these complexes have the common objective of seeking to enhance the fiscal and monetary interests of particular segments of the electorate.
3. The campaign reform laws created the PAC system and "soft money," which is one way these complexes dominate public policy creation, concentrating their resources on the most valuable incumbents and key committee members.
4. The advent of modern campaigning, with its emphasis on mass marketing and television, enhances the value of money in the campaign process, thereby increasing the importance of PAC money, and of keeping PACs happy.

Concentrated Benefits and Dispersed Costs

So, we are left with the question of why this process is so bad. After all, there are some people who seek to make the case that the government money that is spent goes to people who need it; there are still others who say that the deficit really isn't that much of a problem. First of all, the deficit is a big problem itself, but there are other immediate effects that are less understood. The process of influence we have described distorts public policy by leading to the overproduction of certain types of programs, while at the same time, leading to the failure to implement certain policies and reforms that are very much needed. This tendency is the reason why outmoded and ridiculous government programs, like the honey subsidies, are never eliminated, expenditures on entitlement programs can never be controlled, but welfare and educational reform never make it past the inevitable presidential task force. The key to understanding this imbalance is understanding how the benefits of a policy or program are provided to specific groups and how the costs of that benefit are dispersed throughout society.[21]

Generally, the costs and benefits of any given program such as Medicare or medical research can either be concentrated, meaning that a certain segment of society, not the whole of society, either reaps the dominant share of benefits or pays the majority of the costs of that program. Or, a government program can benefit or cost society as a whole, meaning that the costs and benefits are widely dispersed.

Today, the imbalance of influence that causes the most difficulty is when policies are created that have highly concentrated benefits, but whose costs are distributed widely over the vast expanse of American taxpayers. It is in precisely these situations where the American political system is impotent to control the content of policy and the outward flow of federal resources. For example, the overwhelming body of opinion, expert and otherwise, is that this country systematically overproduces agricultural subsidies, entitlements like Medicaid and Medicare, and federally funded local projects. The answer to why we do this should be obvious. These policies produce huge revenue streams—selective benefits as it were—which are highly concentrated. The costs, however, are widely dispersed through taxation and other mechanisms that we will discuss shortly. It is far more costly for a legislator to decrease revenue to a group organized to protect that revenue than it is to disperse the cost among the unorganized public, either by deficit spending or increasing taxes. When costs are dispersed widely, it is highly unlikely that the public will react because each individual voter will pay only a small share of those costs. In addition, in an electoral system in which incumbents always win, the threat of electoral retribution means very little. Once government money is given regularly to *any* group, the recipients will organize and fight dearly to keep it, but the taxpayers—all the rest of us—react not at all.

Conversely, our production of welfare reform, educational reform, criminal justice reform, and gun control fall far short of what the public wants. With welfare, the case is remarkable. Policy experts have known for more than 30 years that the welfare system as we have created it, now aids in the destruction of families and encourages the creation of a permanent underclass in American society. As we will demonstrate in Chapter 7, there are few issues on which the public, both blacks and whites, is more united than the need to change the welfare system dramatically. Nearly every politician in America runs on a program of advocating reform of the welfare system. And yet, one would have to look hard to find an issue on which so little progress has been made in this country over the past 30 years.

Welfare reform is effectively *vetoed* by the group that is the *real* beneficiary. The majority of the money spent on welfare is not spent on the poor. The majority of money spent on social welfare programs is spent on a whole range of middle-class people: an enormous bureaucracy that manages the programs, the public employee unions, community organizations that work with the poor, neighborhood associations, and public housing developers who are experts at turning a profit from public money and local governments. To make matters worse, this money often goes out the door with little supervision or follow-up. For example:

- The city of Troy, New York, used development funds from the Department of Housing and Urban Development (HUD) to enable a local group of investors to buy a minor league hockey team.
- The local government in Jacksonville, Florida, used their $5,000,000 of HUD money to subsidize the construction of a distribution center for Sears, Roebuck & Co.
- Delaware County, Pennsylvania, provided more than $5 million of HUD money to a local organization whose chairman just happened to be the county's representative in Congress.[22]

In 1990, we spent a total of $210 billion dollars in cash and non-cash benefits for people who the government defined as having "limited income."[23] These are the people, whether they deserve it or not, that the government has determined are in need of public money. Assistance is given in just about every imaginable form: medical care, cash aid, pensions, food benefits, housing assistance and low-rent housing, interest reduction payments, community service block grants, senior community service employment, summer youth employment, and more.

According to the government's definition of it, there are 33.6 million individuals "in poverty."[24] A little simple math tells us that we are spending $6,250 for *every individual* that the government has decided is poor and needs help. For a family of four, this would amount to $25,000 in federal assistance each year. This clearly means that if our tax money was all being spent to help "poor" people, we wouldn't have any poor people. Of course, we all know that the number of people designated as "poor" keeps rising each year. So where is the welfare money going? The welfare system feeds an enormous bureaucracy, numerous middle-class beneficiaries, and other networks that make their living off the public assistance programs. According to one estimate, there are almost 5 million public employees across the nation whose jobs depend on public assistance and poverty programs.[25] They are well organized, employing large staffs of legislative liaisons and public relations staff to help protect the agencies, and they are loath to reform the system. Invariably they are successful and nothing changes.

Health care provides another blatant example of the problem. For two decades the American health care system has been the most expensive and least expansive of any system in the world. This is a grave problem because the cost of medical care has had a tremendously adverse effect on our nation's ability to compete economically, as employers are forced to deal with costs far greater than those of our competitors. The cost of health care now accounts for 14 percent of our Gross Domestic Product (GDP) and has made Medicare the fastest-growing part of the federal budget. Yet for decades there has been no true reform of the system. This is because the costs of doing so would once again be concentrated on specific groups that are highly organized and well funded to protect themselves. There is a powerful and sophisticated network of organizations centered in Washington, D.C., whose main goal is to maintain the status quo on health care. According to the National Health Council, the number of health care groups who maintain offices in the capital has increased from 117 in 1979, to 741 in 1992. The industry groups are extremely well financed. By conservative estimates, they contributed over $33.8 million to members of the House and Senate from 1998 to 1992. In addition, according to the Center for Responsive Politics, health care PACs gave 29 percent more in 1992 than in the previous election.[26] Table 1 is a list of contributions given in the 1992 election cycle by the larger political action committees associated with the health care industry.[27]

Not only is the amount of money staggering, but the health care industry also targets that money effectively on the legislators with the most clout in the policy process. Table 2 details conservative estimates of what some of the key legislators with major jurisdiction over health care policy received in 1990 and 1992 from PACs representing the health care industry.

When President Clinton tries to reform the health care system, he will run directly into this type of influence. Any plan will undoubtedly be challenged on each and every detail by the industry's protectors, and it will be picked apart as the bills pass through these committees and the rest of Congress. The result will be far less reform than is promised or is necessary.

The budget game is, in effect, stacked against the public's wishes, regardless of what incumbent politicians promise, largely because of the huge complexes that dominate the political process. With one set of policies, there is a huge imbalance in favor of systematic overspending. With another set of policies, there is a huge imbalance of influence against any and all fundamental reform. In both instances, contrary to the rosy vision provided by pluralist theory, the competitive structure

Table 1   **PAC Contributions by Health Care Providers (1992)**

Organization	Contributions
American Medical Association PAC	$6,263,921
Texas Medical Association PAC	1,721,810
American Dental PAC	1,660,838
American Academy of Opthalmology Inc. PAC	1,185,776
American Chiropractic Association PAC	1,036,150
California Medical Association PAC	1,014,122
Florida Medical PAC	921,779
New York Medical PAC	873,623
PAC of the American Hospital Association	757,825
Pennsylvania Medical PAC	746,248
Illinois State Medical Society PAC	579,525
Independent Medicine's PAC	502,777

Adapted from data collected by the Federal Election Commission.

Table 2   **Health Care Industry PAC Contributions (1990 and 1992)**

Member of House	Position and Committee	Contributed 1990, 1992 Election Cycles
Henry Waxman (D-Calif.)	Chairman, Health and Environment Subcommittee; Energy and Commerce	$315,700
Pete Stark (D-Calif.)	Chairman, Health Subcommittee; Ways and Means	299,251
Dan Rostenkowski (D-Ill.)	Chairman, Ways and Means	228,850
John Dingell (D-Mich.)	Chairman, Energy and Commerce	201,600
Member of Senate	**Committee**	**Contributed 1990, 1992 Election Cycles**
John D. Rockefeller (D-W.Va.)	Senate Finance Committee	319,672
Bob Dole (R-Kans.)	Senate Finance Committee	238,807
Tom Daschle (D-S.Dak.)	Senate Finance Committee	299,624
Daniel Coats (R-Ind.)	Senate Labor and Human Resources Committee	416,663

Adapted from *Congressional Quarterly Weekly Report*, July 31, 1993.

pits powerfully organized and well-financed complexes against weak or nonexistent competitors, whose only strength is that they represent what an overwhelming majority of the American voters want.

The most often cited example of the uneven outcomes caused by this one-sided pluralist system is the current system of federal subsidies for the agriculture industry. Only American farmers will vote to spend enormous amounts of tax money to support the existence of farmers who cannot compete in the open market. Regardless of our nostalgic feelings about family farmers, they are no longer the backbone of the American economy. Yet, for political reasons, the farmer is *singled out of all the other industries for special protection.* They receive price supports, tariff protections, government-sponsored programs to buy their products, and the infamous programs that pay farmers not to grow. All these policies are in direct conflict with the general non-farming public because they artificially raise prices and taxes. Even worse, the rise in prices helps the big-business farmers the most because they have so much product to sell. Although they are not the only group of businesses that receives special subsidies, they are the most subsidized sector. The results are the protection of businesses that are not viable and higher prices in the grocery store for everyone.

In short, the United States agricultural policy is a pathetic joke. In 1991, we spent $54 billion to support the Department of Agriculture's 122,594 employees, who doled out $63.2 billion from 1986 to 1990 in cash subsidies directly to farmers.[28] This money is nothing more than a welfare system for midwestern commercial businesses. In addition, this figure does not include the astronomical number of bad loans the government gives to struggling farmers. One Government Accounting Office report indicated that the Farmers Home Administration suffered an operating deficit of $36 billion in 1988 primarily due to bad loans. Yet, like a nightmare, our politicians claim to be unable to cut this funding or even to talk about cutting it.

This tendency to overspend, as with agriculture, does not imply that we never reduce the size of the budget in a given area. With defense, for example, we will over the next five years substantially reduce defense spending. However, we will not reduce that spending anywhere near as fast and extensively as the public would like. For example, we currently have no practical need for the B-2 Bomber, yet last year we agreed to produce 22 of them at a cost exceeding $40 billion. In the case of military expenditures, more than in most areas, vocal and well-organized groups of people argue against spending in this area, which is why military spending has not gone as wild as other types of spending. What we need are some "entitlement doves" to make similar noise about other kinds of spending.

Chart 3   **Off-Line Federal Spending (1945–1990)**

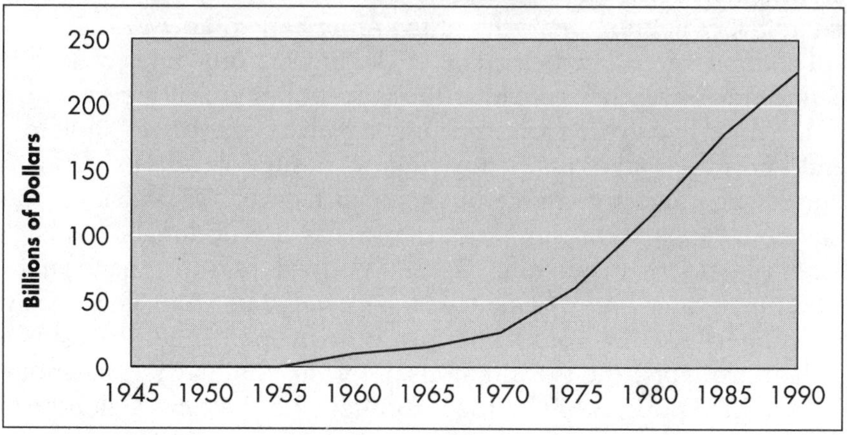

Adapted from the *Statistical Abstract of the United States, 1992.*

How Congress Disperses Cost

Faced with pressure from increasingly effective interest groups, legislators have become very adept at dispersing the cost of these programs in ways that minimize the chance that they will be held electorally accountable. Deficit spending, of course, is the ultimate example of dispersing cost because all the benefits of the expenditure are immediate, but the costs are pushed far into the future. What a perfect deal for a legislator interested in reelection! The only immediate cost even considered is the threat of destabilizing the financial markets.

In addition to deficit spending, legislators at both the state and national levels have devised a myriad of mechanisms that reduce the manifest consequences of their spending policies. The following are some examples of the mechanisms of dispersing costs, and the list is not exhaustive. By moving budgets "off-line," Congress is able to protect spending by simply not accounting for it in the regular manner. Consider the growth in the use of off-line budget items over the years (see Chart 3).

When money is taken off-line the figures are not calculated into deficit projections, but are treated as separate and independent entities. Yet no matter what the politicians say, a buck is still a buck. What kind of spending is taken off the books? For some reason, our legislators think that the following government expenditures do not really qualify as spending:

- The cost of bailing out failed savings and loans, which will come to $300 billion.
- The cost of funding Operation Desert Storm.
- The budget of the post office.
- The cost of federally backed direct loans, loan guarantees, mortgages, and student loans that the government must cover if loans are in default.
- The Federal Deposit Insurance Corporation.
- The cost of the Pension Benefit Guarantee Corporation.[29]

The Systems of Taxation

Usually, systems of taxation have the effect of widely dispersing costs, although sometimes they can be concentrated on specifically targeted groups like smokers or the rich. Every government program is paid for by taxing each individual a small amount. Those who receive the selective benefits of the program have a large financial incentive to organize the protection of that interest. In contrast, those who pay the cost of a program have, at best, only a small incentive to organize in opposition. In the case of income tax, for example, direct deductions from payrolls make this process seem less painful and apparent, and payroll-based income tax deductions receive less public opposition than property taxes, which are often paid in lump sums. The payroll deduction system was justified on the grounds that it is easier on the taxpayer, but the system is even easier on the politicians because the public is less aware of money they never see being taken away.

In addition, states are notoriously effective at instituting taxes that are hidden from the public eye. If we don't see the taxes, we can't fight the taxes. The more obscure the tax is, the easier the government can increase it, and correspondingly, its own power and programs. For example, consider the primary ways that the state of New York collects revenue:

- Alcoholic beverage control license fees and alcoholic beverage tax
- Bank taxes
- Cigarette and tobacco taxes
- Corporation and utilities tax
- Corporation franchise tax
- Estate tax
- Highway use tax
- Insurance taxes
- Motor fuel tax

- Parimutuel tax
- Sales and use tax
- Unincorporated business income tax

The diffusion of revenue sources eases the pressure to increase taxes from just one or two sources, making each individual increase relatively easier politically. We are not arguing here from some naive view against all taxation. We are arguing instead that the easier and less visible we make taxation, the easier it is for those in office to spend more money on *their* programs, many of which voters would find unacceptable.

Indexing and COLAs: Increases without an Increase

To make matters worse, more and more programs became indexed to inflation during the late 1960s and early 1970s, so that the baseline for the budget of these programs became the last year's budget adjusted for inflation, plus whatever increment by which the budget was to be increased. One study found that 57 benefits programs were indexed to inflation, including "Social Security, railroad retirement, veterans benefits, Medicaid, Food Stamps, some federal pay programs, and part of Medicare."[30] In addition, another 42 programs that provided goods and services were indexed, including farm price supports, medical vendor payments, nutrition, and training stipends.[31] Consequently, in all these programs, the budget increases were automatic and the politicians essentially were able to increase funding without having to vote for an increase. To make the process even more hypocritical, what "cuts" were advocated were simply taken off the already-increased base, allowing politicians to claim a reduction when, in fact, there had been an increase. Although an adjusted increase is not an increase in real dollar value, the Cost of Living Allowance (COLA) has the effect of making it procedurally more difficult to control expenditures. As COLAs spread across various programs, the upward pressure to spend is further accentuated. The COLA is no more than a device designed by those in office to avoid accountability to the electorate. The government automatically, by law, has to increase expenditures for any host of programs, while the politicians can claim that they are powerless to do anything to stop it. The fact is, they do have and always have had the power. Withholding increased expenditures on indexed programs is only a matter of changing the law allowing for the COLA. Last we heard, Congress still had the power to make law.

Shifting from Discretionary Spending to Mandatory Spending

One of the great fallacies in politics is that we have gotten into the mess we are in because we spent too much on the military under the Reagan administration. It is true that we spent too much money and we greatly overestimated the Soviet threat; but the fact remains that we have gotten into this mess primarily because of the growth of "mandatory" domestic spending, not the growth of military spending, or even the growth of "discretionary" domestic spending. Even as spending for "mandatory" domestic programs, or entitlements, has eaten up more and more of the budget, it has become a virtual sacred cow. In the current system, legislators claim they are powerless to cut mandatory programs like Medicare, Medicaid, welfare, or Social Security in any serious way, even though all it has to do is change the laws governing them.

The percentage of the budget that consists of direct payments to individuals has risen from 14.4 percent of our total outlays in 1940 to an impressive 49.2 percent of our total budget outlays in 1991.[32] It is precisely these programs, which our leaders profess to be powerless to restrict, that promise to bankrupt this country.

The key is that the entire nature of the budget shifted from a discretionary budget, where lawmakers maintained the implicit and acknowledged authority over expenditures, to a mandatory budget, where lawmakers increasingly delegated their ability to control the nature and composition of the public benefits. In these programs, anyone who meets objective criteria established by Congress has a legal "right" to benefits, and the total mandated payment is determined by the total number of recipients who meet the eligibility requirements as defined by law, as large as this figure may be.[33] (Some programs are capped for total expenditures, but they are the exception, not the rule.)

In short, Congress gave away its ability to budget. It committed budgetcide. Because these payments were written into law, any attempt to limit them promised to be a monumental battle. The more the budget became automatic, the less Congress had the capacity to do anything about it. More and more, through the 1970s, these programs became increasingly insulated from the entire appropriations process. As a result, payments to individuals went through the roof, while Congress found itself fighting over a smaller and smaller piece of the pie. Chart 4 illustrates the transformation from a discretionary budget where lawmakers are forced to make decisions to a mandatory budget where decisions are automatic and require no vote.

Where does most of this mandatory spending go? Social Security, public pensions, Medicare, and Medicaid account for the vast majority

Chart 4   **From a Discretionary Budget to a Mandatory Budget (1965–1990)**

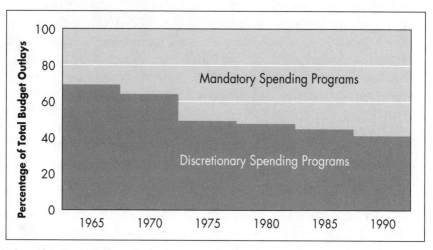

Adapted from Harold Stanley and Richard Neimi, *Vital Statistics on American Politics*, 1992.

of it. This brings us to the sad truth, the truth no one wants to talk about. The fact is that the elderly are the primary recipients and most powerful protectors of these entitlement programs. If we subtract Social Security and Medicare from non-interest domestic spending, what is left accounts for less of our Gross Domestic Product today than what we were spending in 1940.[34]

Most voters today would not criticize the goals of these programs—helping our elderly and handicapped, providing for veterans and the unemployed, and attempting to create a viable national retirement program. If we agree that these are programs we want to pay for, we should be honest with ourselves and raise the funds through taxation to pay their current costs. At $760 billion and rising fast, these programs are the root cause of the budget deficit that is bankrupting this country. It is true that either increasing taxation to pay for these programs or cutting benefits will cause ferocious public outcry and interest-group opposition, but we elect representatives to make tough choices.

The Opening of the Budget Process

As we have seen, all public policy has its unintended effects. Perhaps no policy has been more well intentioned, but ultimately destructive to the policy process than the "opening" of the federal budget process. Before the 1960s, the budget was basically done behind closed doors, in the so-called smoke-filled rooms of Congress. The process was very undemocratic, but it had the perverse effect of protecting legislators who wanted to cut programs. The process was significantly altered with the advent of "sunshine" practices in the late 1960s, and committee meetings were opened to the public in an effort to make the process more democratic. The problem was that the only people who had any interest in attending committee meetings were lobbyists, whose access and impact were greatly intensified by the procedural changes. A good idea quickly went sour. A clerk of the Senate Appropriations Committee gives the history:[35]

> If you wanted to track the growth of the deficit with the opening up of committee markup to the public, you'd find there was a direct correlation. It's very simple: People are against spending in general, but not against it in the particular. So the only people that are interested in the appropriations process, in the details of the process, are those who want more money. And they are very sophisticated and clever in going about getting that money. And the more you open up the process, the more people are paid to come up here and increase spending! There's a whole industry that's grown up whose basic goal is to increase federal spending.[36]

Underfunded Liabilities

The worst offense against reasonable government is not the deficit, which we can at least see, but the gigantic underfunded liabilities that are all but invisible to the general public. The worst of these is the pension system for public employees, at nearly every level of government. The fact is, nobody knows exactly how much the future pension systems will cost. It is difficult to put an exact figure on this debt, because as our life span increases, these figures will rise. The government has previously used out-of-date actuarial figures to determine pension costs in order to foster lower estimates of the obligations. In addition, the estimates as to the future costs of the pension funds are very dependent on the projected rate of return on assets that are assumed by the funds' overseers. A percentage-point difference can mean billions down the road.

These funds, which are supposed to operate independently from regular budget considerations, have become highly political in recent years. The politicians, especially at the state level, have increasingly been playing games with the public pension money to alleviate their own budgetary pressure. Sometimes they change the financial assumptions used to calculate the future cost so the amount of current state contributions to the fund can be reduced. As a result, the vast majority of state pension programs are underfunded. *A recent study found that 69 of the 85 public employee funds surveyed, comprising 87 percent of all the public pension assets, did not have enough assets to meet future obligations.*[37]

Despite the trouble the funds are obviously in, our state governments find it politically expedient to treat the pension funds like a public bank account to be used whenever times get tough. For example:

- California Governor Pete Wilson tried to take $1.6 billion from the California Public Employees Retirement System in order to close his budget deficit, and tried to fire the independent board in order to put the fund directly under his own control. To make matters even worse, California is cutting its contributions on the assumption that it will sharply increase contributions after the year 2001, long after Pete Wilson has left office.
- The state of Illinois, despite the fact that its pension funds are dangerously underfunded at only 46 to 65 percent of future obligations, has chosen to ignore its own law requiring the state to be fully funded by 1996, falling $500 million short in current state contributions.[38]

These debts are every bit as real as our visible national debt, and they have the added problem that future generations will actually have to pay for them out of real tax dollars. Unlike the national debt, on which we pay only the interest at the present time, these underfunded liabilities are designed to provide incomes for millions of people who will retire from our public employment systems.

The issue of hidden future liabilities does not stop with federal pensions. It also includes $5.7 trillion dollars worth of future liabilities in the form of direct loans, loan guarantees, government-sponsored enterprises, deposit insurance, and various federal insurance programs.[39] This figure is from 1990, so it's probably far higher today. In addition, this figure does not include the four trillion in debt we already have. The government is fully and legally responsible for all that debt, and the losses will inevitably be in the hundreds of billions of dollars.

You Scratch My Back, I'll Scratch Yours

The accumulation of debt is actually better understood today, thanks to the special efforts of Ross Perot. During his 1992 October presidential campaign, Perot made the issue of the debt more understandable to more people than at any other time in our history. The systematic accumulation of debt is the political and fiscal device that replaced inflation as a method of increasing spending, after inflation almost ruined us.

Although President Reagan and the Democrats in Congress didn't invent deficit financing, they elevated debt accumulation to heights never before experienced in peacetime. President Reagan wanted to spend the Soviets to death on defense, and the Democrats wanted desperately to maintain and protect their entitlement programs. The classic example of this was the 1985 "Oak Tree" agreement between President Reagan and Speaker of the House Tip O'Neil (D-Mass.). In order to resolve an impasse in the budget negotiations, the two politicians made a classic "you scratch my back, I'll scratch yours" agreement. Reagan agreed to allow the Democrats to restore the Social Security COLA in exchange for receiving the full increase he wanted for defense expenditures. So both politicians got their way and the deficit continued to skyrocket, selling out a generation's future for short-term political gain, despite the ironic fact that Gramm-Rudman-Hollings was being passed at the same time.[40] Working together, the two parties in power managed to flood America in a veritable sea of red ink; all the while, of course, maintaining steadfastly that it is really the other side that is to blame. This is the fundamental truth underlying all that is wrong with Washington. *The system exists to the detriment of us all because everyone in government, both the Republicans and the Democrats, agree to disagree, allowing government spending to continue unabated to protect their own political interests and supporters.*

It is the attitude of mutual complicity that lies at the very core of our spending problems, and leads to the ridiculous pork-barrel projects that have become so infamous. Brian Kelly, in his book *Adventures in Porkland,* provides some excellent examples to illustrate what our congressmen deem are worthy projects in the face of trillions of dollars in debt:

- $2.7 million for a catfish farm in Arkansas.
- $3.75 million for a Poultry Center of Excellence at the University of Arkansas.
- $2 million to promote the sale of Hawaiian handicrafts.
- $5 million to the citizens of the Solomon Islands for a new Parliament building.
- $100,000 to fund a study to determine whether or not the people of New Mexico are in danger of being hit by falling pieces of spacecraft.
- $15 million for states to hire small businesses to plant trees on federal land.
- $10 million to build a ramp for the Milwaukee Brewers.

- $19 million to study the effects of cow flatulence on the environment.
- $20 million to the International Fund for Ireland, including a project to study Irish ancestry and promote the sale of Irish goods.[41]

The point is that the government couldn't spend itself out of control without the tacit participation of both the Republicans and the Democrats. Each project may be harmless by itself, but of course, one bee sting won't kill you. However, a swarm of bees can be quite deadly, just like the swarm of spending that emanates from Washington each year, comprised of hundreds of little spending bees. Our deficits exist, in the end, because the beekeepers have decided it is in their mutual interest to open up the door to the hive. In this case, they disperse responsibility by spreading it around among all the members. Each member has his hand in the honey, so nobody can complain.

The Rhetoric of the Deficit

How do those we elect get away without having to come clean to the public about all this? One answer is the clever rhetoric they use to campaign for office and the way they discuss these issues while in office. Members of Congress and the state legislatures have for years practiced the curious tactic of running against the very institution of which they are a part. They get away with it because they face only token opposition in most of the districts, and without opposition, as we explained in the previous chapter, there is no one holding up an incumbent's record to serious public scrutiny.

In addition, the modern political wonderland is a place where even the English language is carefully crafted to maintain the illusions that the government wants us to see. It is vitally important for us to recognize that President Clinton's new strategy constantly hammers away at investment rather than taxes. In his State of the Union speech, Clinton never mentioned the word taxes, *while proposing one of the largest tax increases in history.* Of course, nothing has changed. Clinton, no matter what he wants to call it, is still taking money from us to spend as he sees fit.

On the lighter side, here is what we predict will become the new vernacular. Call it "Clintonese."

- "Entitlements" will now be called "Mandatory Investment in Our Elderly."
- "Pork-Barrel Projects" will become "Geographically Defined Investment."

- "Welfare" will become "Non-Work Related Investments."
- "Agricultural Subsidies" will become "Non-Production of Food Investments."
- "The Deficit" will now be referred to as the "Insufficient Investment Revenue."
- "Bureaucrats" will become "Investment Managers."
- "Personal Income" will now be called "Individual Investment Potential."
- Congress will be renamed "The National Investment Corporation."
- The IRS will hence be referred to as the "Investment Relocation Service."

The End of the American Dream

If you think the political process is irrelevant to you and your children, consider three graphics we constructed using U.S. Census data. Table 3 is the *annual real growth rate* in the United States. What this table says should sadden us all. Essentially, the leaders of America of the 1950s, both in politics and business, gave the younger generation of the 1960s a world in which *real economic growth* averages 3.6 percent over an entire decade. That growth meant increasing prosperity, opportunity, and incomes, and the rising hope that is the companion to increased prosperity. As President Kennedy said: "A rising tide raises all boats," and the Kennedy and Eisenhower administrations most certainly left us a rising tide.

The leaders in Washington and our state capitals today inherited a marvelously prosperous world in the 1960s. For example, Speaker of the House Tom Foley (D-Wash.) was first elected to Congress in 1964. Senator Robert Byrd (D-W.Va.), the powerful chairman of the Appropriations Committee, became a congressman in 1953. Senator Bob Dole (R-Kans.), leader of the Senate minority, entered the House in 1960.[42] For all their years of service, these political leaders will leave our children a world in which the growth rate is expected to average less than 1.0 percent (see Table 3).

The Power of Political Influence

If you want to see the consequence of political muscle in stark relief, Chart 5 and Tables 4 and 5 should be instructive. Chart 5 compares the wage changes between 1970 and 1990 of entire segments of our work force. The consumer price index between 1970 and 1990 climbed 236 percent, and this is the benchmark. If a group is below the center line in the graph, their wages have actually fallen in relation to inflation.

Table 3   **Rates of Change in Gross Domestic Product**

Decade	Percent Growth Rate
1960s	3.6
1970s	1.7
1980s	1.6
1990s	??

Adapted from the 1992 Statistical Abstract.

Chart 5   **Percentage Point Changes in Average Compensation Compared with CPI (1970–1990)**

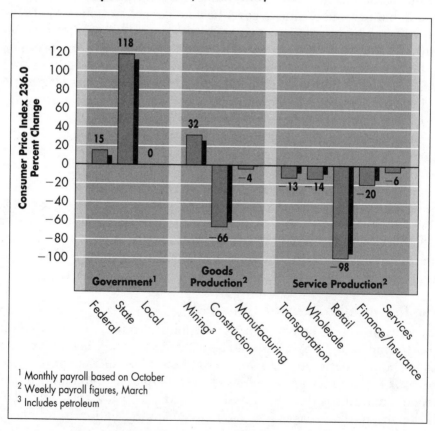

[1] Monthly payroll based on October
[2] Weekly payroll figures, March
[3] Includes petroleum

Table 4   **Percentage Increases in Employee Compensation (1984–1990)**

	1984	1985	1986	1987	1988	1989	1990	Average
CPI[1]	4.3	3.6	1.9	3.6	4.1	4.8	5.4	4.0
State[2]	4.3	4.8	6.8	4.3	5.3	4.9	4.4	5.0
Local[2]	6.0	3.7	5.6	5.4	5.5	5.6	5.4	5.31
Private	4.4	3.7	3.0	2.2	2.5	3.3	4.1	3.31

[1] Consumer Price Index
[2] Changes in negotiated state and local pay
Adapted from the Statistical Abstract, 1992.

Table 5   **Percentage Increases in Total Employee Cost (1985–1991)**

	1985	1988	1989	1990	1991	Average
Private industry[1]	3.9	4.8	4.8	4.6	4.4	4.5
State/local government[1]	5.6	5.6	6.2	5.8	3.6	5.4

[1] Changes in total employee cost, including benefits
Adapted from the Statistical Abstract, 1992.

That means that the group has become worse off economically over the past 20 years. If they are above the line, their real wages have actually increased, meaning that they are better off economically. The only private sector jobs that have improved real wages are in the mining sector, because this sector has undergone a transformation from a low-tech industry to a high-tech/high-skill industry. *Every other private segment of the economy became worse off over the 20-year period.*[43]

However, public employees have prospered relative to their private counterparts during the same period. Local employees held even with inflation and federal employees saw their real wages rise moderately. State employees had increases in real wages that were dramatic. By this point you should have expected these results, because we have already shown you that public employees, as a group, are among the most passionate, powerful, and effective special interest groups in America. Moreover, these figures are based on actual wages. The figures do not include pensions, where public employees have made even more dramatic gains than their private counterparts. *For the past twenty years, America's public employee unions have used their political clout to extort ever-increasing wages and benefits from the taxpayers as the economic prosperity of those same taxpayers declines.*

And if you think that is something in the past, think again. Between 1984 and 1990, the average annual wage increase of state employees increased 1.0 percentage point per year faster than inflation, and the local employees exceeded inflation by 1.31 percentage points per year. During the same period, all private wages fell behind inflation by 0.79 percent per year (see Table 4). Public employees in the United States have become a kind of protected class, whose protection is purchased through campaign contributions and political clout. Total employee cost is rising nearly one percentage point faster as a result (see Table 5). These bureaucrats are the same people who propose most budgets, recommend tax increases, and increase the deficits. They are not only among the most powerful PACs in the United States, but they have also used their power to dominate the Democratic Party. As much as the radical right has an excessive influence over the Republican Party, the major public employee unions exert an almost equal control over the Democratic Party. Is it any surprise that the new administration and Congress are already proposing the most staggering tax increases in history? They clearly know where they get their bread buttered, and whose bread to butter in return.

Do you think Bill Clinton or Congress is going to change this? President Clinton announced a pay freeze as part of his budget plan. An analysis by *Forbes* shows that 60 percent of the federal public employees are going to get raises despite the freeze because all the step and merit increases that are practically automatic for most employees are not included in the freeze. The across-the-board increase is the only raise that has been eliminated. In the government merit system, 99.8 percent of all middle managers are rated meritorious and given raises accordingly. On top of this, according to *Forbes*, another 35 percent are rated "outstanding," which entitles them to another raise. Yet the Clinton plan doesn't touch these raises. As a result, federal civilian pay increased at 6 percent in 1992, "twice as fast as in the private sector." And you can expect to see a continuation of these trends in the future.[44]

What We Must Do

The implications of these processes are depressing. American politics today is structurally flawed, producing a huge bias in favor of overspending at both the state and national levels of government, while systematically favoring the status quo and inaction in other areas such as gun control, educational reform, and welfare reform. The keystone on which this entire process rests is the systematic elimination of electoral choice in American politics, because it severs the relationship of accountability between the voters and their elected officials. If the threat of electoral retribution is very weak, legislators are free to pursue their political interest by satisfying interest group claims. If the officeholders can obscure and disperse the true costs of the revenue benefits they provide, the potential political reaction diminishes again. Therefore, the key to decreasing the power of special interests is to *maximize* the possibility that legislators will be defeated if they choose to satisfy interest groups at the expense of the broader public. In effect, we must restore our democracy before we can hope to restore fiscal sanity. The restoration of real electoral competition, at both the state and the national levels, will do more to control runaway spending than any procedural reform. And as we will argue, the only way to increase the level of electoral competition is through the creation of a new, centrist political party.

The task of undoing the damage that has been done to America is substantial. The people in Washington and the state capitals, who are vested in the current system and derive their livelihood from it, would have you believe that nothing more substantial than what they are doing can be done; or better still, that you should trust them to straighten out the mess. The current political system, with the Republicans and Democrats in control, is simply not capable of taking the action necessary to break the cycle of interest-group politics that has sent spending out of control. As a result, the type of political force needed to reconstruct federal spending policies can be achieved *only* by a direct political movement, backed and paid for by millions of American people, and unified in its goal of sound fiscal policy.

At the same time, the seeds of that revolt can be seen in an electorate enraged by the systematic destruction of the things they care about. There is a very real opportunity to take decisive action, an opportunity created by the dramatic levels of frustration and discontent that engulf the American political system. The potential of this opportunity was dramatized by the striking support for Ross Perot in the 1992 presidential campaign. The historical roots and character of this discontent is the subject of the next chapter.

≈ 4 ≈

Understanding Perot

The death of democracy is not likely to be an assassination from ambush. It will be a slow extinction from apathy, indifference, and undernourishment.[1]

—*Robert Maynard Hutchins, 1954*

The Pyramid of Voter Blame

Despair is a strong word, and some may find it melodramatic as a description of the American people's attitudes toward politics. Despair is a word aptly associated with those mired permanently in poverty, or those helplessly captive in a world of violence. Despair is what people with AIDS feel, or what is felt by the victims of child abuse. Despair is what partially ignited the rage of residents of Los Angeles. But we will use the word nevertheless because it implies a state of hopelessness, coupled with a sense of futility and defeat; and by this definition, an increasing proportion of the American public feels despair about our political system.

Although Clinton's election prompted a bubble of optimism in the first few months of 1993, this momentary sense of hope should not mask the long-term underlying trends in American life that have developed over a period covering seven previous administrations. In fact, shortly after the initial bubble, the approval ratings of the Clinton administration declined faster than for any new administration since the beginning of modern polling. Despite Clinton's earnest exhortations about the need for change, nothing truly fundamental has changed with the new administration, and the public knows this. The forces that produced the rapid decline in Clinton's post-election popularity are the same forces that earlier propelled the candidacy of Ross Perot. Although some would like to believe that each new administration is going to be different, there is no reason to believe that Clinton can reverse the 30-year trends that will be described in this chapter.

In this chapter, we will also show just how broad and deep public discontent is, and we will explain the Perot phenomenon in terms of a historical evolution of American politics. Perot needs to be seen not as a unique event in history, but as an inevitable outgrowth of the recent trends in American politics. We will paint a picture of the electorate that will illuminate the conditions that led to Perot's successful entry into presidential politics.

The success of Ross Perot in galvanizing public support, whether or not one agrees with him, is instructive as a case study of the current state of our party system. This was the first time since modern polling began that a candidate outside the two major parties led both an incumbent president and the defacto opposition candidate in the polls. For our purposes, Perot is interesting because of what we can learn about American politics by analyzing his campaign and the public reaction. What we are interested in is how and why the American people reacted to him the way they did.

The Erosion of the Voting Process

One of the best ways to measure the result of voter despair is to trace the slow, incremental decline in voter turnout since 1960. As Chart 1 shows, between 1960 and 1992, the United States experienced a 13 percentage point drop in the number of adults voting in presidential elections, and

Chart 1   **Voter Turnout in Presidential Elections (1960–1992)**

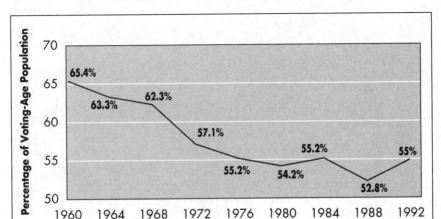

Adapted from Ruy A. Teixeira, *The Disappearing American Voter.*

by 1988 this meant that nearly half of all eligible voters failed to vote in the presidential election. In 1992, turnout rose to 55 percent, a modest gain almost certainly the result of the entry of Perot into the election creating a third choice. Interestingly, this overall decline in voting almost perfectly matches the trend of decreasing electoral choice in American elections, which raises the distinct possibility that the public is all too well aware that its votes matter less than they once did.

One mechanism for looking into the future of American politics is to track trends in the turnout rates of young voters. Chart 2 shows that the voting rates among the 18- to 34-year-old age cohorts have consistently been declining for the past two decades. This raises a troubling specter for the future rate of voting participation. Once individuals start voting, chances are they will continue to vote regularly in the future; voters who start voting later in life, however, are more likely to vote with less frequency and knowledge. Therefore, if young people today are voting *less* than their earlier counterparts, the chances are they will continue to vote with less frequency in the future, continuing the downward spiral in turnout rates. In addition, the willingness of individuals to take part actively in a political system once they reach political maturity is indicative of the political efficacy of the system itself. Unfortunately, voting rates among the young have been falling consistently, and they account for much of the overall decline in turnout.[2]

Chart 2   **Voter Turnout in Presidential Elections, by Age (1972–1988)**

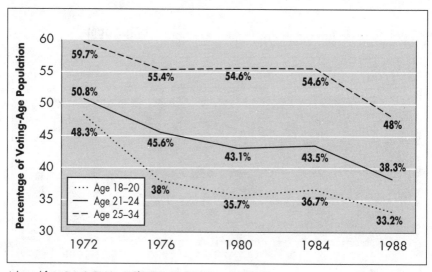

Adapted from Ruy A. Teixeira, *The Disappearing American Voter.*

The fairly significant increase in voting in 1992 is encouraging only because it proves a point. Ross Perot created a reason for many discouraged voters to vote, forcing the other candidates to talk about such issues as the deficit and taxes, which had not been talked about as seriously before. However, this short-term increase does not indicate that the long-term trend in turnout has changed.

Analyses by various experts have found causes for the decline in voting ranging from the procedures used to conduct elections to the changing composition of the electorate and the decline of the per-ceived benefits of voting.[3] We make the case that one of the primary causes of the decline is that the perceived benefits of voting have been decreasing. This perception can be seen in an analysis of the attitudes that underlie American politics. It is precisely the attitudes relating to voters' feelings about their government that have been deteriorating. Deteriorating attitudes may not be the only *direct* cause of decreasing participation, and undoubtedly the reality is more complicated. But these attitudinal changes, in conjunction with the declining turnout rates, present a portrait of a political system teetering on the edges of illegitimacy.[4] In addition, it is precisely the widespread existence of these attitudes that explains why Perot captured the interest of mil-lions of voters, and why there is the potential to create a new political force in American politics.

Alienation of the Voters

Chart 3 documents the long-term rising trends in voter alienation and declining belief in government, which we believe provide the basis for a true political revolt. Even in the late 1960s, academics were already concerned about the evident rise in discontent that was occurring in broad segments of our society, and as Professor Arthur Miller wrote then:

> A democratic political system cannot survive for long without the support of a majority of its citizens. When such support wanes, underlying discontent is the necessary result, and the potential for revolutionary alteration of the political and social system is enhanced.[5]

What we have called despair provides the environment in which an upheaval can take place. Perhaps one of the best measures of despair is captured in the "alienation index" published by the Harris Poll since 1967, which is presented in Chart 3. The alienation index is the average of responses to a series of hard-hitting questions that cover

Chart 3   **Harris Alienation Index (1966–1992)**

The Index is calculated by averaging the number of responses that agree with
the following statements.

1) The rich get richer and the poor get poorer.
2) What you think doesn't count very much.
3) Most people with power try to take advantage of people like yourself.
4) The people running the country don't really care what happens to you.
5) You're left out of things going on around you.

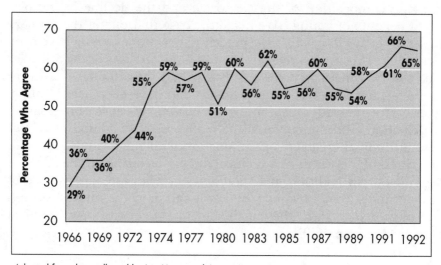

Adapted from data collected by Lou Harris and Associates.

a range of beliefs about the political system. For example, in 1991, 83
percent of those surveyed think "the rich get richer and the poor get
poorer"; 67 percent agree that "what you think doesn't count very
much anymore"; 67 percent think "most people with power try to take
advantage of people like yourself"; 61 percent feel "the people running
the country don't really care what happens to you"; and 50 percent feel
"you're left out of things going on around you."

In December of 1992, just following the election, the index stood at
65 percent, just one percentage point lower than than the all-time high
recorded in January earlier that year.

Usually, one would expect that with the election of a new administration and the rejection of an incumbent president, the public would
have a renewed sense of optimism and connection with the political
system. Instead, the alienation index measured in December of 1992
found that the public did not feel any less alienated from the political
system than they had the year before. The reason: the election did little

that would address the undercurrent of discontent that is still prevalent in the American political arena.

A particularly interesting point about the Harris figures is that although alienation continues to be higher for the groups traditionally most alienated—the poor, African-Americans, Democrats, the less well educated, and Hispanics—the poll showed that *more than half* of the most successful segments of society—college educated, earning over $50,000, and Republicans—were also alienated. And, as Humphrey Taylor, chairman of the Harris organization points out: "That this record level of alienation should come after a year history will remember for the collapse of the Soviet Union, the death-rattle of the Cold War, and a spectacular high-tech victory in Kuwait, is quite remarkable."[6] Taylor concludes, "If it [alienation] remains as high as this, we can expect to see more 'new politics' outside the traditional two-party system, and more populist, antiestablishment, anti-incumbent candidates in the future."[7]

A New Crisis of Confidence

The Harris Poll on alienation is certainly not unique. For the past four years, practically every poll has displayed a near collapse in public confidence and support for the president, Congress, both political parties, and for nearly everyone else involved in the political system. In fact, in 1992, polling research revealed that Congress had reached unprecedented depths of unpopularity. As shown in Chart 4, approval ratings for Congress collapsed from a high of 56 percent in late 1987, to a meager 16 percent by mid-1992. Likewise, disapproval of Congress has risen from 40 percent to 78 percent during the same time frame. By comparison, the percentage of individuals who said that Congress was doing a "poor job" in the 1950s hovered regularly between 11 percent and 16 percent.[8] Particularly important is the fact that during the same period, the percentage of those disapproving of their *own* representative had risen from 18 percent to 40 percent. And even as the new 103d Congress convened for the first time, a remarkable 66 percent of the public disapproved of the institution, according to the ABC News/ *Washington Post* Poll. Considering that this was a newly elected Congress with 124 new members, the high disapproval is evidence that elections are no longer serving to reinvigorate public optimism and belief in the system.

The discontent is not directed only at the institution of Congress. It is also directed at the presidency. Bill Clinton's approval ratings began at 58 percent in January 1992, before crashing down to 37 per-

Chart 4   **Approval Ratings for Congress (1987–1993)**

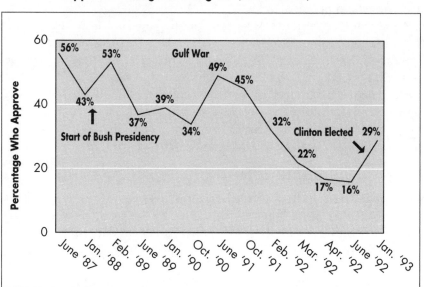

Adapted from ABC News/*Washington Post* and cited in *The Public Perspective*, Volume 4, No.1.

cent in June, according to Gallup.[9] As we noted earlier, George Bush's approval rating had taken a very similar nosedive in the previous year. In addition, strong disapproval is directed at the system as a whole. In a CBS/*New York Times* Poll taken in late April 1992, 78 percent of those surveyed thought public officials represent the "special interests" over the "public interests," and nearly half (44 percent) thought that the government "does not pay much attention to what the people think." Finally, when asked what should be done, a combined 85 percent thought that the government either needs to be "completely rebuilt" or that, at a minimum, it needs "fundamental changes."

Is This Really Something New?

Are people really any more angry and hopeless than they were at other times in history? If the evidence is analyzed, it is clear that this frustration has been steadily accumulating for the last 30 years, and that it is indeed at an all-time high. The National Election Study (NES) is an academic research project conducted every two years at the Survey Research Center of the University of Michigan. By analyzing the responses to two key questions intended to measure political cynicism, which have been used in the NES for many years, one can very accurately gauge changes taking place in public attitudes about politics. These questions are as follows:

- How much of the time do you think you can trust the government in Washington to do what is right—just about always, most of the time, or only some of the time?
- Would you say the government is pretty much run by a few big interests looking out for themselves or that it is run for the benefit of all people?

When looking at Chart 5, note the very consistent and massive increases in both indicators until 1980, followed by a respite during the deficit-fueled economic boom of the mid-1980s, and ending with a resumption of the same upward trends.

The available data displayed from the NES ends in 1988. However, data in current public opinion research shows that the situation has deteriorated further and that cynicism has returned to the levels reached in the late 1970s. Both of the questions tracked in Chart 5 have been asked in public opinion surveys (using identical wording) every year since 1988, and by analyzing the responses to these questions we can see what has happened since 1988. An ABC News/*Washington Post* Poll in February 1993 found that 78 percent of those surveyed feel that government can be trusted only "some or none of the time." During 1992, numerous polls found that from 72 percent to 79 percent of the public basically had little or no faith in the government to "do what is right."[10] These figures are comparable to the levels found in 1980 by

Chart 5   **Key Indicators of Political Cynicism (1964–1988)**

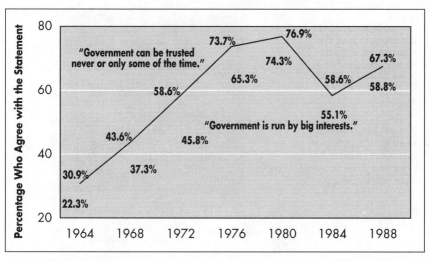

Adapted from data collected by the National Election Study and cited in Ruy A. Teixeira, *The Disappearing American Voter.*

NES. Likewise, the percentage of people who felt that "government is run by a few big interests" has continued to rise since 1988, continuing the upward trend. In 1992, 80 percent felt that big interests run the government, according to a Gallup Poll. Other polls replicate this finding, and from 1989 to 1992 the percentages of people who felt this way commonly ranged from 71 percent to 77 percent.[11]

To add historical perspective to these numbers, public opinion toward the Congress in the 1930s and 1940s was characterized either by general approval or neutrality. The public did not look at Congress with basic, fundamental hostility, as it does now. Chart 6 shows that in 1937, *in the midst of the Great Depression,* almost three times as many people thought that Congress was as good a representative body as possible, as opposed to thinking that members of Congress basically cared only about their own political futures. In contrast, when the exact same question was asked more than 50 years later, the ratio was almost perfectly reversed. Therefore, it is reasonable to conclude that it is not simply tough economic times driving the current levels of discontent with American democracy. After all, the times were far tougher in 1937. By implication, the great reservoir of Americans' good feelings, built up over 150 years, has been dissipated by a single generation of leadership.

Chart 6   **Popular Attitudes toward Congress (1937 and 1990)**

Question: Which one of these statements best expresses your attitude toward the present U.S. Congress as a whole?

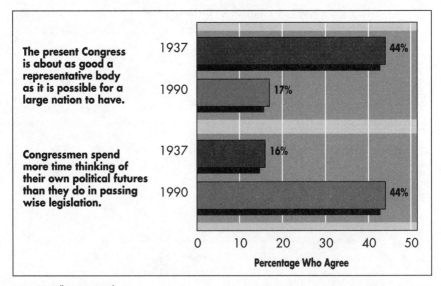

Note: Not all categories shown.
Adapted from surveys by the Roper Organization cited in *The Public Perspective,* Volume 4, No. 1

The psychological distance between the governing elite and the governed has increased dramatically. As we noted before, the percentage of people who think the government is run by "big interests" has skyrocketed in the past 30 years, and the current attitudes regarding Congress provide additional evidence on the degree of voter alienation. By 1990, only a third of the public felt that members of Congress were more interested in serving the public than in serving themselves.[12] It is particularly ironic that the psychological schism between our representatives and the rest of us has coincided with the advent of modern communication technologies, which have vastly improved the flow of information throughout the country. The technological revolution in communications, which might have made people feel closer to the operations of government, instead has helped the public lose the belief that our representatives are looking out for our collective interest. This sentiment is displayed in Chart 7, which shows that the percentage of people who feel that members of Congress pay "a good deal of attention" to the people who elected them has fallen from 42 percent in 1964 to a pathetic 12 percent in 1990, a 30-point negative shift in 26 years. Likewise, the comparison shows that the percentage of people who think that members of Congress pay "not much" attention to the people who elected them has doubled.

Chart 7   **Congressional Attention to Voters (1964 and 1990)**

Question: How much attention do you think most congressmen pay to the people who elect them when they decide what to do in Congress?

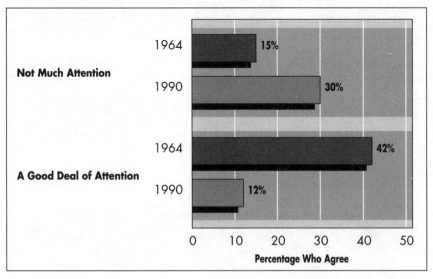

Note: Not all categories shown.

Adapted from surveys by the Roper Organization cited in *The Public Perspective*, Volume 4, No. 1.

This data, taken in a sort of "snapshot" comparison between 1964 and 1990, does not reveal how persistent and gradual the rise in discontent and anger toward the government and politicians has been, regardless of who is president. Data collected by the Center of Political Studies at the University of Michigan reveals that the anger has grown gradually over the last 30 years.

The questions in Table 1 reinforce the ideas we have already discussed. They deal with the attitudes that are central to a healthy, functioning democracy—trust in those who govern, a belief that elections have an impact, and that people are connected to the system of governance. Unfortunately, many of these questions were dropped from the study, but we can use public opinion research from other organizations to bring this information up to date.[13]

The measures in the latter two portions of the table are powerful because they are the results of a completely random sample of people being asked the exact same question over a long period of time. As a

Table 1 **Political Frustration in the American National Election Studies**

Question: Do you feel that almost all of the people running the government are smart people (who usually know what they are doing), or do you think that quite a few of them don't seem to know what they are doing?

Response	1964	1966	1968	1970	1972	1974	1976	1978	1980
Don't know what they are doing	27%	**	37%	44%	40%	46%	50%	51%	62%

Question: (Agree/Disagree) I don't think public officials care much about what people like me think.

Response	1960	1964	1968	1970	1972	1974	1976	1978	1980	1982	1984	1986
Agree	25%	36%	43%	47%	49%	50%	51%	51%	52%	47%	42%	52%

Question: How much do you feel that having elections makes the government pay attention to what the people think—a good deal, some, or not much?

Response	1964	1966	1968	1970	1972	1974	1976	1978	1980	1982	1984	1992
A good deal	65%	62%	60%	58%	55%	50%	52%	56%	51%	**	42%	33%

Note: All response categories are not shown in the interest of brevity.
** Indicates that this question was dropped from the study.

Chart 8   **Honesty and Ethics Ratings, by Profession (1976–1992)**

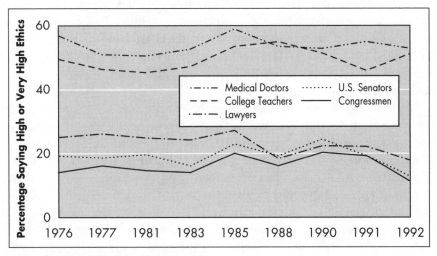

Adapted from *The Gallup Poll Monthly*, July 1992.

result, the slow decline in our democratic public faith over the last 30 years is obvious. By 1992, polls showed that only 33 percent of the electorate felt that "elections make the government pay attention to what the people think"—a drop of 32 percentage points in 28 years.[14]

The collapse of faith in government shows up in other types of measures of public opinion as well. The Gallup Organization has been asking a series of questions about honesty and ethics since the mid-1970s. When rated against other groups and professions in society, the perceptions of the ethical standards of congressmen and senators rate slightly above used-car salesmen, but below lawyers. Chart 8 shows the low regard we have for our own popularly elected officials.

America Loses Interest

As the elected and appointed leaders of our governments—state and national—failed to deliver on their promises, all the while permitting spending to run entirely out of control, another logical deterioration started to occur: Americans started to lose interest in politics. According to data from the National Election Study, from 1960 to 1988, *the percentage of the public who did not read a single newspaper article on the election increased 31 percentage points*. Perhaps one could pin this trend on an increase in people who received their political information through television. Unfortunately, the same data show that the percentage of the population who watched "many programs" on the campaign decreased from 47 percent in 1960 to a meager 25 percent in 1984, before inexplicably rebounding to 41 percent in 1988. Yet the overall trends clearly indicate a gradual withdrawal of the electorate from the political scene.[15]

At the same time, as Chart 9 indicates, the measurement of belief in government responsiveness declined dramatically as well. The percentage of people who perceived the government as being fundamentally unresponsive increased 27 percentage points, from 16 percent to 43 percent, while those who perceived the government as responsive decreased from 62 percent to 30 percent (not shown on graph). Again, this is more evidence of the dramatic break between the governing elite and the governed. Likewise, the percentage of people who indicated that they are "very interested in the campaign" dropped 11 percentage points, from 39 percent to 28 percent.

Is There a Legitimacy Crisis?

All the data we have presented in this chapter tell the same story using slightly different words. We have tried to show that however one measures discontent and frustration, the answer is consistently the same—the American people no longer believe in their government. The connection between the governing elite and the governed masses has de-

Chart 9　**Campaign Interest and Government Responsiveness (1960–1988)**

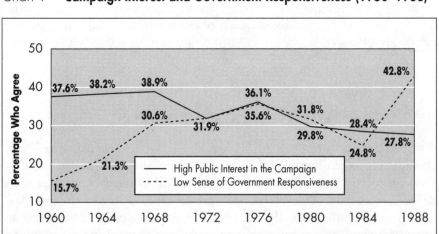

Adapted from The National Election Study and Ruy A. Teixeira, *The Disappearing American Voter.*

teriorated to a pathetically shameful state, although we are certain that some national elites will argue that such sentiments are not very meaningful or useful. This is not some short-term transient phenomenon that can be changed with a quick fix from some glib politicians.

Indeed, there has been a running debate in the academic community since the early 1970s about what the sharp rises in the indicators of cynicism and discontent mean—if anything. Academic studies have found that some fundamental values about our political system have *not* decayed in the same manner as some of the attitudes we have cited.[16] For example, the percentage of voters who feel that it is a citizen's duty to vote, and that voting is important, has not changed much in the last 30 years. However, a belief in the fundamental importance of political participation and voting does not contradict the belief that one's vote is worthless and a waste of time in a system without political choice. It is logical to hold both of these beliefs at the same time, and the first only serves to underscore the disturbing nature of the second. In addition, trends in improving educational attainment have increased the general knowledge of the importance of participation among the electorate. This countervailing trend, which would supposedly encourage political participation, has probably slowed the deterioration caused by the increased frustration and alienation.

Despite the high levels of voter anger, voters generally do believe in the primacy of democracy and don't want to change our constitutional form of government. In their book, *The Confidence Gap*, Seymour Martin Lipset and William Schneider trace a similar decline in confidence to the one we have presented here. They trace the decline using multiple sources from survey research, measuring the various components of confidence in America's institutions, and they effectively connect that decline with the perception of governmental failure and the actions of the media. We certainly agree with their analysis on this point. They argue, however, that there is no legitimacy crisis because Americans continue to believe that the political system is basically sound—that is, they don't feel the need for some sort of major constitutional changes in our form of our government or *severe* alteration of the power structure. They say that people have simply lost confidence in the leadership of our institutions, not the institutions themselves. Therefore, they conclude that

> Helping to sustain the legitimacy of the country's institutions is the public's belief that, since the failures of the system are the fault of incompetent power-holders, the situation can be greatly improved by changing the incumbent authorities. The cure for a government and an economy that are performing poorly is a change of leadership—brought about by the democratic process.[17]

For our purposes, we agree with their assessment of the public mood—that leadership is the problem—but disagree strongly with the implication of their conclusion. Lipset and Schneider assume that the system and public confidence can be redeemed by changing the leadership through the current system of democratic processes. Yet we have already shown repeatedly, and in detail in Chapter 2, that it is practically impossible to change the "incumbent authorities" in the current system. Therefore, if the only cure is a change in leadership, but the leadership cannot be changed, then the system is indeed in a crisis of legitimacy.

Of course, the leadership in the executive branch can be changed because the system provides adequate competition at that level, as we have seen with the defeat of two of the last three incumbent presidents. Also, most governorships are at least moderately competitive. But this only proves the point that if the legislatures cannot be changed, true reform cannot take place because the executive branch cannot achieve success on its own. Indeed, we have changed presidents eight times since 1960 and the decline continues unabated, despite some momentary recovery after each election.

The excessive focus of attention on campaigns for the presidency and governors by the media directs our attention away from the source of the greatest failure of our democracy. The crisis of legitimacy, therefore, is not that the public doesn't believe in democracy any longer; it is that a large portion of the country no longer believes that our democratic process will ever bring the changes they desire. They can voice that sentiment through presidential elections, but they cannot through legislative elections. This sentiment is displayed in the responses to the questions shown in Table 2, which were identically asked in two na-

Table 2   **Disillusionment with Politics (1992–1993)**

Question: Do you agree/disagree with the following statement?	% Who Agree	
	May 1992	May 1993
The current incumbents will *never* reform the political system.	69	67
Special-interest groups have more influence than voters.	83	84
Congress is largely owned by special-interest groups.	74	74
If the Democrats and Republicans continue to run things, we will never get real reform.	46	45

Adapted from data collected by a Gordon Black Poll.

tional polls conducted in May of 1992 and after the election of Bill Clinton in May of 1993.

The table shows that the election of Bill Clinton did nothing to convince the public of the *possibility* of genuine reform. Even when we ask the question specifically mentioning the two parties, almost half of all adults in the United States believe that the existing parties are incapable of real reform.

Who Drove the Voters Away?

Political research has produced a large body of knowledge attempting to document the causes of these declining attitudes, citing issues ranging from the procedural aspects of voter registration to the loss of electoral competition.[18] Yet given these deep feelings of resentment, as well as the corresponding decline in participation rates, we should ask more than just why, but also, who is to blame? One distinguished scholar, Walter Dean Burnham, places much of the blame directly at the doorstep of the political parties:

> The evidence is pretty overwhelming that the current low levels of participation correspond no longer to sudden inflations of the eligible population base, or to the piling up of procedural barriers designed to discourage participation. They correspond instead to a degeneration, now very far advanced, in the collective structures of electoral politics: in short, to the degeneration of the political parties.[19]

If we accept the idea that these data document the severe deterioration of the representational relationship between those who govern and the 250 million people who depend on them, then we must ask whose role it is to provide that link. Over the past 15 years, as a market research firm, we have seen the results of more than 200 customer satisfaction studies, conducted for many different products and services. *We have never, not once, seen consumers in the private sector in the United States as unhappy with a business or a product as Americans are with their government and political leaders.* The members of our state legislatures and Congress could not last three days in the competitive private sector with this kind of performance. They last in the public sector, by contrast, only because they have unethically created a hegemony over government that is virtually unassailable.

Of course, these are the same people who use their positions in government and their access to the media to go after American business, to abuse those who have successfully built whole industries. These are the same people who attempt to tell the rest of us where we have gone wrong. Based on their records in public life over the past 30 years, these are people who do not know how to tie their own shoelaces. As monopolists, they are an unqualified success. As leaders and public servants, they are a tragic failure.

But where has the failure in the system occurred? Certainly one prime pair of candidates for this dubious honor are the Republican and Democratic parties. To the extent that they claim the mantle of responsibility for representation, they have failed and failed miserably. As we shall see later in this book, today there is very little relationship between what the public actually wants and what the parties provide. At the same time, the political parties are the only effective means to connect voters with their government in a meaningful way, and they have failed in this capacity. In the process, the parties have invented modern politics and destroyed the role and beliefs of millions of voters in the pursuit of short-term political advantage.

The Lessons of 1992: Term Limits and Ross Perot

What does the election of 1992 tell us about our political system? Have the rules of the once comfortable two-party game changed? In 1992, there were twin movements unlike anything ever seen on the American political scene—term limits and Ross Perot. Both movements were the logical result of the deterioration of the public's attitudes about its leadership. By analyzing the public's reaction to term limits and to Perot, we can learn some important characteristics of the newly emerging cleavages and tendencies in American politics and what they mean for the party system.

The Struggle to Limit Terms
In 14 states in the election of 1992, the voter discontent found a politically viable, non-partisan outlet: the term limits movement. This is a perfect example of how American discontent extends beyond the leadership to the structure of the political system itself. The idea behind term limits is simple. If we cannot succeed in voting elected office-holders out of office, we can limit the degree to which they stay in power by legally and constitutionally limiting their tenure in office. The movement was possible because 22 states, mostly in the West and Midwest, have the right of the initiative, which permits citizens to bypass control of the legislature to place a measure directly on the ballot. Only in Florida was the action a result of a legislative vote. The movement started with a successful drive in Oklahoma and then spread to California and Colorado. It sputtered a little in 1990 in Wash-

ington State, when Speaker of the House Thomas Foley (D-Wash.) organized a highly financed, successful effort to frighten the Washington voters with the notion that they would lose billions in defense funds if they lost their powerful members in Congress (including the speaker himself).

In 1992, despite powerful forces aligned against them, grassroots organizations succeeded in passing an unparalleled 13 initiatives and one referendum in the 14 states where the issue was put to the test. Nearly 21 million Americans voted for term limits, resulting in the specter of 181 members of the House serving automatically limited terms ranging from 6 to 12 years (see Table 3). The slogan in Florida, which passed a measure easily, was "eight (years) is enough." The percentage of the voters supporting the limits was overwhelming, averaging from 66 percent to 34 percent.[20]

The movement was successful because angry voters were presented with a way to bypass the legislature and undermine the power and con-

Table 3   **Results of Term Limit Referendums (1992)**

State	Senate	House	Percentages	
			For	Against
Arizona	12 years	6 years	74	26
Arkansas	12 years	6 years	60	40
California	12 years	6 years	63	37
Florida	12 years	8 years	77	23
Michigan	12 years	6 years	59	41
Missouri	12 years	8 years	74	26
Montana	12 years	6 years	67	33
Nebraska	12 years	8 years	68	32
North Dakota	12 years	12 years	55	45
Ohio	12 years	8 years	66	34
Oregon	12 years	6 years	69	31
South Dakota	12 years	12 years	63	37
Washington	12 years	6 years	52	48
Wyoming	12 years	6 years	77	23

Adapted from data collected by the Associated Press.

trol of the incumbents in Congress and the state legislatures as institutions, instead of as individual legislators. Term limits gave voters a mechanism by which they could get at all those "other congressmen," while still voting for their own. In addition, they obviously felt that it was more important to increase turnover in Congress by limiting terms than it was to prolong the career of their own representative, regardless of whether or not they liked him or her. In addition, millions of these voters undoubtedly voted to *reelect* their own congressman, while at the same time they voted to limit their terms. While this may seem ironic, in light of the poor quality of challenging candidates in most districts and the lack of effective electoral competition, it makes perfect sense.

There also seems to be a widely circulated fallacy that somehow the movement to limit terms suddenly appeared on the political scene only in the late '80s. Term limits were actually used in the Articles of the Confederation in 1781, when delegates to the Continental Congress were limited to serving for only three years in any six-year period.[21] In addition, the data on public opinion illustrates the longevity and depth of the issue. The support for term limits has been near or above 50 percent since the 1960s, rising steadily to its current levels of support in the 80 percent range.[22] The opportunity for action on this issue was always there, waiting for someone to organize and capitalize on it. However, the 1992 effort that mobilized across 14 states to gain access to the ballot was prodigious, and the size of that effort itself is an expression of the degree of discontent in American politics today.

The major obstacle stopping institutionalized term limits was the problem of enacting them as law at the federal level. It was commonly thought that term limits could be enacted only through the creation of a constitutional amendment, which would require a two-thirds vote in the House and Senate. Instead, the supporters of term limits decided to attack the issue at another level, arguing that individual states had the right to limit their delegations' terms without a constitutional amendment. After the 1988 election, various groups started to place the issue on the ballot in the upcoming elections. They were extremely successful. This should not be surprising—the term limit groups were like Sunday morning ministers preaching to their flocks. As the public opinion data illustrates, the public had long since been converted to their cause.[23]

The term limit movement should be seen for what it is—positive proof of the American people's desire to reform their institutions and limit the accumulated power of incumbent legislators. The question of whether or not these initiatives will pass the court test is not yet resolved. If the voters feel powerless within existing institutions, it is rational for them to turn to extra-constitutional means to regain that power. It is a sad comment on the state of the American system that they have been forced to do so. At the same time, successful initiatives are possible only in the 22 states possessing the right of initiative. In the remaining 27 states, minus Florida, it is highly unlikely that intransigent legislators will put such measures on the ballot.

Ross Perot and the Summer of Our Discontent

By the summer of 1991, more than a year before the election, we were convinced through our polling that American politics was entering a phase that was qualitatively different than what we had seen earlier. Polling organizations have been tracking two additional dimensions of presidential popularity (besides overall approval) since the late 1930s. It is fairly standard practice to ask one question that measures the approval of the way the president handles foreign policy and foreign affairs, and a second question that measures the approval of the way the president handles the economy. While these questions are independent of the overall approval measure, they effectively measure different components of a president's overall support.

During the invasion of Kuwait, Bush was clearly at his best, and his overall presidential job approval rating and his approval on foreign affairs rose to nearly 90 percent, a level of presidential approval never before attained in polls (see Chart 10). At the same time, however, the approval of his performance in managing the economy was much

Chart 10   **Bush Approval Ratings (July 1990–December 1991)**

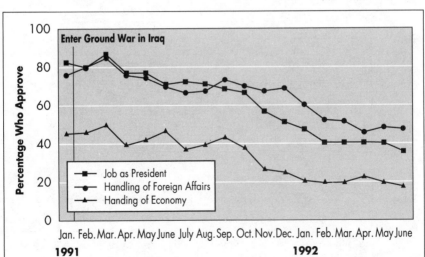

Compiled from The Roper Center Poll Database, surveys from Gallup Organization for Overall Approval, and surveys from CBS News and ABC for Economy and Foreign Affairs.

lower, around 42 percent and declining. As the attention of Americans turned back to the economy after the Persian Gulf War, President Bush's overall approval began to be shaped more by economic issues than by his foreign successes. Bush continued to have relatively high ratings on foreign policy, but the concern of the public had shifted decisively to domestic issues. This resulted in the fastest decline of presidential approval ratings in history.

Bush's drop in approval wasn't merely a reflection of specific discontent with his handling of the office, but was part of a much broader-based discontent that came to the surface of American politics at this time. The war had simply masked the frustration that had been there all along. Other measures—the approval rating of Congress, consumer confidence, and future economic outlook—were indicating that it wasn't only government that was the problem, but that growing numbers of people felt angry and dismayed at the state of the entire nation. One measure of this angst commonly used by pollsters is the "right track/wrong track" question. For the entire year following the summer of 1991, as Chart 11 displays, the percentage of the population who felt that the country was "on the wrong track" continued to increase.[24]

Pollsters saw these signals, but the political elite exhibited a remarkable insularity about them. Every potential major Democratic

Chart 11   **Country on the Wrong Track (1991–1992)**
Question: Do you think things in this country are generally going in the right direction or do you feel things have gotten pretty seriously off on the wrong track?

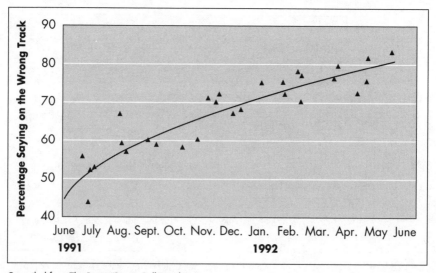

challenger—Sam Nunn, Bill Bradley, Al Gore, Mario Cuomo—failed to smell the scent of Bush's vulnerability. Outside the Beltway, however, Americans were extraordinarily vocal about their unhappiness, and some even began to take action. For example, a retired Florida investment counselor, Jack Gargan, took $45,000 of his own money and placed six full-page advertisements in regional newspapers calling for Americans to "Throw the Hypocritical Rascals Out" (T.H.R.O.). When the mail in response finally subsided, Americans from all walks of life had sent Gargan more than $250,000 to continue his efforts, and by late 1993, he had placed over 630 full-page newspaper advertisements paid for entirely by voluntary contributions. Another disaffected citizen, Lionel Kunst of Kansas City, organized a national effort called the Coalition to End the Permanent Congress. His organization has encouraged more than 100 candidates to seek office in an effort to change Congress.

Although the national media paid scant attention to the expressions of frustration, there were signs all over the country that the 1992 election was going to be different. The underlying political conditions were ripe for a "revolt of the moderates," but the difficulty of organizing such a movement prevented widespread expressions of discontent. Usually, people who are angry most of the time do not organize to take action. In fact, successful organization is extremely difficult to achieve under most circumstances because of what is known as the "free rider problem." The free rider problem is simple: as long as individuals will receive the benefits of organizing for a specific purpose, without paying any of the costs of organizing, rational people will abstain from participating in that collective action.[25]

For a political movement to occur, some people have to be so highly motivated that they are willing to pay most or all of the costs of organizing. Under most circumstances, this impediment makes organizing a large-scale, national organization very unlikely unless there are specific economic incentives at stake. Another factor that stands in the way of organizations of this kind is the negative perception that success is very unlikely. Organizing the entire country is an enormous task, and there are only limited historical precedents to support a belief that success of any significance is possible. Under most circumstances, people will not by themselves generate the effort necessary to make such a success possible, even when discontent is widespread. And, of course, there are few people who could generate this kind of effort. The presumption of failure discourages all but the most ardent organizers.

The failure of the national media to appreciate the deep desire for a real alternative like Ross Perot makes the success of an outside candidate even more unlikely. Perot, however, offered to solve these organizational impediments. The most important quality about Ross Perot, at the outset, was that he could pledge to pay *all of the costs* required to run a campaign. His pledge, coupled with his ability and willingness to spend his own resources, immediately solved the free rider problem for everyone who was unhappy, and the normal barriers to organizing became irrelevant. In addition, Ross Perot, for all of his billions, was also in touch with the concerns of Americans in a manner almost totally outside of the experience or possibility of those who lived and worked inside the Beltway. From the first moment of his campaign on "The Larry King Show," Perot spoke the language of revolt and reform that reflected the unexpressed sentiments of millions of Americans. His words were the embodiment of the public's frustration and discontent.

When Perot avowed that he might be willing to run, one million potential volunteers attempted to reach the Perot headquarters during the next three days. Between February and May, Perot became the most important feature in American politics, as both of the traditional political parties promoted the candidacies of men whom most Americans did not like. Yet the polling on the Perot candidacy still did not capture the magnitude of his support, and much of the polling failed miserably to ask the kind of questions that would explore the depth and passion of this support. As usual, the national media, and their pollsters, viewed Perot only in the short term, and not in the much broader context of 30 years of rising discontent.

Support for Perot in the polls rose steadily during April and May, and in June he actually surged ahead in several polls. In late May, Perot was a strong second and looked like he could actually win in November. The reason for the breadth of his support is that Perot was gathering support from the center. He was a centrist candidate, not a radical. The most significant advantage of the centrist candidate traditionally is being the second choice for the supporters of both the more liberal candidate and the more conservative candidate. Because Perot was taking over the center position, he stood to take the moderates' vote away from both Bush and Clinton. If either of the other two candidates found themselves in third place in October, that candidate would suffer the "wasted vote" problem, and they would suffer the defections that would occur as the actual election approached. Those defections would go to Perot from either Clinton or Bush (see Table 4).

The wasted vote problem is a very simple voting dilemma that confronts the voters who support the weakest of three candidates in a three-candidate race. The issue for the voter is simple: should they vote for their preferred candidate, who seems to have little chance of winning, or should they switch to their second choice in order to keep the

Table 4 **Voters' Second Choices (1992)**

Group	Date	Candidate Named as Second Choice (in percent)			Organization
		Perot	Bush	Clinton	
Clinton voters	June 14	51	25	**	CBS
Bush voters	June 14	41	**	33	CBS
All voters	Oct. 28	40	20	19	NBC/Hart
All voters	Oct. 11	33	19	18	Times Mirror
Registered voters	Oct. 22	46	21	17	Times Mirror

Adapted from data collected by The Roper Center. Date cited is day interviewing was completed.

person they like the least from winning? In 1968, voters defected from George Wallace toward the end of his campaign, dropping his vote from a high of about 22 percent in the polls to a final vote of 13 percent. That did not mean that the Wallace supporters in the polls suddenly stopped liking George Wallace, only that a Wallace vote was a wasted vote. John Anderson in 1980 suffered even worse defections, dropping from more than 25 percent in some polls to a final vote of 6 percent. The meaning of this is of considerable importance. If Perot could run second in the polls in mid-October, he would be the recipient of the defectors from one of the other two candidates and his vote would surge. As the centrist candidate, Perot would pick up voters regardless of which of the other two was the weaker candidate. We will return to this issue in more detail in a moment, when we examine some voter data from the November election.

In June, we released a national survey, and we argued that it appeared likely, barring a major stumble, that Perot's support would continue to surge upward to somewhere in the 40 to 45 percent range. In a sense, the campaign was his to win, or lose, depending upon how he would handle the myriad of pressures and problems that arise in the course of a presidential campaign.

Missing the Mark

What happened to Perot? Why did his campaign start to weaken, even before he dropped out of the race? We would guess that no one, perhaps not even Perot, anticipated the remarkable outpouring of effort and sentiment that he provoked initially. Certainly the meager Perot organization in Dallas was not prepared for the volume of phone calls, mail, and faxes it received. The result was chaos, with the Perot organization doing its best to meet the requirements for mounting a successful national campaign, but often falling short simply because the demands were excessive by any standard. It is not surprising in retrospect that Perot and his organization made mistakes. But the moments of opportunity in American politics are extremely infrequent, and the mistakes probably cost Perot the presidency.

Perot built the first phase of his campaign using his access to the free national media with extraordinary skill. He appeared on most of the national talk shows and television magazines repeatedly, and until he was a declared candidate, the networks did not have to guarantee equal time to the other candidates. Although Ross Perot was already well known to opinion leaders, his name was far from a household word. Using the free media almost exclusively, he accomplished the first task of a candidate—building awareness of who he was among the American people.

Public awareness of Perot grew consistently from late March through late May. During this period, the public greeted him favorably, according to the polls. Table 5 shows that the ratio of people with favorable opinions of Perot, as opposed to unfavorable, was usually 2 to 1, if not more. Comparing favorability among different sets of polls should be done with caution. The various polling organizations word

Table 5 **Perot Favorability Ratings (1992)**

Date	% Favorable	% Unfavorable	% Neutral/Haven't Heard Enough/No Opinion	Organization
March 20	20	12	69	Gallup
March 26	16	8	76	CBS/NYT
March 31	32	10	58	Gallup
April 9	30	15	55	Yankelovich
April 20	21	9	70	CBS/NYT
May 7	47	15	38	Gallup
May 13	35	16	49	Yankelovich
May 21	30	15	55	Gordon Black
May 28	53	26	29	Times Mirror

Adapted from data collected by The Roper Center Poll Database.

the questions somewhat differently and place the questions in different points in the survey. The list of surveys in Table 5 is meant to provide a sample of Perot's favorability ratings during the spring of 1992, not to provide a trend line.

The Failure to Use Paid Media

The free media has a central limitation. It requires the voluntary activity of tuning in to a specific program on the part of the public. As a result, as of mid-May, around 50 percent of the electorate still did not have enough information on Perot to form an opinion, either positive or negative. Moreover, a poll conducted for NBC News/*Wall Street Journal* in the third week in May found that even those who knew about him didn't know very much[26] (see Table 6).

That "lack of awareness" made Perot uniquely vulnerable to the counterattack that was bound to emerge as the other two parties began to perceive that Perot was a serious threat. The free media was a perfect strategy to build initial awareness, but it was a poor vehicle both for countering these attacks and for building a central focus for the campaign in the minds of the electorate. In the free media format, a candidate cannot dictate the questions and cannot guarantee that the right people will see the message. The continued use of the free media format did not permit Perot to provide a consistent focus on reform to the voters, particularly those who did not know much about him, and did not permit Perot to effectively counter the charges that were being made against him daily. As a result, Perot was vulnerable in June, and the counterattack that month caused his polling numbers to slip as voters began to have doubts about his character as a presidential candidate. As both Bush and Clinton started to challenge Perot's statements,

Table 6   **Voter Knowledge of Perot**

Question: How much would you say you know about Ross Perot and what he stands for?

Response	Percent
A great deal	4
Quite a bit	13
Just some	34
Very little	30
Nothing at all	18

Adapted from data collected by The Roper Center and NBC News/*Wall Street Journal* Poll, May 1992.

stories started to appear on Perot as a dictator in his firm, an auto-
cratic with employees, and so forth.

The purpose of our discussion here is not to rehash the events that
took place from July through September. In mid-July, Perot withdrew
from the campaign and remained largely on the sidelines until late
September, when he reemerged as a candidate. During the same time,
the organizational effort continued—with his financial support—to
secure a place for him on the ballot in all 50 states. That effort was successful before the end of September, and Perot returned as an active
candidate. His withdrawal, however, was a bitter pill for the huge numbers of people who had quite literally put their own lives on hold and
joined the crusade to get Ross Perot on the ballot.

The Surge in October

Perot entered the October campaign in a deep hole, which he had
largely dug for himself when he pulled out of the race. In his spring
campaign, his competitive advantage over the other candidates was
that in general, people believed him and trusted him. In April, an NBC
News/*Wall Street Journal* Poll asked voters the reasons why they would
consider supporting Perot. The most common response (28 percent)
was that "He is honest and says what he believes."[27] In contrast, after
he pulled out of the race, the public opinion data showed that Perot's
supporters felt that they had been deceived. An October 4, CBS
News/*New York Times* Poll asked people who had supported Perot in
the spring why they no longer supported him. The poll found that 80
percent of his one-time supporters, who now intended to vote for other
candidates, "didn't trust him" because he had quit the race.[28]

However, Perot's support in the polls, which had declined to as low
as five to seven percent in September, started to climb back up with his
first debate and with his initial infomercials (see Charts 12 and 13). By
the next-to-the-last week before the election, Perot's percentage in several polls exceeded 20 percent while Clinton's lead was shrinking badly,
even though it remained substantial.

Conventional wisdom says that once an individual forms a negative opinion of a candidate, it is difficult to convince that person to vote
for the candidate. This concept is the rationale behind negative campaigning—the goal being to drive up a candidate's "negatives." The
election of 1992 offers a serious challenge to this theory. We witnessed
the formulation and reformulation of Bill Clinton in the summer, and
the re-creation of Ross Perot during the debates in the fall.

Certainly, one reason for the rebirth of Perot was that he ran a
campaign that largely avoided the negative tone of the other two campaigns. He forced the other candidates to stay on the issues and he

Chart 12   **The Perot Polling Results (October 1992)**

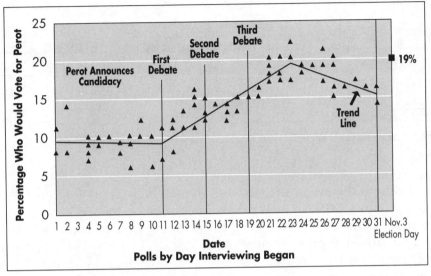

Adapted from *The Public Perspective*, Nov./Dec. 1992.

avoided attacking the other candidates personally, even when he had easy opportunities to do so. The response to the question in Table 7, asked in late October by Lou Harris & Associates, demonstrates the reaction to this campaign style.

Chart 13   **Popular Opinion of Perot (October 1992)**

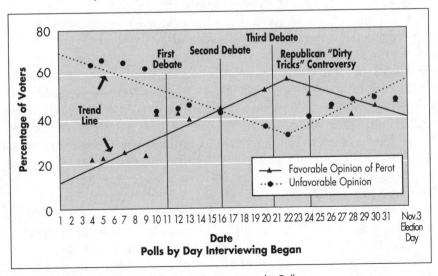

Compiled using The Poll Database, The Roper Center; surveys by Gallup.

Table 7   **Popular Perception of Campaign Style**

Question: Who would you say ran the most positive campaign focused on the issues?

Candidate	Percent
George Bush	16
Bill Clinton	32
Ross Perot	46

Adapted from data collected by Lou Harris and Associates, October 30–November 1, 1992.

Even on the eve of the election, the public support for Perot was quite strong. A CBS News/*New York Times* Poll on the weekend before the election found that 34 percent of the public felt that Perot would do the best job solving the country's economic problems.[29] This response, on the single most important issue of the campaign, is indicative of the support he held throughout the month. This percentage did not translate into more votes for one good reason—nobody thought Perot could actually win. That same CBS poll in late October found that only 4 percent of registered voters thought that Perot would win.[30] If a voter perceives that their candidate cannot win, many will be rationally unwilling to "waste" their vote on the losing candidate, even if they might have preferred him to the other candidates.[31]

Toward the end of October, we witnessed one of the most bizarre weeks in the modern history of political polling. The Gallup Organization, which is the oldest and best-known name in public polling, suddenly switched the base group on which it was reporting poll results from "registered voters" to "registered and likely voters." This change reduced the Gallup Poll's margin for Clinton to under three percentage points, and they and their clients CNN and *USA Today* declared the presidential race now too close to call. This was disastrous for Perot because George Bush suddenly became a competitive candidate, putting further pressure on Perot voters to choose one of the two other candidates. Then, a few days later, Gallup declared Clinton the probable winner by a huge margin, 48 percent for Clinton, 38 percent for Bush, and 13 percent for Perot. The actual vote count 24 hours later was 43 percent for Clinton, 38 percent for Bush, and 19 percent for Perot.

From "too close to call" to an "electoral landslide" in just four days; it was not a good week for Gallup, their clients, and the entire polling industry. Gallup was wrong by the largest margin in its history. Something was very wrong at the House of Gallup, and that something detracted from the campaign and the polling enterprise.

How Polling Can Influence Elections

If Perot had been in second place in the polls in late October, we noted before that he would have been well positioned to benefit from the voters who would defect from the other two candidates. However, because he was in third place in the polls, it was his voters who were under the pressure to defect rather than waste their votes.

The wasted vote problem is one of the few instances in which the character of the polling conducted during the campaign can actually shape the character of voting on election day. Without public opinion polls, the voters really cannot be sure which of three candidates is losing, although they well might guess based on history that the weaker candidate is likely to be the independent candidate such as Ross Perot (or John Anderson, or George Wallace). With polling, however, this problem should be reduced or eliminated, if the polling is conducted properly.

Polling contributes to this problem, in part, because the division on the primary voter choice question used in polling can become a self-fulfilling prophecy, shaping the very behavior that it is trying to predict. The "voter choice" question commonly used by pollsters does not ask which candidate the voters actually *prefer*, but asks instead how they would vote if the election was held at that particular moment in time. The act of voting reflects more than just preferences. It also reflects a "strategic choice" *based on which candidates voters think are likely to win or lose the election.* After all, if a vote for your favorite candidate will result in the election of your least-favorite candidate, you may be better off voting for your second choice. But how do voters determine the relative strength of the three candidates? From the polls! In other words, the polls provide voters with information on the likelihood of outcomes, and this information affects the decisions of the voters, making the likely outcomes "more likely" to occur.

Because there were three viable candidates in 1992, polling organizations should have been consistently asking instead: "Regardless of who you think will win, which candidate would you prefer to be president?" If they had done so, perceptions about Perot's strength would have been different. Gallup, which asked a preference question two weeks before the election, found that Perot had reached 28 percent and was statistically tied with Bush, but the media chose not to explain the meaning and importance of the finding.[32] As far as we know, the finding was never published, except in professional journals after the election. There was a chance that President Bush would have been perceived as the third choice among the three candidates, and it would have been *his* voters facing the wasted vote problem. Bush's voters, if they had defected, would have gone overwhelmingly to Perot because, as we showed before, Perot was the second choice among both the Bush and the Clinton voters.

More than any third-party candidate in modern history, Perot fell victim to failed polling that did what polling is *never intended* to do—actually shape the way people vote by supplying the voters with misleading information. The national polls did not intend this outcome, but it happened because the polls were done the way they are *always* done in two-candidate races, without thinking about the consequences.

There is an important lesson in this. Candidate polls should be altered in three-candidate situations at all levels of office to include a preference question along with the candidate choice question. The question is simple: "Which candidate would you actually prefer to win the presidency—Republican George Bush, Democrat Bill Clinton, or Independent Ross Perot?" The question can also be asked in the form: "Will you vote for [?] if you think he has a chance to win?" If the media companies refuse this request for fairness, the third-party candidates should force the issue in whatever manner they can. This issue is far too influential to our democracy to leave its resolution to the chance good will or understanding of an editor or a pollster.

Perot, during the month of October, defied nearly every expert opinion regarding the campaign. Despite his earlier withdrawal (which he acknowledged as a mistake), despite his choice of a vice presidential candidate (who was not successfully cast for the role), and despite the mistake in discussing threats against himself and his family during the last week of the campaign, what Perot accomplished in October has the potential to rewrite presidential campaigns.

- His use of 30-minute infomercials defied predictions of failure. The media and advertising people said that the American people would never watch. In the final analysis, however, he was named "Advertiser of the Year" by *Advertising Age* magazine. How did the people react to the infomercials? According to a survey by Lou Harris & Associates, 73 percent of the public thought the infomercials were effective, with 34 percent saying they were "very effective."[33]
- He conducted his entire campaign without the usual criss-crossing of the country, concentrating instead on the production of his half-hour presentations.
- His conduct in the campaign avoided invective, innuendo, vicious charges, and unfair characterizations. He set a standard for clean campaigning that took us back to the era before spin doctors and advertising advisors.

- He entered the debates without a staff of trainers, coaches, media experts, and debating teachers. He held his own in the first two debates, and in the final debate won decisively in the polls of public opinion.
- He managed to make the federal deficit a major voting issue of the campaign.
- He forced the other candidates to deal with issues in greater specificity than ever before, and he forced both candidates to give pledges for reforms that both parties had heretofore ignored.

In terms of dollars spent for votes cast, Perot ran one of the most successful campaigns in history. He spent $65 million and secured 19 percent of the popular vote. In comparison, Bush and Clinton each spent more the $200 million when both hard and soft moneys are counted.

The Radicalized Moderates

There is one important reason why we want to understand the support that Perot received. The people's willingness to vote for him even though they knew he would lose, and the large portion of his electorate that supported him during the spring are important issues. Understanding the nature of his support illuminates the key groups that the present political system has alienated, and the issues that have driven those individuals and groups to break the long-held bonds of the two-party system. Indeed, this analysis shows that the current two-party system has radicalized the moderates. Despite fervent campaigning by Bill Clinton and George Bush to woo moderate support, the moderates did not return to the fold as predicted, and they are just as alienated today as they were in the spring of 1992.

A "centrist revolt" in American politics is almost a contradiction in terms. Historically, most political revolts occur on either the extreme left or right of politics, and not in the center. Centrists are moderates in most respects, and they tend as a group to lack the intensity of preference that makes those on the extremes so formidable organizationally. The Republican Party began as a movement of the extreme on the issue of slavery. Populism was a left-wing movement politically, and the Dixiecrats and the Wallace Movement were propelled from the right. People who are political centrists aren't usually angry enough to form a movement. The exceptions are the Progressives from the first two decades of the twentieth century, and the Anderson independent candidacy from 1980. Anderson is really a very direct precursor of Perot.

In fact, the best analogy to the Perot phenomenon doesn't come from the United States. It comes from France in the 1950s, when General Charles DeGaulle returned from retirement to lead a centrist movement of political reform to restructure the political system. Like the Gaullists, the supporters of Ross Perot came from the political center. *The main importance of Perot is that he illustrated that the American political system has, in the terms of political scientist Theodore Lowi, "radicalized" that portion of the electorate that should never be radical—the political middle.* Traditionally, the two parties compete for the middle, where the largest bloc of voters is located. These votes are crucial in forming a governing coalition, which is why the Perot appeal is so significant. Perot illustrated that the middle is willing to desert the parties if given an effective alternative.

A poll we conducted in May 1992 showed distinct differences between Perot voters and supporters of Clinton and Bush. These voters were:

- More likely to be independent or without party affiliation. (A in Table 8)
- More disillusioned and angry with the government and the existing political parties. (B in Table 8)
- More outraged by the role of money and lobbyists in politics, and more committed to institutional reform and democratic reforms of every type. (C in Table 8)
- More committed to reform of education, welfare, and other programs. (D in Table 8)
- More centrist in terms of political philosophy. The Perot movement was not skewed towards either conservatives or liberals. Perot was the first choice among self-described moderates, and 53 percent of his supporters identified themselves as moderates. (E in Table 8)

If a new party is to emerge in American politics, it is important to establish who that party would appeal to and what issues drive those participants. Any vital political organization depends ultimately on an issue base for sustenance. The 19 percent of the electorate who voted for Perot clearly indicates that there is a large number of people eager

Table 8   **Supporter Profiles for the 1992 Presidential Election (May 1992)**

	Question	Response	Bush	Clinton	Perot
			Percent Who Intend to Vote for:		
A	Party Affiliation	Democrat	9	71	28
		Republican	61	5	29
		Independent	26	22	39
B	Performance of: The President	Angry or dissatisfied	27	92	82
	The Senate	Angry or dissatisfied	66	70	78
	The House	Angry or dissatisfied	67	63	75
C	If Democrats and Republicans continue to run things we will never get real reform.	Agree	35	36	64
	Special interests have more influence than voters.	Agree	77	84	88
	Congress is largely owned by special interests.	Agree	68	71	84
	Prohibit campaign contribution from PACs.	Agree	64	63	72
D	Areas of the federal government that should be completely overhauled:	Welfare system	58	53	64
		Public education	33	39	42
		Trade policy with Japan	33	41	39
		Agricultural policy	22	25	29
E	**Political Philosophy**		**Bush**	**Clinton**	**Perot**
	Conservative		50	14	32
	Middle of the Road		34	23	36
	Liberal		22	41	32

Adapted from data collected by The Gordon Black Poll.

to look beyond the choices provided by the two-party system. The analysis shows that these voters are centrist, moderate, and have a commonly shared anger. All they need to break from the current system is leadership and opportunity.

One of the best sources of data on the Perot movement comes from the national exit polls conducted for the news networks by Voter Research & Surveys. The exit polls constitute nationally representative samples of the 55 percent of eligible voters who actually made it to the polls on election day. We already showed you some of what the Perot movement looked like in May of 1992. However, we need to understand a little bit more about Perot's demographic and geographic appeal.

Like all candidates, Perot's support varied significantly by region and state. In terms of percentage of the vote, his top ten states all have one thing in common—they are all far from the Beltway (see Table 9). They are representative of parts of this country that have been left out of modern power politics. In general, these states are mostly rural.

Overall, Perot's support was slightly more likely to come from the West and the Midwest and tended to run slightly higher in the suburbs and rural areas than in cities (see Table 10). However, the differences in his support by region and population aren't enough to make much of a difference.

Demographically, the Perot voters are surprisingly representative of the public as a whole. There simply are no clear demographic attrib-

Table 9   **Perot's Ten Best States**

State	Percent of Supporting Vote	Total Vote
Maine	30	205,076
Utah	29	202,605
Idaho	28	129,897
Kansas	27	310,458
Nevada	27	129,532
Alaska	27	55,085
Wyoming	26	51,209
Montana	26	106,869
Oregon	25	307,860
Washington	24	470,239

Adapted from data collected by VRS, *Congressional Quarterly*, November 7, 1992, p.3552.

Table 10   **Geographic Profile of Perot Voters**

Region	Percent All Voters	Percent Perot Voters
East	24	22
Midwest	27	29
South	29	25
West	20	24
Community		
City: Pop. Over 500,000	9	6
City: Pop. 250,000–500,000	3	3
City: Pop. 50,000–250,000	12	10
Small cities & towns (Pop. under 50,000)	11	11
Suburbs	41	44
Rural	24	25

Adapted from data collected by VRS.

utes within the group, as is found with most political organizations (see Chart 14). They are balanced economically, though they are more likely to be middle class. They consider themselves moderate in political philosophy and, not surprisingly, they are far less likely to have a political affiliation than those who vote for the other candidates.

Unlike both the major parties, demographic and socioeconomic factors are not the glue holding the Perot constituency together. What makes Perot voters different is their desire for reform and their concern over fiscal issues such as the economy and the debt. On election day, VRS asked voters what issues mattered most in deciding their vote. Table 11 details what the most important issues were for the supporters of the three candidates.

Perot supporters picked the budget deficit as one of their most important issues, which is dramatically different from the other candidates' supporters. This means that the budget deficit is fast becoming a defining issue in American politics. A significant group of voters are starting to use the deficit issue as the primary determinant of their voting choices, much like abortion is a defining issue for some voters, both liberals and conservatives.

The fiscal conservatism of the Perot voters showed up in other measures as well. One question in the exit poll asked voters to choose between a large activist government or a smaller, less active govern-

Chart 14   **Demographic Profile of Perot Voters**

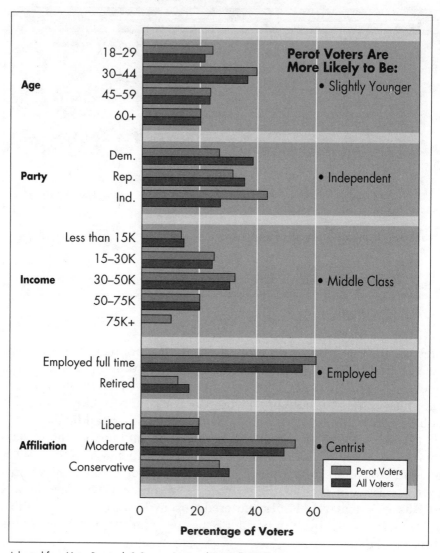

Adapted from Voter Research & Surveys National Exit Poll, 1992.

ment. Although this question doesn't delineate which services would be cut from today's large government, it is useful as a general gauge of attitudes about the role of government in our society. On this question the Perot voters look much more like Bush voters than Clinton voters (see Table 12).

Although the Perot supporters are fiscally conservative when it comes to government spending, this conservatism does not necessarily translate to social conservatism. While the Perot voters are certainly

Table 11   **Issues Most Important to Voters**

Question: What issues mattered most when deciding how to vote?

Response	Percent Clinton Voters	Percent Bush Voters	Percent Perot Voters
Health care	30	10	14
Federal budget deficit	18	15	42
Abortion	10	18	5
Education	17	8	10
Economy/jobs	50	28	52
Environment	9	2	4
Taxes	8	22	13
Foreign policy	1	18	2
Family values	7	27	9

Adapted from data collected by VRS.

more socially conservative than Clinton voters, they lack the stridency of many of the Republican partisans. For example, Table 13 displays the opinions of the voters on the issue of abortion. The relative distribution of the Perot voters' opinions about abortion falls between the Clinton supporters and the Bush voters, although they are decidedly more pro-choice than the Bush coalition.

At the end of the election, the Perot voters appeared much the same as they did in June, when they were first defined in the Gordon Black Poll we described earlier. They are more likely to be independent, moderate on policies, centrist, and passionately committed to the revolutionary idea that a government should balance its books and create

Table 12   **Voter Preferences for Government Services and Taxes**

Question: Which of the following would you rather have?

Response	Percent Clinton Voters	Percent Perot Voters	Percent Bush Voters
Government provides more services but raises taxes?	55	26	20
Government lowers taxes but provides fewer services?	36	66	72

Adapted from data collected by VRS.

Table 13   **Voter Positions on Abortion**

Question: Which comes closest to your position on abortion?

Response	Percent Clinton Voters	Percent Perot Voters	Percent Bush Voters
Abortion should be legal in all cases.	46	37	19
Abortion should be legal in most cases.	31	32	27
Abortion should be illegal in most cases.	14	21	35
Abortion should be illegal in all cases.	5	6	15

Adapted from data collected by VRS.

processes that are fair. Other than this, the Perot constituency is a remarkably accurate reflection, demographically, of the country as a whole. Perot was not a normal presidential candidate and his constituency was not a normal constituency. These voters share the fiscal conservatism of the Republicans, and the social moderation of the Democrats. On issues of political and governmental reform, however, they are angry and disillusioned with both parties and with those in power. Moreover, they are inclined to reject the interest-group domination of the Democratic Party and the moral majority domination of the Republicans. Given the domination of both parties by special interests, these voters have no where to go politically.

The success of Perot can be understood as a siren call that the political center is now ready to act decisively to get what it wants out of the political system, if they are provided with leadership. The candidacy of Ross Perot has identified a segment of the electorate that refuses to accept the status quo any longer. Perot has demonstrated that it is possible to energize the political power of the middle to launch serious races for office. The nature of the Perot constituency did not change in character from May to November, and, as we will see later, his constituency remained very much the same well into the summer of 1993. The constituency appears to have the stability necessary to grow into a more potent force. It is not changing in response to short-term political stimuli. It remains to be seen, however, whether this force can be focused politically to achieve the reforms necessary to repair the damage of the last 30 years.

The New Politics of Disorder

What does the success of Ross Perot tell us about the nature of our political system? Ross Perot was successful precisely because he operated in a system in which all the institutions that once provided order, loyalty, and stability no longer do so, and because he had a message that appealed to the core of voters who no longer have loyalties tying them to either political party. He was both the benefactor of that disorder and the recipient of the hope for a better system. In the end, Perot emerged because the attitudinal structures of American politics created a detached political constituency that was a ready market for him. Ross Perot must be understood, in the final analysis, both as the result of history, and the maker of history.

The broader effects of the deterioration of the loyalties to the two-party system can also be seen in the public's reaction to Bill Clinton. The quick collapse of public support for Bill Clinton means the president can no longer count on a window of opportunity to enact even parts of his program. In this atmosphere, individual legislators have even less motivation to cooperate toward broad-based goals and more motivation to use the weakness and uncertainty to advance their own narrow interests. Public opinion rises and falls in response to short-term events and media attacks, with no central core of loyalties to stabilize it. This is the politics of electoral disorder.

We started with despair. We started with the growing sense of powerlessness and hopelessness in the face of indifference by our elected officeholders. If there is no choice at the polls, why should we vote? If we have no choice at the polls, why should elected officeholders pay any attention at all to what we think and feel? If our elected officials scorn the bond of honesty and candor we expect of them, why should we trust them? If the special interests can control the progress and content of public policy with a few million dollars of campaign contributions giving them access to the policy process, why bother to participate? In the face of certain defeat, why struggle? Who will look out for the interests of either the majority of current voters or for the generations that are to follow?

If the current democratic processes are not producing either the leadership or the potential for change necessary to legitimize our institutions, then we must look outside the current paradigm to find both. The only institution capable of providing leadership and the potential for change in a democratic system is a political party. Only the political party, as an institution, can aggregate the dispersed, unfocused public sentiment into political action on a scale broad enough at both the state and national levels of government. A successful political party restores competition and political choice by running candidates to challenge incumbents. Neither an interest group nor an educational group like United We Stand, America can do this. The restoration of fiscal responsibility and public confidence can occur only if we restore choice. Political parties promote electoral choice. *The implication of this logic, which will be supported in great detail later, is that the only way to restore the legitimacy of our institutions is the creation of a new, centrist political party of reform.*

Nowhere in the existing literature does anyone put forth a rationale for why we should expect the current officeholders or party system to solve the basic problems in our political system. Supporters of the current system ignore one central truth: if the accountability between the public and the government officials has failed, then the political parties as vehicles for conveying public sentiment have failed by implication. Why they failed, and why we cannot expect them to reform themselves, are the subjects of the next chapter.

5

The American Two-Party System in Decline

> Any analysis of where the American party system is heading must include the possibility that it is headed into oblivion.[1]
>
> —James L. Sundquist

A common myth about political parties and the two-party system emerged during the 1992 presidential election. Listening to the experts from the national media and to prominent figures in the two major parties, one would have thought that the two-party system, dominated by the Republicans and Democrats, was a creation of the Founding Fathers, sanctified in the canons of the Constitution. When Ross Perot had the temerity to threaten the tight little game controlled by the two parties, the Washington pundits came forward to warn of the dire consequences of his assault on the two-party system. We heard predictions of a constitutional crisis caused by a deadlocked electoral college and the spectre of a Democratic House voting to thrust the then third-place Bill Clinton on an unsuspecting populace.

As we noted in Chapter 1, public opinion research demonstrates that support for the two-party system has been declining slowly since the 1930s. In 1938, a mere 13 percent of the electorate felt there was a need for a new party to challenge the major parties. By October 1992, on the eve of the presidential election, 63 percent of the electorate favored the creation of a third political force.[2] What happened to our belief in the political parties and the two-party system?

The reality of the party system is in fact very different, both historically and currently, than what many party politicians would have the public believe. As is familiar from the accounts of the Constitutional Convention, our ancestors were profoundly suspicious of factions, organized minorities, and other entities that might become tyrannical. In fact, George Washington was positively disdainful of parties and warned against their formation. A. James Reichley, a former Brookings Institution scholar and author of the *Life of the Parties*, described the feelings of the Founding Fathers this way:

> Parties, by framing every issue in terms of winners and losers, the Founders believed, undermine this indispensable willingness to seek at some level the common good rather than the satisfaction of special interests. Parties, therefore, are socially destructive and must be considered, as Madison wrote, a potentially "mortal disease"; as Hamilton claimed, an "avenue to tyranny;" and as Washington insisted, a source of "frightful despotism."[3]

Despite the concerns of our first president, the original political parties quickly formed around the conflicting views of Hamilton, who believed in a strong federal government, and of Jefferson, who wanted to preserve the prerogatives of the states. Some political theorists have argued that the persistence of a largely two-party system in the United States, as opposed to multiple parties, is a product of three key factors:

1. Regional differences in culture, ethnicity, and social class are relatively small in this country.
2. Elections are conducted in "single-member districts" in the United States.
3. The two parties, operating as a cartel, have created powerful constitutional, legal, and administrative barriers that discourage the formation of effective third parties.

In terms of regional variations, America has not traditionally been characterized by the clustering of large concentrations of politically powerful ethnic minorities in distinct regions, as Canada has with the French in Quebec. African-Americans, for example, conducted a long migration out of the South in search of jobs, diminishing their potential for a regional party. Hispanics, Asian-Americans, and African-Americans have clustered in some regions, but they have not developed the kinds of distinct, unified, and separate political programs needed to sustain a third party. Instead, they have opted to form coalitions with the major parties. Also, class-based parties have not emerged as distinct entities, except for such minor parties as the Socialists and Communists. This is not to say that regional, ethnic, and class voting is not an important part of American politics. Indeed, when regional differences have become crucial in the United States, political efforts outside the two-party system have been more likely to emerge. The political movements that emerged from conflicts over civil rights are prime examples. Both the Dixiecrats in 1948 with Strom Thurman and the American Independent Party of George Wallace in 1968 are reflections of this regional variation in the modern era. Also, interest in the Socialists rose during the economic dislocation of the Great Depression. But these types of regional movements are not a constant and enduring factor in American politics.

The lack of breakaway parties is also significantly due to the logic of political organizing in a single-member district system. A single-member district means simply that only a single candidate can win in any given district's election. Most federal and state legislative districts are single-member districts. By building coalitions, based on some temporary common goal or view, the various factions in a single-member district increase the probability of electing public officials responsive to their cause. This produces a pressure for two distinct coalitions to emerge in each district. With single-member districts widely in use in the United States, particularly at the presidential level, there always exists the pressure to merge multiple-party efforts into two, thereby maximizing the chance of success.

Finally, in order to make their hegemony over the voters' choices complete, the two parties have conspired in most state legislatures to create a wide variety of impediments to the formation of new parties. In some states, such as New York, a political party can't have a line on the ballot until it has won some 50,000 votes in the race for governor. This means the proponents of creating a political party must wait four years for the opportunity to form, making organization based on immediate political events extremely difficult. Other impediments include very large registration drives required in very tight time frames, voters' inability to register as members of a party unless that party is certified statewide, and all kinds of formal reporting criteria for money and organizational character. Florida, for example, requires 196,255 signatures for a party to gain access to the ballot.[4] These restrictions are justified as providing "reasonable requirements" for regulating the electoral process, but their real effect and intent is to make it difficult for a national, or even regional, third party to form.

The Republicans and Democrats in Decline

Why is the domination of the current parties such a problem? Because the parties have lost touch with the main concerns of the majority of Americans and have been captured by minority elements within their ranks. These minorities warp their priorities and render them impotent to act as positive forces for reform and change. We have already shown how interest groups, through the PAC system of funding, have come to dominate the electoral process and translate their financial support into legislative victories of great value to the myriad of special interests they represent. But what about the political parties? Why don't the Republican and Democratic parties live up to their promise to serve the general public by converting public sentiment into public policy representing the majority of Americans' wants and needs? Why don't the parties channel and contain the unbridled self-interest represented by the special-interest groups? What role do the parties play in the continuing dissatisfaction of the American electorate?

The crucial problem of the two parties is precisely this: they have failed as a system of popular representation. Historically, the parties mediated between the governors and the governed, between the elected aristocracy in Washington and the voters on which they rely. As we have noted before, however, the officeholders in the existing party system no longer need to represent the interests of the voters, and they no longer serve as a counterweight to narrow special interests, who are therefore able to rule the policy process for their own ends.

In a narrow sense, the two parties do govern, or rather present the *trappings* of governance to the public. They do control positions of power in state and federal government, and they do sometimes behave with a high degree of cohesiveness in Congress and the state legislatures. However, when it comes to the actual content of decisions, the members of both parties protect their own interests first, the needs of the special interests second, and those of the general public last, if at all. After all, the current party system is the creation of the parties themselves, and it is designed to do two main things: protect incumbents and try to win one major office—the presidency. Of course, to some extent the parties try to increase their seats in Congress and in state legislatures, but these efforts are concentrated on a tiny minority of races. To truly understand why the two parties have become so aloof from the average voter, we need to understand a number of changes that have taken place in party politics over the last 30 years.

The Changing Character
of Party Organizations

We have argued throughout this book that 1960 can be seen as a turning point in modern American politics. And again, we see an important development that begins about this time. Prior to 1960, almost all party organization was local. Except for the periods during presidential election campaigns, state and national party organizations simply did not exist outside a small handful of dedicated professionals. The state and national parties that did exist consisted largely of the members of the legislatures and Congress and their staff; the governors and their administrations; and the presidency. The suggestion that the two national parties could maintain national staffs in the hundreds would have been viewed as preposterous by most students of government at the time.[5]

In general, until 1960, the national political parties were essentially coalitions that consisted of the independent elements within legislatures and administrations.[6] Within the legislatures, party discipline (the ability to force members to vote with the party) was significantly weaker than in the parliamentary systems of most Western democracies. American legislators were elected locally and subject to local influences. They defected from their respective parties when a vote with their party would jeopardize their opportunity for reelection. The literature on political parties of that period was deeply concerned with the need to have "responsible parties," which is to say, parties in which legislative voting and issue cohesion could be enforced and maintained, and in which the candidates ran on the party platform.[7]

The reason for a lack of national or state party organizations was that the national parties simply had no ability to raise the kind of money needed to maintain full-time permanent organizations. Full-time employees cannot exist without money to pay their salaries. In 1959, the Democratic National Committee (DNC) had an income of approximately $750,000 and a debt of $3.5 million following the 1960 elections, and the Republican National Committee (RNC) was $255,000 in debt in 1963.[8] Until 1960, the national and state party organization simply lacked resources. Therefore, national and state party organization was trivial by today's standards.

The political parties of 1993 look radically different in almost every important respect. The national party organizations and many state organizations have expanded enormously, to the point where they are a major source of funding, expertise, and support for candidates. (However, the amount of money provided by PACs still dwarfs that provided by the parties.) The amount of money raised and spent by the national parties based in Washington has increased dramatically since the 1970s. In 1976, the national Democratic Party organizations raised and spent around $18 million, but by 1988, that figure increased to $100 million. The Republicans have been even more successful at mastering modern fund-raising techniques. They raised around $45 million in 1976, and they increased that figure to almost $300 million in

1984 before falling to $267 million in 1990 and about $243 million in 1992.[9]

According to staff estimates, both the RNC and the DNC have between 220 and 250 full-time paid staff members working in Washington, D.C. year-round. This number does not include a cadre of consultants hired for various projects, or the people working in the respective congressional committees, or the party outside Washington.[10] Also, there is a significant number of party operatives who are paid by the parties but work in the presidential administration, the state parties, or Congress. The base number nevertheless indicates the size of the operation.

At the same time, local party organizations have declined equally dramatically, reducing their influence with candidates and officeholders. The Republicans started this transformation by mastering modern fund-raising techniques in order to raise huge sums of money, primarily via direct mail. The Democrats soon followed suit. As the money concentrated in Washington, so did influence over the decision making of elected officials. The entire nature of the parties shifted. They became large bureaucratic electoral machines whose main goal was to reelect their incumbents, while they failed to provide active political leadership on the important issues of the day. In the process, the connection between the voters and the national elected elite was greatly diluted as the grassroots character of the parties all but disappeared. Moreover, the parties ceased to have any role in translating local sentiments into influence with the representatives.

In addition, the centralization of party power contributed to the lack of electoral competition in legislative races at the local level. As we have shown in Chapter 2, the vast resources solicited by the parties are not, by and large, used to challenge incumbents of the opposite party, and are restricted by campaign finance regulations that were written by the lawmakers themselves. This includes hard money contributions, and also the large contributions of services, support, and research that are part of the "soft" money contributions. Because the flow of power to Washington has left the local parties too weak to put on viable challenges, incumbents are able to reign at will, seriously eroding the choices available to voters.

America is, in most places, really a one-party system dominated by two national party organizations operating in entirely separate districts. Each election cycle, the two parties fight in a small number of races they have determined will be competitive. In the rest, they simply concede to the other party, leaving any candidate who runs under their party flag to his or her own devices. The most visible exception is, of course, the fight for the presidency, for which competition is fierce. But the intensity of the race for that one office creates the entirely incorrect impression that there exists a competitive two-party system in the United States, which simply is not the case.

Some studies have been done to analyze the nationalization of the political parties. In the 1980s, an academic, Paul Herrnson, administered a questionnaire to 500 congressional candidates asking them to rate how important the main political organizations were to their campaigns.[11] Though Herrnson used the study to show how the national party organizations were playing an increasing role in congressional campaigns, the findings also illustrated how independent of their local base House candidates had become. Some of the findings included the following:

- The Democratic congressional candidates rated the congressional campaign committees, the unions, interest groups, and PACs as *more important* in issue development than either the local party or the state party. So, according to this data, the local party had less influence over a candidate's issue stands than Washington political operatives and narrow interest groups.
- For Democratic congressional candidates, the unions and PACs were rated as far more important than the local and state party in terms of assistance with fund raising.
- The data showed that Republican candidates rely more on the National Committee and congressional committees for campaign support than on local parties.
- Overall, the study found that "local party organizations no longer play a dominant role in many phases of the campaigns."[12]

The two parties have become, at the local level, "the paper tigers" of American politics, to use the famous words of Chairman Mao Tse-tung. The party organizations are powerful, if at all, only because citizens accord them a power that no longer exists. The parties' incumbent candidates are powerful only because of the monopoly of money that pours into their candidacies from the PACs and from state and national fund-raising efforts. These parties persist in power largely because they are unchallenged by the voices of discontent. The parties may indeed be powerful as national institutions, but they are becoming less powerful as organizing forces in the electorate. They persist because the voting districts are designed (gerrymandered) to give one party or the other sufficient voters to make a challenge by the other party improbable.

Certainly, one of the most costly results of the hegemonic lock of the two national party organizations and their state counterparts has been the alienation of the voters from participation in partisan politics at the grassroots level. As the national organizations thrive, they increasingly depend on modern campaign technology at the expense of the local party activist. Although no causal relationship can be empirically proven, some of the alienation of the voters has undoubtedly come from the national parties' dependence on technology as a substitute for grassroots party politics. Senator Paul Laxalt of Nevada echoed this sentiment when he said, "We've got too much money, we've got way too many political operatives, we've got far too few volunteers. . . . We are substituting contributions and high technology for volunteers in the field."[13] The major technological developments have all pushed the emphasis away from the people and diminished the role of the voter and local party activists. In this light, the volunteer support for Ross Perot's United We Stand, America (UWSA) is more understandable.

From Ward Leaders to Washington Pollsters

Before pollsters, voters' desires were communicated up through the party hierarchy by local party officials who knew what was important. Today, voters are poked and prodded by pollsters, not to find out what reforms they want or to engage in what can ideally be called a high-tech channel of communication, but to test which messages will motivate them. Campaign strategies are tested and themes are sounded out to find the best way for the campaign to *manipulate* the voter. Rather than being participants in the process, the voters are treated more like lab rats, tested and analyzed to find the magic sound bite that will get them to pull the right lever.

From the National Convention to the Free Political Advertisement Convention

In the not-too-distant past, conventions had an impact on the policies and direction of the parties. From 1974 to 1982, the Democrats even had midterm conventions to debate party policy. These were discontinued so the public would not see the party members bickering amongst themselves.[14] In contrast, at the 1992 Democratic Convention, both Governor Bob Casey (D-Penn.) and presidential candidate former Governor Jerry Brown (D-Calif.) were shunned because they wanted to express points of view that didn't conform to the official positions of the Clinton entourage. Now, the conventions are so staged and unimportant and so little real politics occurs that major networks resist covering them. What was once high political drama has been reduced to a carefully choreographed opera that is over well before the fat lady sings. In the process, another vital connection between the party and the people has been cut, and another once-colorful facet of democratic participation has been destroyed.

From Voter Participation to the Voter's Pocketbook

The organizations that used to involve millions of people in the process of selecting those who govern have become organizations that ask people for their money and then run the entire process without them. For example, the Republicans have a computerized list of 60 million names from which they solicit money. Do they use these lists to involve people in the process? As one RNC staffer noted, "Parties used to be people oriented, but now they no longer have the people so the computer has to some extent filled the gap."[15] It's the money they are after, not the activity of the people.

The Vulnerability of the Parties to Special Interests

The weakness of the local party organizations, and the corresponding emphasis on their Washington-based organizations, have left both parties especially vulnerable to nationally organized interests seeking very narrow and parochial objectives. These interests operate outside the party, but in many instances they have infiltrated it to control the content of party debate and public policy. By centering much of the party power in Washington, the parties became as easy to lobby as Congress. As more power has become vested in the national party organizations, the effect of that lobbying is magnified. The influence of these interests has been devastating on the ability of the two parties to mobilize majorities to deal with the major problems confronting America.

On the Republican side, the problem is exemplified by the advocates of what has been called the moral majority. In 1992, these elements dominated the Republican National Convention, producing an event that appeared as right wing on social issues as any convention in history. The 1992 convention adopted the most restrictive position on abortion possible, calling for a constitutional amendment to outlaw abortion in *all* circumstances, even those involving rape and incest. The support for this position was measured on election day by Voter Research and Surveys (VRS), which found that a mere 9 percent of the public agreed with this extreme position.[16] The symbolic importance of a major political party taking a position so obviously at odds with the public should not be underestimated. How can such a party pretend to represent the broad national interest when a small minority interest is able to control the content of the party's policies to such an extent?

Research on Republican convention delegates has shown that for nearly three decades these activists were more conservative than the electorate as a whole, particularly on such so-called social issues as abortion, school prayer, the rights of those accused of crimes, and civil rights.[17] During the 1980s, however, the mobilization of the new religious right in American life shifted the activist base of the Republican Party even further to the right at the local level, largely because these new, highly motivated, and ideologically committed activist groups were challenging a party of declining vitality and participation at the local level. As a result, the Republican organization serves as a platform for conservative morality far to the right of the general public, while basing the rest of their appeal on simpleminded anti-tax populism. Many voters who may agree with the party on economic issues are alienated by the vitriolic cultural debate.

The Democrats have a different problem. The Democratic Party has been a coalition of diverse special interests since the Depression. Up to the early 1960s, however, the party was a composition of opposites: Blacks, Jews, Hispanics, and liberals in the North, and a Southern Democratic Party that was much more conservative. Between 1960 and today, however, the conservative southern whites have largely left the Democratic Party in presidential elections, switching to the Republicans, and they have been replaced by black voters who were denied participation until the Voting Rights Act of 1964. The shifting Democratic alliance pushed the activist base of the party to the left, and the dominance of the liberals in the party was ratified with the nomination of George McGovern in 1972.[18]

A second shift is of equal importance. Organized labor was a vital component of the Democratic coalition that emerged in the 1930s, and it was at its peak of power during the late 1940s and early 1950s, when there were as many as 18 million unionized voters in the United States. During the past three decades, however, the blue-collar elements of organized labor have watched their base of support erode as the economy shifted toward white-collar and nonunion service industries, and as manufacturing jobs were shifted overseas. The organized union movement in this country was and is pragmatic, moderately liberal on social and economic issues, and interested in such broad social programs as Social Security, health care, and labor legislation.

As blue-collar organized labor declined, new segments of organized labor became increasingly powerful in the Democratic Party. These major national organizations, which also operate extensively at the state level, include the American Federation of State, County, and Municipal Employees (AFSCME); the American Federation of Teachers; the National Education Association; and the American Postal Workers Union. Although these organizations appear to espouse broad programmatic policies, they are united and intensely focused on a particular special interest: the protection and promotion of the jobs, salaries, and pensions of people employed by governments and on public payrolls. These organizations have become more powerful as local party organizations have decayed. They are huge contributors to political campaigns. As shown in Table 1, in the 1990 and 1992 election cycles, government and postal worker employee unions (not including teacher organizations) contributed over $8,349,000 to political campaigns, $7,443,419 of which went to Democrats.[19] In addition, these organizations also provide tremendous numbers of volunteers to work in political campaigns. These workers are articulate, sophisticated, middle-class, with strong organization and leadership, and they are highly motivated since they are working to influence the very people who decide their salaries and benefits.

Not many people realize that public-employee organizations spend more money trying to influence legislators than some of America's more prominent special interests. For example, all four of the organizations detailed in Table 1 gave more money to federal candidates than the Association of Trial Lawyers, the National Association of Life Underwriters (Insurance), the American Bankers Association, or even that paragon of corporate influence-peddling, the AT&T PAC.

The Democratic Party has fallen under the control of a coalition committed to expanding the role of the government, protecting the jobs of public employees, and promoting the pensions and benefits of those

Table 1 **Political Contributions by Public Employee PACs (1990 and 1992)**

1990 Rank Out of All PACs	Political Action Committee	1990	1992
4th largest	National Education Association PAC	$2,349,575	$5,817,975
6th largest	Committee on Letter Carriers Political Education	$1,790,912	$1,919,475
7th largest	American Federation of State, County, and Municipal Employees	$1,533,970	$4,281,395
8th largest	National Association of Retired Federal Employees PAC	$1,533,000	$1,826,190

Adapted from data collected by the Federal Election Commission.

in the public sector. They are among the largest contributors to political campaigns, largely out of state fund-raising efforts, and they can mobilize a large number of volunteers whenever and wherever they are threatened. Today, through their influence within the Democratic Party, the public employee unions have a virtual veto power over reforms of education, welfare, or the pension and benefits systems in the public sector.

Special interests of all kinds had a more difficult time influencing national public policy when the resources that shaped elections were local rather than national. When the majority of campaign funds came from local interests, candidates were forced to be sensitive to the local interests that supported them. Today, however, many congressional candidates receive a *majority of their campaign funds* from outside their district, from the state and national party organizations rather than from the local party. At the same time, the "nationalization" of the interest-group structure enables the interest groups, with the PACs, to use their funds and resources much more strategically, aiding those incumbents in places pertinent to their interest in the legislative process.

The net result is a shift of influence of profound importance for understanding the failure of the party system. *The only way the public as voters can have an impact on the debate over public policy is through the election of representatives sensitive to and concerned about the broader views of the voters in the district from which they came.* That broader public interest is diminished by all the changes that have occurred since 1960 in the operation of the party system—by the dependence of incumbents on outside money from PACs, by the intrusion of the state and national committees in funding local elections, by the constant communication between the lobbyists and the representatives, by the ability of the PACs to mobilize local sentiment in support of special-interest legislation, and by the near-elimination of electoral competition and choice. These changes permit officeholders to ignore the broader public interest in their districts while placating the special interests that fund their election campaigns.

The national party organizations are vital, growing, and increasingly influential largely because they have secured access to large sums of money by administering faithfully to special interests. The flow of funding, in turn, sustains a large staff, which adds to the importance of the national organizations. The local party organizations, by contrast, have decayed both because the local parties have fewer funds available to them and because the other motivations—ideological and civic—have been undermined by a pervasive system of one-partyism which proves daily that participation and volunteerism are futile, worthless, and ineffective. The net effect is to make fundamental reform almost impossible in American politics within the confines of the current system of party government, as each reform initiative will invariably threaten a special interest on which one or the other party depends.

The Public Reacts

In Chapter 3, we documented the rise in despair and discontent with the general political system. We did not, however, detail how the public has come to view the political parties and what this means for our political system. Basically, the public has become as increasingly frustrated and disenchanted with the political parties as they are with the government. With government failing at every level, the voters recognize that the parties are failing as well. The alienation of the parties from the voters is, therefore, a double-edged sword. A poll we conducted in May 1992 found that 59 percent of the voters said they were "angry" or "dissatisfied" with the Democratic Party, 60 percent said the same thing about the Republican Party, and 83 percent of the voters agreed with the statement that "special-interest campaign contributions have more influence than voters."[20]

In addition to the centralization of party power in Washington, an equally important contributing factor is the political divergence from the center of electoral opinion of the two parties at the national level. One of the supposed virtues of the two-party system is the tendency for the parties to converge ideologically to attract the centrist voters. America, with its large middle class, historically has been a system in which most voters consider themselves moderate or centrist on most issues. Anthony Downs, in his famous work, *An Economic Theory of Democracy*, provided the theoretical rationale for why parties and candidates must converge to the center in a two-party, two-candidate race.[21] What Downs, writing in the 1950s, did not appreciate was the potential for the capture of each political party by a coalition of activists whose views were markedly at variance with both the party and the country as a whole. In 1992, however, the moral majority representatives within the Republican Platform Committee wrote a plank on abortion, later ratified by the convention, that was supported by only nine percent of the American people as a whole.

Before the 1964 election, through the use of the party convention, both political parties nominated candidates who were fundamentally moderate and centrist in tone. While the primary system was supposed to be a reform, the low turnout, multi-candidate elections had the ironic effect of greatly increasing the ability of fringe and ideological groups to elect sympathetic candidates by decreasing the threshold of support necessary for the nomination. Until 1964, the chief complaint against the political parties was that they never offered the electorate much of a choice because they consistently selected candidates of the center: John Kennedy and Richard Nixon, Dwight David Eisenhower and Adlai Stevenson, Harry Truman and Thomas Dewey, etc. After 1960, the parties begin to offer ideologically divergent candidates with greater frequency: Barry Goldwater in 1964, George McGovern in 1972, Ronald Reagan in 1980, Walter Mondale in 1984, and even George Bush and Michael Dukakis in 1988. As we have already noted, this divergence was demonstrated most graphically in 1992 by the strident morality of the Republican Convention and the overwhelming presence of the public employees and their organizations in the Democratic Convention.

The result is a profound shift in the meaning of the parties to average Americans. In a fundamental sense, the Republican and Democratic parties, as organizations and as elected officeholders, have both deserted their voters. They have left them vertically, moving power from local districts to the state and national capitals; and they have left them ideologically, moving far to the left and right of where the voters really are on most issues.

In the same way that any product manager depends on brand image and brand loyalty for long-term economic success, political parties depend on partisan loyalty for long-term political success. However, the flight of the parties from their roots has, for 30 years, made party labels more and more meaningless for voters. This trend has been well documented, and there has been considerable academic work done on the subject.[22] For our purposes, there are a number of trends directly related to the need for and the potential success of a centrist, value-driven third party.

The Rise of Independents

As Chart 1 illustrates, the number of people who do not identify themselves as belonging to either political party has been consistently rising for the past 30 years. This trend is a powerful piece of empirical evidence that the relevance of party labels has seriously declined. Some academics, like political scientist Larry Sabato, try to rationalize this trend by noting that "research clearly demonstrates that Independent 'leaners' in fact vote very much like real partisans."[23] While this may be true, identifying oneself as an Independent indicates a willingness to assess individual candidates on merits and positions with far less consideration to party. From the standpoint of creating a new party, this is an important cognitive process that must be present for an indepen-

Chart 1   **Trends in Partisan Identification (1952–1988)**

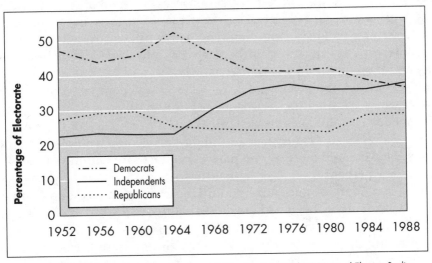

Adapted from Wattenberg, *The Decline of American Political Parties.* SRC/CPS National Election Studies.

dent candidate to succeed. Independent voters and "leaners" supported Ross Perot at a much greater rate than strong partisans, indicating that these independent voters are likely to vote for third-party candidates when they are provided a centrist choice.

The decline in the use of partisanship as a voting cue simply means that political customers have become less loyal, more willing to change their votes, more difficult to hold together in a coalition, and more willing to abandon the two-party system altogether. A study conducted by University of Michigan professors in the earlier 1980s found an important connection between party allegiance and third-party voting. The study's authors noted that:

> Between 1952 and 1980, when a nationally prestigious third party candidate ran, voters with weak ties to the major parties were 37 percent more likely than the most attached to cast their lot with a third party candidate. . . . The impact is indirect: attachment to the major parties boosts voters' evaluation of the Democratic and Republican nominees, which in turn reduce their probability of third party voting.[24]

The potential for the establishment of a successful new party depends on voters' willingness to consider alternatives to the major parties. The trends in partisanship over the last 40 years illustrate how the bonds of attachment to the major parties have weakened, providing the opportunity, we argue, for a third party to be successful on a mass scale. Other academic research, particularly by Martin Wattenberg, echoes this argument by showing that political parties have simply become less relevant to the political process. Wattenberg's concern is that with the decline of partisanship "many citizens have been set adrift without an anchor in a political world full of strong eddies and currents. As a result, some no longer vote; others are swept first one way and then another by the currents."[25]

In contrast, the electorate prior to 1960 was composed mostly of voters who identified themselves as being Republicans or Democrats, who tended to vote fairly consistently for the candidates of their party at every level of government. The straight-party voter, who voted exclusively for the candidates of one party, was far more common then. In 1960, 26.1 percent of congressional districts were carried by a presidential candidate of one party and a House candidate of another. By 1984, as a result of Reagan's landslide, that figure peaked at 45 percent before falling to 34 percent in 1988.[26] The data shows that the purposeful straight-party voter is almost nonexistent in American politics, except among African-American voters, leading one academic observer to lament that "voting the man, not the party, has now become part of the American consensus or creed."[27] A study in 1986 found that only 14 percent of the electorate agreed with the statement "I always support the candidates of just one party."[28]

Another factor driving voters from the parties has been the rise of negative campaigning. Obviously, the parties did not invent negative campaigning in the 1980s. Indeed, President Lyndon Johnson was a master at it, and his vicious campaign against Barry Goldwater in 1964, culminating in a famous TV ad in which a beautiful little girl disappears in a nuclear explosion, was especially effective in portraying Goldwater as a "dangerous extremist." However, during the past decade, led by the religious right wing, the candidates of the two political parties have taken off the gloves of civility and decorum and have gone after each other with baseball bats and slime. Although such tactics appear successful in the short run, the voters have become disgusted with both parties and their candidates in the process.

The disrepute of politics and politicians in the modern era did not happen by chance. Both parties brought it on themselves. Imagine, if you will, General Motors and Ford spending ten years and a billion dollars in harsh, negative advertising toward one another. The Japanese would be ecstatic, of course, and that fact restrains both companies. But the impact would be the same—we would learn to dislike both. The effect of this harsh negative campaigning on the two parties is clear: the brand labels of "Republican" and "Democrat" are so debauched today that all around the country candidates commonly avoid carrying their own party label on their advertising and promotional materials.

Within the academic community there has been much debate on whether the declining partisanship is due to increased anger at the parties or simply to the declining relevance of the parties in the individual voter's life. For our purposes, we can accept both interpretations. This weakness is captured in the SRC/CPS National Election Studies, which ask respondents what they like and dislike about the parties. Over the last 30 years, people simply have had less and less to say about the parties each year. The voters have fewer important feelings one way or the other, as demonstrated in Chart 2.

Decreased partisanship in the electorate is a logical, though not demonstrable, result of the centralization of political parties when coupled with the increasing distance between the parties and the voters over issues. The further removed the parties became from the local roots, the less meaningful participation became at the grassroots level, as more and more people did not seem to fit into a party anymore. The old machine tactic of trading Christmas turkeys for votes may be morally questionable, but turkeys are certainly more meaningful to voters than negative campaign commercials.

Voters' perceptions of their connection to the government correlate significantly with their perceptions of their party as an active political voice. One of the most interesting findings of the NES studies, shown in Table 2, is that the perception of the parties as a voice of the people has declined. If the parties are no longer a voice, what are they?

As we showed in Chapter 1, the deterioration of the collective attitudinal structure of American politics has caused voters to question the efficacy of the two-party system itself. Although we will present more

Chart 2   **The Rise in Neutral Feelings about the Parties (1952–1988)**

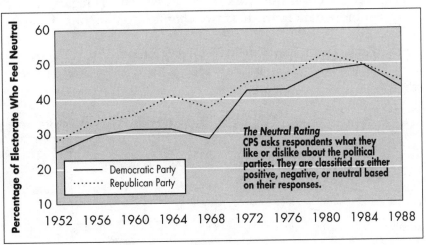

Adapted from Wattenberg, *The Decline of American Political Parties*. SRC/CPS National Election Studies.

Table 2   **Public Perception of Political Parties as a Voice of the People**
Question: How much do you feel that political parties help to make the government pay attention to what the people think—a good deal, some, or not much?

Response	Percent in 1964	Percent in 1968	Percent in 1970	Percent in 1972	Percent in 1974	Percent in 1976	Percent in 1978	Percent in 1980
Not much	13	16	19	18	19	26	22	28
Some	39	41	43	52	55	53	53	51
A good deal	41	37	33	26	22	17	21	18

Adapted from data collected by SRC/CPS National Election Studies.

data in the next chapter, the deterioration of the two-party system in the electorate was studied in a significant survey conducted by Lou Harris and Associates in July of 1992.[29] The Harris poll found that while people felt the two-party system had served the country well in the past, a large majority felt it was no longer working. Harris's president, Humphrey Taylor, wrote that "less than a third (29 percent) of all adult Americans would like to see the continuation of the two-party system."[30] In addition, the poll found that a surprisingly large number (38 percent) wanted elections in which candidates ran without party labels. However, to put this response in context, Taylor accurately notes that "party politics has been an inevitable consequence of free elections." So this response should be understood as a measure of frustration and disgust with politics in general. Table 3 provides some partisan breakdown of who is most frustrated with the two-party system.

We can see from Table 3 that the Perot voters are more likely to feel the two-party system is not working very well. This is logical, and we will present more data in the next two chapters to illustrate this trend.

Table 3   **Public Frustration with the Two-Party System**
Question: Right now would you say that the two-party system is serving this country well, or not?

Response	Percentage of All Adults	Percentage Who Plan to Vote for:		
		Bush	Clinton	Perot
Is serving this country well	39	55	39	25
Is not	59	53	60	74
Not sure	1	2	1	1

Adapted from survey taken by Harris, July, 1992.

If the public is generally in agreement that the two-party system is no longer working, it is not in agreement on how to solve the problem. Roughly a third of the public indicated that it directly advocated the creation of a third party, and another 30 percent advocated the continuation of the present system. The question, therefore, given the distribution of the responses in Table 3, is what would happen to the 38 percent that doesn't want partisan labels. We can't tell from this data what their feelings toward a third party would be, given that parties are inevitable.

Table 4 illustrates the support for the two-party system, grouped by age and race. This table reveals some remarkable deterioration of faith in the two-party system. The groups most likely to abandon the two-party system are the middle-aged and younger voters. This is logical, because they have reached their political consciousness in an era in which politics has become increasingly devoid of meaningful party affiliation and is characterized by negative campaigns and policy failures. In contrast, the older voters developed their political views when party affiliation was stronger and it meant something to be a Democrat or a Republican. However, the younger voters provide more support for nonpartisan politics, while the voters aged 30 to 50 give more support for a new party. It is precisely these voters who are the key to the success of a third-party movement. An analysis of the differences in ethnicity also reveals an interesting, though not surprising, tendency. African-Americans are more likely to believe in the continuation of the

Table 4 **Support for the Two-Party System**
Question: Which do you prefer?

Responses	% All Adults	% by Age Group						% by Racial Group	
		18–24	25–29	30–39	40–49	50–64	65+	White	Black
A continuation of the two-party system	29	26	20	18	26	44	41	28	37
Elections in which candidates run without party labels	38	49	52	44	40	25	29	39	31
The growth of one or more new parties that could effectively challenge the Democrats and the Republicans	30	26	28	37	32	27	22	31	29

Adapted from a survey by Harris.

two-party system, which is logical given their bloc support of the Democratic Party. However, if one considers the situation strategically, it is ironically in the best interest of minorities to advocate the creation of a new party because it would most likely increase the minorities' power within the Democratic Party. Assuming a percentage of moderate Democrats would defect to a moderate third party, the influence of the minorities, who would make up a larger share of the remaining Democratic Party activists, would increase proportionately.

In short, the public opinion data presents a mirror of the decline of the political parties in the electorate. The two-party system, once a vital part of our culture, has slowly deteriorated in the opinion of a majority of Americans. Political parties and political systems exist because people believe in them as active concepts. The less people believe in the two-party system as a needed institution, the more that institution depends on legal barriers and electoral tricks to maintain its existence. At the same time, these institutional laws and barriers, once justified as procedural necessities, are profoundly antidemocratic and exist simply as a means of suppressing and limiting public choice in elections by denying ballot access to candidates. The oldest tactic of monopolists is to deny access to the market, and the Democrats and Republicans are the ultimate monopolists when it comes to their own market dominance.

Can the Party System Be Challenged?

Reshaping the party system is no easy task, but it does have its precedents in American politics. Though cynics commonly deride the efforts of third parties, these efforts have been extremely important in the development of modern American democracy. Many important reforms first appeared on the platforms of third parties, only to be incorporated later into the practice of two-party politics. These developments include the following:

- The convention system of nomination
- The primary elections for delegates to national conventions
- The extension of suffrage to women and African-Americans
- The direct election of senators
- The abolition of slavery
- The income tax[31]

The situation facing voters in the 1990s is similar to that of voters who lived under the tyranny of the urban party machines of the 1890s.

Those political machines used every technique available to rob the voter of choice. After they eliminated political opposition, they used their unilateral control of the political institutions to enrich their friends and punish their enemies, all at the public expense. Sometimes the machine politicians operated with audacity and style, and voters admired them in the same manner we sometimes glorify mobsters and pirates. At other times, however, the rule of the tyrant bosses was savage, ugly, vicious, and brutal. When the politicians turned nasty, there really wasn't anything the average voters could do about the situation.

Imagine yourself as a citizen in nineteenth-century New York City at the height of the Tweed Ring dominance. Boss William Marcy Tweed and his army of patronage workers have an iron lock on the nomination process in the Democratic Party. The Republicans cannot hope to compete for control of the city because of the control of voters purchased through favors, public programs, jobs, and even outright gifts. As a result, electoral choice is gone and there exists no countervailing force to hold Tweed and the other politicians accountable for their actions. The description of what happened in New York then sounds a lot like what is happening in America today.

> Cash flow problems drove Tweed and his cronies to dig deeper and deeper into the public till. Between 1867 and 1871, New York's municipal indebtedness tripled, finally arousing concern among members of the city's financial community, who "through purchase of municipal bonds during the period of the Ring rule" had permitted their interests to "become intimately intertwined with that of the city government."[32]

If we substitute the federal debt for the municipal debt, the situation sounds fairly familiar, and the situation looks pretty hopeless to you as a voter. What could you do? You have few real choices at the polls, so you really have no way to express your discontent with a political machine that is raping the city for the personal benefit of those who control it. These bosses have worked up deals with the business community, the labor unions, and the ethnic organizations. Your only alternative is to take on a pervasive system of alliances, fueled by enormous profits, for the purpose of producing political reform.

It is not outrageous to say that we have substituted an "incumbent machine" for the political machines. The analogy between the machine era and the modern system of one-party districts is a fair one. In both periods, the two parties worked together to divide the political map into one party's sphere of control. In both periods, the outcome of unilateral and uncontested control by a single party was runaway budgets and huge deficits as the two parties vied with one another to pass out the financial resources of government for the purpose of maintaining their political control. In both eras, the large, organized interests found it more in their interest to buy into the political machines rather than to oppose them. In both instances, the parties worked to rig the system to reduce or eliminate political choice. In both instances, those in office routinely substituted lies, distortions, and half-truths for reality. When political competition is destroyed, truth is always the first casualty.

The downfall of political machines came about partly as a result of a national reform movement that began in the last two decades of the nineteenth century. A similar reform movement is required today. First, the movement was fueled by the work of such crusading journalists as Lincoln Steffens, whose book, *The Shame of Our Cities*, was a bestseller.[33] He was joined by the architect of the urban reform movement, Richard Childs. Work by crusading journalists and urban intellectuals was intertwined with movements inside and outside the party system itself, most notably the successful national electoral efforts mounted by such Progressives as Senator Robert LaFollette of Wisconsin and Governor Hiram Johnson in California. The Progressives sought to restore voter involvement and participation through the initiative, the referendum, and the recall.

These reform movements were enormously successful by any standard. They restored competition and fiscal integrity to our urban centers. They broke state-level control over public policy by the railroads, the oil lobby, and other large economic interests. They dramatically reduced graft and corruption at the local level. And, perhaps most importantly, they restored the public's confidence that it could democratically control its destiny through the rule of law and the exercise of political rights. By the middle of the twentieth century, direct democracy had taken root in many of the states around the country:

- Twenty-one states have the initiative that allows proposed state laws to be placed directly on the ballot by citizen petition. Fourteen of these states require no legislative action be taken to put proposed laws on the ballot, while seven require some form of legislative action.
- Fifteen states have processes to recall elected officials.
- Twenty-five states have processes to hold referendums on state laws passed by the legislature before they are enacted.[34]

The importance of these reforms was in evidence in the 1992 election. Of the 21 states possessing the right of the initiative, 13 passed term limitation measures in the largest single-issue referendum in the history of American politics. Among the 29 states without the right of initiative, only the Florida legislature has seen fit to permit its citizens to vote on term limits. Nor are the states likely to provide such an opportunity in the future. *If every state in the United States had the right of initiative, the vast majority of states would today pass term limitations on all of its state and federal offices.* Support for term limits nationally ranges between 65 percent and 78 percent depending upon the length of time officeholders are allowed to serve. Unfortunately, the reform movements of the past were not successful enough to win the right of initiative in every state in the country, and the voters in most of the remaining 29 states will never get the opportunity to vote on term limits if state legislators are required to vote on the issue.

The reform movements of the past succeeded because a number of forces created the conditions in which the opponents of political machines could mobilize public sentiment in the face of highly organized opposition, frequently from both political parties. First, the political machines generated local and state opposition within the business community. This opposition was not a product of civic virtue on the part of business. The opposition arose because the price of compliance to the dictates of the bosses got too high.

In addition, local newspapers were almost always at the forefront of reform. In most communities, there was serious competition among the daily newspapers in uncovering corruption, graft, and favoritism. As a result of zealous newspaper coverage, the educated citizens were barraged with information negative to the interests of those in power.

Also, the machines themselves blocked the political ambitions of certain groups of people. The machines were often, although not exclusively, ethnic—Irish, Italian, Jewish, or English Protestant. Those in control from one ethnic group favored that ethnic group in opposition to the aspirations of young men in other groups. Those whose ambitions were blocked joined the efforts to "reform" the political machines.

Finally, most of the worst political machines were local or statewide, and certainly not national. The costs of organizing to oppose an oppressive local political machine are dramatically smaller than the costs of organizing on a national level. The Urban Reform Movement and the Progressive Movement were largely local or statewide efforts, and they generally did not focus on national issues except for the issue of directly electing senators and gaining women's right to vote.

These circumstances created a set of conditions that were extremely helpful in achieving opposition to the dominance of political machines:

- Public outrage fed by competitive and aggressive journalists, who could use corruption and graft to sell newspapers.

- An economic elite so squeezed by the machines that they became willing to help pay the cost of organizing the opposition to the machines.
- Political leaders whose ambitions were frustrated by the control of the machine and the unwillingness of the machines to support their advancement.

These forces fueled a long nationwide struggle to free local and state politics of the kind of dictatorial and corrupt politics that existed in political machines. This struggle began during the period just after the Civil War, and it persisted until the end of the Daley machine with the death of Mayor Richard Daley in Chicago in the early 1970s. It was a uniquely colorful period of American history, but it was also a period without precedent for its corruption and politically inspired violence. *Although it took a long time, the forces of reform eventually prevailed and changed the way our cities across America are governed, proving that challenging the party system is quite possible if the circumstances are right.*

Why No Reform Movement in the Modern Era?

The scale of fiscal corruption of the modern era, starting in the mid-1960s, dwarfs anything the political machines attempted to do. Instead of million-dollar deficits, we have billion-dollar deficits. Instead of handing out dinner baskets to impoverished immigrants, our politicians hand out tens of billions of subsidies to defense contractors, farmers, the elderly, and special interests of every kind and description. Instead of direct bribes to politicians, we allow special interests to contribute tens of thousands to the campaign coffers of those who will hand out the goodies of government. Instead of taking thousands of dollars directly out of the public till, we allow our politicians to take millions in pensions and perks for themselves. Modern politicians have elevated corruption to a level that would make machine politicians envious, and they have legalized it. They have taken our best motives— the desires to reduce suffering, improve opportunity, and protect democracy and freedom, and they have twisted those values to serve the ends of their own advancement, power, and permanence in office.

There are many factors that make it difficult for a third (or fourth) party to be successful electorally, but they do not make it impossible. These impediments did not stop Ross Perot from getting on the ballot in all 50 states, nor did they stop Dr. Lenora Fulani of the New Alliance

Party from gaining access with much smaller resources. Both John Anderson in 1980 and George Wallace in 1968 were successful in getting on the ballot in all of the states, despite the efforts by the Republicans and Democrats to keep them off.

The point here is that third-party candidates and new political parties can and do evolve from intense dissatisfaction with the operation of the party system that exists at a given point in time. The formation of a new, successful political party is a bit like a great earthquake; it may not happen very often, but the potential is there when conditions are right.

Moreover, the existence of the single-member district did not stop the newly formed Republicans from capturing the White House and Congress in the middle of the nineteenth century. The historical durability of the two existing parties, which have persisted now for more than 130 years, is no guarantee that this situation will be perpetuated indefinitely into the future. Both Great Britain and Canada have multi-party systems, and they have single-member districts.

Finally, centrist, third-party movements came to dominate politics in France under the Gaullists and in India under the Congress Party. Almost certainly, sometime in the future a new, successful, nationwide third party will emerge in American politics, and the experts will fail to predict its success, largely because most so-called experts in Washington have an emotional and political stake in the existing paradigm of the two-party system.

Of course, the central question is, why have we tolerated everything that has occurred? Why did the earlier reform movements succeed while we have yet to begin to organize in the face of threats to our freedom and security far worse than anything posed by the political machines?

These are questions of central importance. Unless we understand the answers, we do not have a chance of doing anything to change the condition of the governance of the United States. There are many answers to why we haven't seen the emergence of a truly effective reform movement, and they can be summarized as follows.

First, the costs of organizing increase as one moves from the local to the state level, and from the state to the national level. The Urban Reform Movement was directed primarily at abuses at the local and state levels. The reforms needed today are at the state and national levels, where the task of organizing is much larger and the probability of success much lower.

The political machines of the nineteenth and twentieth centuries arose at a time when local and regional newspapers were locally owned and often openly partisan in their political views. The Hearst and

Pulitzer newspapers thrived on scandal, and muckraking was common to most urban newspapers. These papers fed the informational needs of those who supported reform and change, and they gave voice to the outrage felt by voters. Today, by contrast, most regional newspapers are owned and controlled by large chains, with editorial staffs that are far more cautious than in the past and with little or no local news competition. As competition between newspapers diminished, it reduced the incentive to spend a lot of money on complex issues and the "newsholes" (the space available for news, as opposed to ads) of most newspapers have declined as papers reduced costs to improve profits. Reporters are younger, less vested in their communities, less knowledgeable, and less qualified as salaries have declined.

At the same time, the national newspapers and electronic media have become closely tied to the existing political parties and officeholders, depending on good connections to sources who are aligned with the parties. They show little zeal for crusading against the abuses of power by people whom they know well and on whom they depend. There is considerable movement of reporters and so-called experts into the political arena, and then back into journalism, with a corresponding loss of objectivity and interest in reform.

A third constraint is the degree to which the leaders of very large corporations, associations, and labor unions are "bought off" by the need to promote the narrow interests of the organizations they lead. The huge corporations routinely require a cooperative government—with trade issues, regulations, federal contracting, etc.—and these leaders are not likely to vigorously support broad scale reforms when their act of support might jeopardize their access and interest in other issues. With these people on the sidelines, the financial resources that are available to a reform movement are limited.

Finally, the political operatives who manage campaign and public relations for the parties have become increasingly adept at telling the public what it wants to hear. Through the use of opinion polls, media management, staged events and other public relations ploys, the establishment has refined the art of maintaining the illusion that change will occur, even when it doesn't. This constant manipulation lulls the public into acquiescence.

There simply has not been enough independent leadership in the American system to sustain a full-blown and vital political and economic reform movement up to this point, regardless of widespread agreement over the need for it. As a result, those in politics operate as if they believe the public will *never* react with hostility. Almost no one, with the exception of people like Ross Perot, Connecticut Governor Lowell Weicker, or Jesse Jackson, wants to rock the boat. It is more profitable, individually, for the powerful interests in America to go along with the present decline than to take arms against the processes and change them. Individual self-interest dictates caution.

The Propagandists of Defeat

One of the most difficult hurdles in the emergence of a new political party is that it must organize in the face of intense propaganda from the existing parties, which gets picked up uncritically by the media. Most of this propaganda is aimed at discouraging angry Americans from investing their time and effort in the enterprise of creating a new party. Two of the arguments used by propagandists are paramount. First, opponents declare that the new effort can never succeed, so why bother? Second, they argue that the existing parties will respond by resolving the problems producing the intense discontent.

The first argument is designed to undermine the confidence of voters in the potential success of the new party. This will reduce people's willingness to contribute their time and effort. The logic of participation is essentially circular. People need to participate if they are to have an impact, but they are disinclined to participate if they feel their activities will be unproductive and unsuccessful. The opposition always seeks to persuade those in a movement that what they are doing is a waste of time, even when there are enough motivated people to create change if they only believe in their own potential.

The second argument is designed to divert participation into the existing party system. Again, the argument is circular. In general, third-party movements have been taken over by one or the other of the two major parties. This has been the case for such third-party efforts as the Populists, Progressives, Socialists, Dixiecrats, American Independents, and others. This argument is a kind of simpleminded historicism; since these takeovers have been frequent, then the pattern *must persist* always and indefinitely. By and large, the argument is made by the proponents of the two parties. It is self-serving, as most of these arguments are. Simply because the creation of a full-scale national party has not happened since 1854 is not sufficient to demonstrate that it can't happen in 1993, or that it can never happen.

Both arguments have some basis of support historically, but we believe they have relatively little applicability to the current period. A successful new political party will almost certainly arise someday in American politics, just as the Republican Party did in the 1850s. When that happens, the historical evidence against its success will seem just as convincing as it does now, but the party will arise despite the historical evidence. The conventional wisdom emanating from the political elite and the media will prove decidedly wrong at that point, because some individual or group will have figured out why the ancient precedents don't apply.

The real issue is missed in most of the debates about the potential for and viability of new political parties. A political party is an organized activity of intentional, motivated people, directed at electing people to office. Many organized political parties have been successful in electing people to local and state offices. In fact, these earlier party efforts have been unsuccessful at only two major goals—electing a president and electing a majority in the House or Senate. In recent years, we have had two successful Independent candidates for governor in Connecticut and Alaska, and we have an Independent member in Congress from Vermont. What we are arguing about, therefore, is the degree of success, not the possibility of success.

≈ 6 ≈

The Potential
for a New Party

The most important distinction in modern political philosophy, the distinction between democracy and dictatorship, can best be made in terms of party politics.[1]

—E.E. Schattschneider

The two parties—Democrats and Republicans—have failed both to protect our right of democratic choice and to protect us from the unbridled self-interest of the special-interest complexes that exist to perpetuate their right to a entitled position in the flow of federal and state dollars. Incumbents of both parties have joined a Faustian pact to mortgage our future in exchange for the tidal wave of PAC money in which they drown their opponents. The exchange is simple: The incumbents gain electoral invulnerability in exchange for policy payoffs that the general public would never approve of if they had a voice.

At this point we come to the most important question in this book: "What is the most effective way to make a real difference in how our government operates?" There are two fundamentally different strategies for attempting to influence the behavior and direction of the government. They are not mutually exclusive, and they can in fact go hand-in-hand, but one strategy is much more effective where issues of broad scope are concerned. The first strategy is that of petitioning and pressuring the government through the use of an army of volunteers. This is the strategy currently being followed by Ross Perot and United We Stand, America. The second is the strategy of running candidates for public office at every level of government. This is the strategy of creating a new, nationwide political party of reform.

The Potentials and Limits of Petitioning the Government

Petitioning the government is a time-honored method of changing public policy. It is done every day, for nearly every conceivable cause. Moreover, it has been done for many centuries, probably for as long as people have lived in organized societies. Today, most of these efforts are financially stimulated by some organization. But periodically the general public really does become aroused, and letters and calls spontaneously pour into Washington. The public outcry over the check-bouncing scandal in 1992 is an instance of real public outrage. It persuaded the Democratic leadership in the House to release all of the names of those involved, not simply a few as they had wanted. Sometimes the results of these efforts are very humorous. There was once a union in Michigan that held a mass meeting to get every member to write his or her congressman. The president of the union stood before the members, who were waiting with pencil and paper in hand, and told them: "Tell that (#@#@#@#@) that we expect him to vote against that (#@#@#@#@) bill." Both the congressman and the union president were surprised when more than four hundred letters ended up in the congressman's office several days later with the exact same language, including the (#@#@#@#@)s.[2]

The impact of such petitioning efforts ranges from little or none to very great, depending on the circumstances of the policy conflict, the quality and volume of those contacting their legislators, and the other political and legislative factors involved in the particular issue. Generally, efforts to influence a specific policy change through petitioning are most successful under the following circumstances:

1. The organized opposition is minimal.
2. The petitioners represent a voting bloc in the congressional district.
3. The petition concerns a specific policy item that does not threaten a competing group.
4. The member of Congress being petitioned is vulnerable in the next election.

Virtually all of the special interests in American politics use petitioning as one tool among several for influencing legislation. In addition, the visible tactics of petitioning include direct pressure in the form of phone calls, mail, and personal visits by constituents, which are orchestrated by the full-time organization; and such direct assistance as providing information for speeches and position papers, arranging public appearances, placing positive stories in the local newspaper, or even prompting constituents to organize fund-raisers to buttress the organization's PAC contributions. Yet, while these are powerful tools, petitioning has a number of distinct and important limitations.

These efforts by interest groups are most successful when their legislative goals are narrowly focused on a particular subject. Where broad changes are desired, it has traditionally been the political party that has been the most effective vehicle of such objectives, both here in the United States and in the other democracies. One problem is that the issues plaguing American politics today are too broad to be represented by any single lobbying group. These issues—electoral and political reform, welfare reform, health care cost containment and coverage, to name a few—simply can't be dominated by any one particular reform group. The policies are too complex, they are national in character, and they invade far too many competing interests for petitioning to have the desired effects. The general and diffuse reform lobbying effort faces a multitude of highly concentrated interests that need to dominate only one small part of the legislative action, while the reform effort needs to influence the entire process. In addition, the narrow special-interest organizations use something very simple to mobilize their members— the expansion or preservation of their revenue stream from the government. That revenue stream is a very powerful motivational force. In comparison, the broad general-interest organizations, such as Common Cause and taxpayer groups, cannot offer their members similar benefits. Therefore, their supporters are less politically potent in their lobbying efforts. However, to be fair to Ross Perot and United We Stand, America (UWSA), they are attempting to build the largest and most thoroughly organized citizens movement of its kind, and the size may alter the normally expected impact from such a broadly organized group.

Another serious limitation of the petitioning process, however, was demonstrated by the news media's indifference to the efforts by Perot and UWSA in the spring of 1993. Perot's nationwide television and radio effort, beginning in the spring of 1992, is unique for such a group, and each of the first two Perot broadcasts on NBC-TV appears to have reached more than 25 million adults, a huge number for a political broadcast. Even his last broadcast on the North American Free Trade Agreement, arguably a much less appealing subject, reached about three quarters of that number. UWSA itself is growing at a rate that could take it well beyond 5 million members in the near term, and a membership of 5 million would produce an average of 11,500 members in every congressional district across the United States. This should be enough people, if they are well organized, to gain the attention of most people in Congress.[3]

During Perot's first television broadcast in March 1992, he asked Americans to send in a ballot responding to 17 questions he raised during the broadcast. The ballots were distributed by UWSA in *TV Guide*, the publication with the largest circulation in the United States. Within two weeks, UWSA had counted more than 1.3 million ballots. It announced the results at a national news conference, but the media coverage of the announcement was almost nonexistent. Although Perot's organization did present the results to members of Congress, the impact of the ballots was minimized by the lack of news coverage. Members of Congress are sensitive to what is in the news. They, like everyone else, use the volume of news coverage as a measure of the importance of an event.

During the next half-hour program in April 1992, Perot took the unusual step of asking Americans to call the congressional and White House switchboards to register their discontent with Clinton's proposed budget plan. There were so many calls that the switchboards were overloaded for days afterwards. By the Wednesday following the broadcast, nearly a million attempts had been made to call the White House, and both the White House and congressional switchboards were all but impossible to reach.[4] These millions of calls were not even mentioned in the national media, and the effect of the media silence was that for all the public knows, its overwhelming petitioning effort simply never happened. The absence of media coverage makes the lobbying effort smaller than it was. Also, the more attention given these efforts, the more likely that Perot supporters will continue to make the effort.

Like it or not, what is real to Americans is what is in the news.[5] If the media does not cover events, those events effectively did not happen for most Americans. The bottom line is that the ability to sustain success in any large-scale petitioning effort depends on the media to cover the efforts of the group. It is clear that this will not consistently be the case for UWSA, and given the unprecedented size and national prominence of the Perot movement, *we have to seriously doubt that it could be for any comparable group.* While Perot has found extraordinary access to the talk shows, the national news media has not been as interested.

However, the most fundamental weakness with the petitioning process, whether by actual petitions, letters, phone calls, or personal visits, is that it is a difficult process to sustain without direct economic self-interest for the petitioners involved. For example, a public employee union or a major industrial association has direct economic benefits to promise its members. These benefits are ongoing and the price of membership in the organization is the cost of sustaining the long-term lobbying effort with which politicians will have to contend permanently. By contrast, it will be very difficult for any lobbying organization that does not seek such economic benefits to succeed on a large enough scale for a long enough time to be successful on broad issues of reform. Those in opposition to the petitioners can follow the tactic of simply waiting the petitioners out. The member of Congress being petitioned will be polite, respectful, cordial, and even supportive. He or she will tell the group exactly what it wants to hear. But as professional politicians, most know that they are electorally invulnerable and that the motivation of the petitioners is subject to erosion over time.

That electoral invulnerability is another central limitation of petitioning the government. Since most incumbent members of Congress are virtually invulnerable because the electoral process provides them with practically insurmountable advantages, what reason is there for them to listen to any particular constituency interest, no matter what its size? In an economic market, one condition that makes us powerful consumers is that we can choose another product anytime we like. In the political marketplace, the condition that makes broad-based petitioners and voters weak is that we cannot choose another product anytime we like. Electorally invulnerable incumbents, as nearly all of them are, will bow first and lowest to the interests represented by the PAC money that makes them invulnerable in the first place. Without a serious electoral choice, UWSA is simply not a serious threat.

The contention by many Perot supporters when the budget fight was lost in Congress in 1993 was that it was the citizen lobbying effort of UWSA that made the vote so close. Although the desire to claim success in defeat is understandable, this view represents a serious misunderstanding of the legislative process in Congress. Close votes are more a product of the desire by a president and his administration to avoid paying more than is required for a political victory. With contentious issues, it is irrational to win with more legislative votes than the minimum number necessary, and Clinton was buying left and right with commitments to gain the support of legislators who threatened to defect. If Clinton had needed additional votes, he most likely could have had them. But why pay for what is not needed? In Congress, it is standard operating procedure for the winning coalition to allow members who might be adversely affected by the vote to defect.[6]

The Answer: A Political Solution to Political Problems

The alternative to the petitioning effort is the strategy of directly challenging the incumbents of both parties. A political party is not interested in converting officeholders to its point of view; rather, it is interested in replacing those officeholders. A political party achieves its goals by the accumulation of enough political power to force the institution to make the changes desired. A party does not depend on the acquiescence of those in power because it is an equal or at least a seriously competitive power, not a supplicant like the petitioner.

Whereas a petitioning organization is rarely able to profoundly affect the political agenda of Congress, a political party with sufficient numbers of representatives is able to greatly influence the agenda, both in the electoral and legislative arenas. The ability to set the agenda is a power not to be underestimated. On a whole range of issues—from welfare reform to electoral reform—large portions of the public have been denied the policies they want precisely because the major parties have failed to even place these issues on the table for serious consideration.

Contrary to conventional thinking, a new political party's assault on Congress need not succeed in winning a majority in Congress and the state legislatures to have enormous, even controlling influence over policy outcomes. If a new party could win 40 or 50 seats in the House of Representatives, or 10 seats in the Senate, it could provide the balance of power on a whole range of policy issues and, more importantly, on the crucial issue of who gets the leadership positions in both the House and the Senate. For example, on the issue of spending cuts, this bloc might support Republican calls for deep cuts. On tax issues, the bloc might vote with the Democrats, providing hope that we can find a long-term solution to our spending problems. A new voting bloc could provide the pivotal votes on a whole range of political issues, casting its votes consistently on the side of institutional and political reform and fiscal responsibility. The same is true for the state legislatures. One vote by a congressman is worth far more than the uncertain threat of 10,000 votes in a member's district, especially when those votes could rarely affect the outcome of a typical congressional election.

Also, the power of a centrist party arises precisely because it is centrist. A left party really would have no choice but to vote with the Democrats most of the time, and the same condition is true for a very conservative party and the Republicans. A centrist party can pivot either way, depending upon the issue. Like the Gaullists in France, who never achieved a majority in the Assembly, a successful centrist reformist minority in a legislature would be more powerful than taking over the Republicans or the Democrats and would be considerably easier to achieve.[7]

In this book we have introduced four major failures in the American political system. It is our contention that the creation of a new party, representing the radicalized center, presents the best opportunity to significantly address all of these failures. Problems caused by political failure demand a political solution. These failures must be understood as interrelated and cannot properly be addressed and solved one at a time. For example, the lack of democratic choice in America is a root cause of the power of special interests and of chronic overspending. Likewise, the deterioration of public attitudes about our democracy and ourselves as democratic citizens is a result of the lack of choice in elections, the failures of the parties in connecting the government with the governed, and the failure of the system to present the policy choices desired by a large part of the populace. The creation of a new party—centrist in orientation and focused in its purpose—is the only solution broad enough in scope to cope with all of these structural deficiencies.

For clarity, it is useful to consider each of the these main failures individually, so we can see how a new party could have a significant effect in addressing the problems.

Failure 1: The Lack of Democratic Choice

As we have shown in Chapter 2, the United States is not really governed by a two-party system. With the exception of the presidency and some statewide races, we have a one-party system in which party factions operating under different names exert nearly permanent control over particular seats. *A new political party, particularly a centrist party, would restore competition in many of these districts simply through the act of competing.* In this area, the mere existence of a new party would accomplish more, faster, than any electoral reform that the two parties could ever come up with. This assumes, of course, a proposition that we will have to prove—that a political party of the center could raise enough money directly from the public to fund a campaign against an entrenched opponent able to open the spigot of Washington PAC money.

In the hundreds of districts where one party currently dominates, a centrist party can effectively provide viable alternative candidates that have not been provided by the other major party. The result will be that many one-party districts actually become two-party districts for the first time, giving those voters real electoral choice. For example, a centrist party can effectively provide alternative candidates in suburban districts dominated by Republicans, where there is no Democratic party to speak of. While a Democratic candidate might never be competitive under any circumstances, a new centrist party could produce fiscally conservative legislators that could effectively compete. The same could be said for the many urban and middle-class districts in which the Republicans fail to field viable candidates to compete with Democrats, eliminating voter choice in those districts.

In addition, the creation of a new party would greatly increase electoral competition and true choice because it would introduce a degree of uncertainty into practically every race. Uncertainty is what drives electoral competition, and when races are uncertain, more candidates are willing to risk entering the fray because they perceive an opportunity to win. In contrast, if the incumbent is perceived as being unbeatable, there is little incentive to run. Encouraging more candidates to run would give the voters more choice and hopefully would lead to improvement of the candidates from all the parties. The introduction of competition in the political marketplace would likely have the same effect that increased competition has in the economic marketplace—all products are forced to improve in response to an innovative new product.

One additional benefit of the new party would be that truly competitive candidates would restore communication with voters by increasing the number of serious electoral campaigns. The resulting debate would present voters with more information toward their voting decisions. Suddenly, voters who have never had the information necessary to make informed choices in legislative elections would be genuinely brought into the debate, reconnecting them to their legislators and increasing their sense of connection to the political system.

Perhaps most importantly, by increasing the number of competitive races, the political control of legislative institutions would become more sensitive and responsive to changing public sentiments. As we have shown, the control of Congress and the state legislatures rarely shifts with changing public sentiment. By increasing electoral competition, a new party can decrease the average winning margins that legislators enjoy, increasing the probability that shifts in voting and attitudes can have an impact on the makeup of the legislature. In other words, if margins are decreased, smaller shifts in the electorate are needed to result in a change of power. The control of the legislature would no longer be electorally insulated from trends in the electorate. In the process, the connection between legislative performance and electoral success would be greatly strengthened.

Failure 2: The Deterioration of Public Attitudes

How can we involve people in the modern political process? Are we to expect that the current parties are capable of changing the processes that have succeeded in driving millions of people from involvement in politics? A centrist political party, committed to real solutions, would help both voter preferences and the broader public interest to return as the basis on which political contests are decided. This would have a tremendously positive effect on restoring voters' belief in the importance of their involvement in the system. For three decades, the public has had their expectations raised, only to be disappointed time and time again. A new party would give people a reason to participate and encourage the reentry to the political system of thousands of people who have been driven away by the failures and scandals of the two major parties. The increase in voting in the 1992 presidential campaign is almost certainly the consequence of having Ross Perot on the ballot and the additional campaigning that he contributed.

In addition, a new political party would permit the unorganized voices of discontent to become connected organizationally, thereby strengthening the alienated voters' sense of involvement and creating a momentum for reform that is impossible if reformers must depend on the support of those already in power. Cynicism is related to the voters' lack of involvement in and connection to the system. By providing additional choice in partisan affiliation, we can involve millions of voters directly in the process instead of allowing them to stand on the sidelines, angry and discontented.

And in contrast to the vast system of organizations that seem to control the political debate, a centrist party, electing candidates without PAC money, would create a political force entirely independent of the special-interest system. In response, the general public confidence would improve greatly if the public perceived that PAC money need not inevitably be the dominating force driving national politics. If the country believes that officeholders are primarily beholden to *them*, not to special interests, they would be more likely to support the complex process of reform necessary to reinvigorate our political and economic system.

As a corollary to increased public involvement, a new political party could potentially recruit a new generation of leaders into the political process, people whose loyalties and values are not shaped either by the requirements of participating in the two existing parties or by the requirements of PAC money for campaigns. Because the new party would inevitably support term limits, it would attract nonprofessional but politically concerned individuals desiring to serve their country for a limited period of time rather than serve only their own career.

Another effect of creating a new party would be that by greatly increasing the number of three-candidate races, the methods of modern campaigning would need to change. In a three-candidate race, negative campaigning drives voters away from both the candidate who throws mud as well as the candidate who is muddied, helping the candidate who stays above the fray. This is often the case in hotly contested primaries. A new political party, determined to avoid negative campaigning, would raise the level of political debate because its presence would create a strong disincentive for the other candidates to engage in negative campaigning. In other words, three-candidate races provide an electoral incentive for all candidates to stay out of the slime.

Failure 3: The Structural Inability to Control Spending

The hard, cold reality is that we will never get rid of the deficit without first eliminating the Democratic control of the House of Representatives. The Republicans have proven incapable of achieving this goal. A new party that can align with the Republicans on spending cuts and the Democrats on tax issues will provide the hope for a long-term solution to overspending. The spending debate has fallen irretrievably into a bitter partisan debate. By breaking a one-party lock on the issue, there will be far more room to build coalitions instead of one party dictating the outcomes of fiscal policy.

One of the main reasons why a new party could apply effective pressure for fiscal responsibility would be that it would increase the electoral risk of pandering to the needs of special-interest groups. Special interests' influence through campaign contributions would become a major campaign issue to the disadvantage of both the Republicans and Democrats, *if the new political party avoids the need for such funding.* Those Democrats and Republicans who have relied the most heavily on the PACs would become politically vulnerable against a centrist candidate who refuses to accept PAC funding or campaign contributions of over $1,000. Rather than trying to control the money with legislation, a political party that could fund its own candidates would be far more effective in making special-interest money a political liability instead of a political virtue.

As we noted in Chapter 3, legislators can engage in reckless policies because they can disperse the accountability for their actions. When legislators are forced to take clear stands on fiscal issues that can then be used against them electorally, they are far more likely to side with the broader interests of the general public. A new party, operating in Congress and the state legislatures, can use the powers of the institution to create new electoral pressure on recalcitrant legislators. Political scientist R. Douglas Arnold, in *The Logic of Congressional Action*, argues that there are two conditions that need to be satisfied for Congress serve the needs of the general public—which he call "inattentive citizens"—rather than specific interests:

> First, legislators feel electorally pressured to serve inattentive citizens only if an issue is salient or potentially salient to substantial numbers of those citizens. Second, legislators feel electorally pressured to serve inattentive citizens only if there are talented leaders who will champion the interests of inattentive citizens by introducing the necessary amendments, demanding roll call votes at the proper time, and doing everything that is procedurally necessary to create a connection between individual actions and both collective actions of Congress and the resulting policy effects.[8]

A political party is the only institution that can make reform issues salient to large numbers of citizens and introduce new leaders who can use the procedures and institutional powers of Congress to force individual legislators to be accountable on reform issues. In short, a political party is the only institution that can satisfy both of Arnold's requirements. The ability to force accountability extends deeply into the legislative process, not just on the final vote. The power of party members in a legislature to challenge rules, call for votes, and introduce legislation are more powerful tools of reform than any signature drive could ever dream of being.

Perhaps more importantly, many people fail to realize that the entire dynamics of the operation of Congress would be altered if a new party could block the formation of a Democratic majority. The election of the speaker of the House and the chairmanships of the legislative committees would suddenly be uncertain. The Democratic Party would lose its unilateral power over the internal operations of Congress. The new party could, in fact, form coalitions with either of the major parties in order to elect legislators responsive to their issues to chair committees. In addition, committees could no longer operate like the fiefdoms of the individuals who chair them. Instead, any legislation emerging from committee would need the support of at least two of the three parties, ending one-party domination of the policy process. Most people fail to realize how much power the committees and subcommittees wield over the content of legislation. By the time legislation comes to the floor, the deal is usually done. The wording of statutes and the form, breadth, timing, and rules of the ensuing debate are all determined by committees and subcommittees. This is where the power is, and people who are serious about reform need to be involved at this level. If one party can't automatically control the outcome of the committees, then both minority parties would have an opportunity to participate positively in the policy process, instead of always playing the negative role of blocking the process.

Finally, a new party that could break Democratic control would most likely attract enormous amounts of media attention, which it could then use to further its cause of fiscal and electoral reform and increase the electoral pressure on legislators from the two major parties. The media can easily ignore a petitioning group, no matter what its size. The media will find it far more difficult, however, to ignore a sizable voting block in Congress and the state legislatures. Indeed, the formation of a new party that could break Democratic domination of Congress would probably be one of the biggest stories in the history of American politics. The ensuing media coverage could create the political pressure and momentum necessary for Congress to undertake fundamental reform, instead of window dressing.

Failure 4: The Failure of the Washington-Based High-Technology Parties

The creation of a new party would also present a unique opportunity to use the best of both modern technology and grassroots politics to involve voters in the political process. The new party should, therefore, be both a social and a political institution. The founders of such a party would have the opportunity to apply what we know is wrong with party politics to craft an effective institution of participatory democracy.

Also, by creating a party centered on specific solutions rather than on candidates, the issues that the party stands for would be clear to all voters, making the choice more based on issues and less on personalities. This is a traditional function of the party that has been all but forgotten. The creation of a clear brand image is vital to the ability of a new party to enact positive change and is vital to the proper operation of any party system. The success of a new party that has clearly staked out the center would create a strong incentive for the other parties to concentrate on reformulating and strengthening their own brand images.

This reformulation would most likely mean that the other two parties would be encouraged to fully embrace the powerful minorities within their ranks that have held sway over the internal positions taken by the party apparatus yet have threatened each party's ability to appeal to the middle. For example, the Democratic Party could become the true champion of minorities, the poor, and the public employees unions, with the liberal wing in power. The Republicans could then pursue their conservative solutions to issues like taxation, abortion, and limits to homosexual rights without having to worry about alienating moderates. The moderates would already have left. In the process, all the parties would take positions consistent with the interests of their core, enabling the voters to better know what a candidate stands for simply by knowing which party that candidate belongs to. At the same time, the parties would be rid of the deep divisions within their ranks.

Winning a three-candidate race in individual districts, of course, requires new and different mathematics from that governing a two-candidate race. The winning candidate need not win 51 percent in a three-way race. Many of the races could be won with 40 percent or less, and that reduces the electoral barrier to the entry of a new political party. A new party, and the major parties, would approach the tactical issue of winning very differently than any party in a two-party system.

The Potential for a New Centrist Party

Perhaps we make the process sound too simple. We say that competitiveness can be restored simply by creating a political party able to compete for seats that are subject to one-party dominance, and the rest of the solutions will naturally follow from there. In reality, of course, the task of creating a serious and competitive political party out of whole cloth is anything but simple. The two current political parties have created roadblocks at every step along the way. In the same way that powerful corporations often behave, the Democratic and Republican parties won control of the electoral marketplace. They have used that control to enact rules that make it extremely difficult for competitors. They regulate everything from the name of a new party to the conditions under which it can be placed on the ballot, as well as how one can register to vote for the candidates of that political party. The parties cooperatively enjoy and exercise monopolistic controls over competition that would never be tolerated in the economic marketplace.

These roadblocks are serious. However, what used to be the main impediment to the successful formation of a competitive party—the existence of widespread loyalty to the two existing parties—has seriously declined. Today, there are more people who think of themselves as independent than there are in either of the two parties, and we have never had so few people expressing positive feelings about either of the parties. Voters are free to a degree that is unprecedented in modern times, and given this, the organizational impediments created by the Democrats and Republicans to control ballot access are probably not sufficient to keep a truly determined effort off the ballot. Finally, the existing parties simply do not have the organizational strength to keep a new party from emerging. Both parties appear to be "aging," and voters under 35 years old have especially weak ties to the party system in general.

The Basic Requirements for a Political Party

There really isn't anything magical about creating a political party.[9] Certain basic conditions must exist for a party to form, and the degree to which they are present will shape the size and success of any effort. In the broadest sense, a successful political party, whether new or old, will necessarily possess certain attributes. The basic requirements are as follows:

1. A "market" of voters willing to support the candidates of the party.
2. A cadre of leaders who are willing to run for public office.
3. A cadre of activists who are willing to provide the organizational core for the party.
4. A financial base that permits the party to compete fairly for many, if not most, offices.

The issue of a market of voters involves a set of conditions that define the role the voters play in the overall process. In previous chapters we have presented ample evidence that enough of the public is sufficiently dissatisfied with the existing parties and governmental leadership to form a market for the creation of a new party. However, it will take more than just being angry at the parties to sustain a political movement. People must be convinced that there is no option other than to create a new political party. They must be willing to actively support a new party in elections, and there must be a core group of citizens who will financially support the party's candidates.

The Belief in the Impossibility of Reform

The level of contemporary pessimism about the ability of the current system to deal with our major problems is demonstrated by the responses to a series of questions that were asked in polls we conducted in May and August of 1992 and during February and May of 1993. This latter period should have been a honeymoon for the Clinton administration. Especially after the removal of an incumbent president, one would expect that the public's faith in the system would be improved. This was not the case. The pattern of the responses is dramatic and rather depressing. At first, the 1992 election did have a slight positive effect on the public mood. Skepticism about the future declined from June 1992 through February 1993, as the mood of strong Democrats improved with the success of Bill Clinton. However, as it

Table 1 **The Impossibility of Reform (1992–1993)**

Question: Do you agree/disagree with the following statement?	Percent Who Agree			
	May 1992	August 1992	February 1993	May 1993
Current incumbents will *never* reform the political system.	69	62	52	67
Special-interest groups have more influence than voters.	83	79	79	84
Congress is largely owned by special-interest groups.	74	71	68	74
If Democrats and Republicans continue to run things, we will never get real reform.	46	38	36	45

Adapted from data collected by a Gordon Black Poll.

became clear that Bill Clinton would renege on the spending cuts he proposed during the election, the disillusionment and skepticism returned near to the pinnacle of discontent experienced in May of 1992. As shown in Table 1, between February and May 1993, there was a 15 percentage point increase in those who believe that "current incumbents will *never* reform the political process," with 67 percent of the voters expressing this view. Almost half, 45 percent, believe that if the Democrats and Republicans continue to run things, we will *never* get real reform—a 9 point increase from the past poll and near the same amount from a year earlier.

The resurgence of confidence among Democrats was short-lived indeed. With less than five months of governing, the Democratic administration and its allies in Congress managed to return America to the condition of extreme skepticism recorded a year earlier. This discontent and skepticism is becoming an enduring part of our political landscape. The momentary hope of an election accomplished nothing but a slight downward blip in an otherwise constant trend.

Willingness to Support a New Party

We undertook an original study that forms the basis for this section of the book. It was designed as a feasibility study for a new political party, researching the political party the same way one would research any complex new product before it is brought to market. There are, of course, similarities between launching a major new product and

Table 2   **Willingness to Support a Third Party (1992–1993)**

Question: Do you agree/disagree with the following statement?	Percent Who Agree			
	May 1992	August 1992	February 1993	May 1993
We need a new political party to reform American politics.	47	44	40	48
Democrats and Republicans are not capable of getting the country going in the right direction— we need a new party.	50	43	43	48
I am angry at both political parties right now.	56	44	39	49
I would vote for reform party candidates.	65	57	53	50

Adapted from data collected by a Gordon Black Poll.

launching a political party. Just as success in the economic marketplace requires consumers who are willing and able to buy the new product, success for a new party requires political consumers who are willing to vote for the party's candidates. It also requires an activist core that will work for these candidates, to be the marketers as it were. In Chapter 5, we showed a series of questions dating back to the 1930s concerning the willingness of voters to embrace the candidates of a new political party. That willingness increased sharply in the 1980s and early 1990s. We first conducted a poll on this issue in May 1992, and since then we have asked the same questions on the issue of a new political party on four separate occasions with the following results. On each question, about half of all American adults indicate support for a new political party (see Table 2). This remarkable level of support exists just four months after the election of a new president and Congress.

In writing our questions, we specifically used extreme language such as "not capable" or "angry" precisely to test the intensity of the sentiments. These responses indicate that large portions of the public are truly ready to look beyond their current political choices, toward solutions that originate from outside the system they distrust so deeply.

The Role of Partisanship

When the original study was completed in May 1992, it revealed that a new reform party would draw almost exactly equally from both the Republicans and Democrats. With the Democratic victory in the election, Democratic support for a new political party declined fairly sharply among the 17 percent of the electorate who consider themselves to be "strong Democrats." This is logical given the success of the party in regaining the White House and the hope that Bill Clinton would be a "new democrat." However, support for a new reform party remained very strong among the 67 percent who consider themselves Independents or were weakly attached to the Democratic or Republican parties. Also, in February 1993, the attraction of a new party was stronger among Republicans than Democrats, although the new party clearly continues to attract voters who are less strongly affiliated. Even so, 36 percent of the "strong Democrats" indicate they would vote for the candidates of a reform party, and nearly three in ten want a new political party created, as shown in Table 3.

The rapid disillusionment of the Democrats with the Democratic Party was clearly in evidence in May 1993, according to the polling data reported in Table 4. In contrast to the earlier poll, on every question the Democrats are almost as unhappy as the Republicans, exemplified by the large percentages: 40 percent of the Democrats and 46 percent of the Republicans would vote for candidates of a new reform political party. The more weakly attached Republicans and Democrats appear vulnerable to the appeals of a new centrist party. We believe both groups will respond to new leadership.

Partisan Hostility

Another interesting issue concerning partisan loyalty is the relative degree to which the voters attached to one party are willing to cross party lines and vote for the other party or a new political party. Republicans are Republicans not just because they like the Republican Party, but partly because they dislike the Democratic Party. The intensification of negative campaigning during the 1970s and the 1980s has had the logical consequence of intensifying inter-party hostility among the partisans of the two parties. Voters have developed negative attitudes toward both parties, and the voters of each party develop even more negative attitudes toward the party against which they are regularly competing. These negative attitudes toward the other party greatly reduce the other party candidate's chances of successfully competing in the many one-party districts across the United States. One of the primary advantages of a third party is that it can appeal to voters from both major parties in contests where there is only one major candidate to compete against.

We looked at this issue with two questions we included in a poll in February 1993. Overall, as shown in Table 5, 75 percent of the strong Republicans and 51 percent of the weak Republicans have a negative

Table 3   **Partisan Basis for a New Political Party (February 1993)**

Question: Do you agree/disagree with the following statement?	Percent Who Agree				
	Strong Democrats (17%)	Weak Democrats (14%)	Independents and Others (38%)	Weak Republicans (15%)	Strong Republicans (14%)
Current incumbents will never reform the political system.	30	50	55	66	69
Special interests have more influence than voters.	62	79	84	88	80
Congress is largely owned by special interests.	55	74	68	71	74
If Democrats and Republicans continue to run things, we'll never get reform.	17	34	45	43	33
We need a new party to reform American politics.	20	42	48	46	35
We need a new party: Republicans and Democrats are no longer capable of moving in the right direction.	18	42	53	50	38
I am angry at both parties and their candidates.	15	38	43	43	38
I would vote for candidates of a reform-oriented party.	36	52	61	61	45

Adapted from data collected by a Gordon Black Poll.

view of the Democratic Party; they would have difficulty voting for Democratic candidates. Conversely, 79 percent of the strong Democrats and 68 percent of the weak Democrats have a negative view of the Republican Party. Therefore, overall about 24 percent of the electorate, on average, is not available to Republican candidates, and 20 percent of the electorate on average is not available to the Democratic candidates. In many individual congressional districts these percentages are much higher.

Table 4   **Partisan Basis for a New Political Party (May 1993)**

Question: Do you agree/disagree with the following statement?	Percent Who Agree		
	Democrats	Independents and Others	Republicans
Current incumbents will never reform the political system.	50	69	83
Special interests have more influence than voters.	76	90	89
Congress is largely owned by special interests.	64	80	79
If Democrats and Republicans continue to run things, we'll never get reform.	34	58	42
We need a new party to reform American politics.	40	58	45
We need a new party: Republicans and Democrats are no longer capable of moving in the right direction.	39	61	43
I am angry at both parties and their candidates.	38	60	50
I would vote for candidates of a reform-oriented party.	40	63	46

Adapted from data collected by a Gordon Black Poll.

Through years of negative campaigning, the two parties have each managed to alienate a segment of the electorate, such that:

- 24 percent of electorate find it difficult to vote Republican.
- 20 percent of electorate find it difficult to vote Democratic.

A new political party, by contrast, would have none of the negative images of the two existing parties, at least certainly not in the early years. From the standpoint of attracting voters, a new political party would be more able to challenge entrenched Democrats in Democratic districts than the Republicans, and more able to challenge entrenched Republicans in Republican districts than the Democrats. The new party would be like the Japanese car manufacturer in our earlier analogy. A new political party might be willing to subsidize the inane negative campaigning of the other parties, simply so that the electorate would dislike both of them even more than they already do. Today, the dislike of both parties is so great that the candidates of both parties across the United States often avoid using their own party label on their advertising materials.

Table 5   **Hostility Between Republicans and Democrats (February 1993)**

Question: What is your attitude toward the Democratic/ Republican Party?	Percent Who Agree				
	Strong Democrats	Weak Democrats	Independents and Others	Weak Republicans	Strong Republicans
Attitude Toward Democrats					
Very positive	53	25	14	2	1
Somewhat positive	42	55	45	43	22
Somewhat negative	3	15	21	39	47
Very negative	—	3	9	12	28
Not sure	2	2	11	4	2
Attitude Toward Republicans					
Very positive	—	1	6	17	48
Somewhat positive	17	26	37	65	44
Somewhat negative	37	51	37	15	5
Very negative	42	17	10	2	2
Not sure	4	5	10	1	1

Adapted from data collected by a Gordon Black Poll.

The implication is that there can be no solution to the problem of inadequate competition within the current party system because of the negative party images. This is a fundamental reason why the solution to the lack of competition cannot come from within the current system. Any hope for an increase in competition has to come from a new force that will not have to fight the long-standing negative images created by 30 years of negative politics.

Counting Third-Party Voters

Predicting who would support a third party can be tricky. However, the 1992 campaign afforded us the unique opportunity to ask a series of questions precisely probing the willingness of the public to support and vote for a new political party. The goal of this research was to identify people who would comprise the "core" of the party. Any political party is inherently a loosely structured organization. Most people only identify with a party rather than join it in some official sense. As a result, individuals align with parties with varying degrees of intensity, ranging from the parties' most loyal supporters, who will vote the party line regardless of the candidate or situation, to voters who vaguely consider themselves a party member, but whose behavior swings back and forth with the changing tides of the public mood. In order for a party to be successful, there has to be a base group of people who profoundly believe in the party and will support the parties' candidates with little prodding or argument. Therefore, we set out to find these people.

In order to create an honest measure of an activity that might happen in the future, we staggered four questions at different sections in our survey. All of the questions had to do with support for a new party. By using multiple measures at multiple points in the survey, we analyzed the various components of partisan activity that would make it likely that an individual would support a new third party.

These four questions were used to ascertain the respondent's willingness to support a third party:

1. Do you agree or disagree with the following statement? We need a new political party to reform American politics.
2. Some people are saying that the Democrats and the Republicans are no longer capable of getting this country going in the right direction and that we need a new national political party. Do you strongly agree, moderately agree, moderately disagree, or strongly disagree?
3. Some people are angry at both political parties and their candidates. Would you say that describes how you feel right now?
4. Suppose that a new reform-oriented political party was created to run candidates for Congress, the Senate, and even your state legislature. Assuming for a moment that this new party was supporting your positions on many issues you cared about, would you be most likely to vote for the candidates of the new reform party or would you be most likely to vote for either the Republican or Democratic candidates?

In order to be considered a likely supporter of a third party, respondents had to answer all the questions indicating support for a third party. In doing so, they indicated that they believed a new party was needed, that reform was not possible with the current parties, that they were angry at both parties, and that they would be willing to vote for a third party. This group is identified in Charts 1 and 2 as the core members of a new party.

Chart 1   **Core Loyalists of a New Party (May 1992–May 1993)**

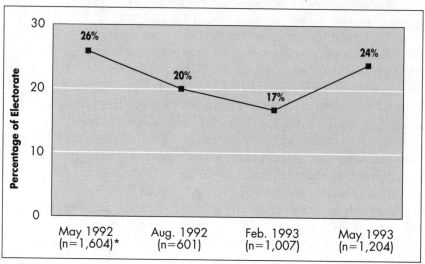

*n = number of cases or interviews.

Note: Projected new party voters answered all four questions regarding the establishment of a third party affirmatively and stated that they would vote for a new party.

Adapted from data collected by a Gordon Black Poll.

In May 1993, our analysis of the poll indicated that approximately 24 percent of the electorate constituted the minimal level of support a new national reform party could expect to receive, as shown in Chart 1. By asking these questions at four different points from May 1992 to May 1993, we were able to track the stability of this base over time. Keep in mind that these voters represent the core of support for a third party when one does not even exist. This is, therefore, the lowest likely level of potential support, rather than an upper boundary. The true upper boundary would ultimately depend on the ability of the new party to succeed electorally and achieve the goals of reform to which it aspires.

The core partisans for a new party are equivalent in type to those who actively call themselves Republican or Democrats.[10] As Chart 1 shows, the support for a new party was highest (26 percent) at the height of the discontent during the 1992 primary elections. As the public invested its hope in Clinton, and Perot dropped out of the race, the core third-party support as measured by these questions declined to 20 percent in August. It is important to note that in August, Ross Perot was extremely unpopular with the public after dropping out of the race. Yet, one out of five voters still indicated a deep and abiding support for a third party. This proves that America's discontent is larger than Ross

Perot, or any one man, which is a point Perot himself makes repeatedly. The third-party movement is not about Ross Perot. He is simply providing the most visible leadership for this group of frustrated individuals. In February 1993, with a newly elected Bill Clinton coming off an effective State of the Union address, the core loyalist measure dipped to 17 percent. As Clinton's troubles began, however, the measure quickly returned to very near its original level.

In order to project what the new party system would look like, we subtracted these individuals from their current party preferences (Republican, Democratic, Independent, or something else). In Chart 2, we see that the new political party would shrink the Democrats to 27 percent of the electorate and the Republicans to 22 percent of the electorate. These numbers suggest that a new party would create three parties of roughly equal size. Many electoral battles would be won or lost in the competition for the 24.3 percent who still consider themselves Independents. However, the number of Independents would actually be much smaller than we project because we are not controlling for likely voters or registered voters. A large portion of the leftover Independents are actually people who are simply not interested in politics and do not vote. They, therefore, would not factor into political competition in a new party system. Also, a large number of these Independents would lean toward one party, acting very much like self-identified partisans. Chart 2 projects what the core party affiliation in the three-party system might look like.

Chart 2   **Projected Party Affiliations (May 1993)**

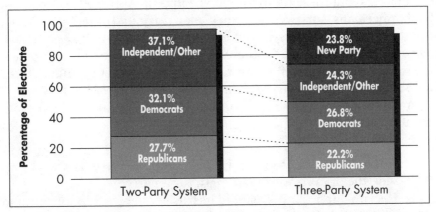

Note: Projected new party voters answered all four questions regarding the establishment of a third party affirmatively and stated that they would vote for a new party. Categories not shown: "Don't know" and "Refused." Adapted from data collected by a Gordon Black Poll.

Organizing a Political Party

The numbers required to displace the establishments in Washington and the state capitals are far less than a majority, and these numbers should be kept in perspective. Current estimated levels of political participation are provided by the National Election Study, supervised and conducted at the Survey Research Center of the University of Michigan.

- Less than ten percent of all adults go to political rallies, meetings, or dinners.
- Less than five percent work for one of the parties or for candidates.
- About ten percent give money, buy tickets, or do something to help a political campaign.
- By the mid-1980s, the combined number of Americans who thought of themselves as *strongly attached* to either the Republicans or the Democrats had declined to 29 percent of the electorate.

Politics-as-usual is based on a very small minority of people in America. These are the percentages to keep in mind when assessing the potential for a new party. Those in the existing establishment would prefer potential adversaries to focus on the number of offices they control, the resources at their disposal, their access to the media, and the historic improbability of the success of efforts such as those sparked by Ross Perot. When examining the potential for the creation of a third force in American politics, however, the most relevant figures are those concerning the strength of the status quo base, and they are remarkably small. To put these figures in perspective, in April 1993, 24 percent of all Americans surveyed say they plan to join United We Stand, America, and by the time this book appears in print, more people will have sent a check to UWSA than to both political parties combined. This is not to say, however, that establishing a new party would be easy. There are many challenges that must be taken quite seriously.

A new political party must solve three major organizational problems if it is to have any success:

1. Recruit a cadre of leadership and volunteer activists who provide the organizational strength for a party.
2. Recruit high quality candidates to challenge Republican and Democratic incumbents.

3. Raise sufficient money to support the party's candidates independent of the PAC system of special-interest funding.

At the time of this writing, there are two different rivers of effort moving in the direction of creating a centrist, national political party.

The first is a series of efforts, aimed at creating new parties, that emerged during the 1992 presidential election. Most (but not all) of the activities are a product of the forces set in motion by the Ross Perot candidacy. These go under different party names, depending on the state, but they share a centrist policy perspective. In some states, these efforts operate under the name of the Independence Party, while in other states they operate under the name of the Patriot Party, or some variant. These party efforts are joined by independent organizations such as A Connecticut Party, which emerged out of the successful gubernatorial candidacy of Lowell P. Weicker, Jr., as well as other independent parties in Utah and Alaska. By the spring of 1992, centrist party organizations were developing in a number of states across the country.[11]

These efforts, although operating under different names, share similar characteristics. One common element is that they are centrist and their major agendas are directed toward political and electoral reform. Next, they are all looking toward the creation of a political party that will run candidates for national and state offices. And finally, they are all local, grassroots organizing projects, working from the bottom up.

Unfortunately, they also share the characteristic of being underfinanced and without strong organizational support. Currently, the problem these parties face is that, as we have pointed out before, the costs of entering politics—money, effort, recruitment of candidates—have risen dramatically over the past 30 years. The central problem is credibility. *If those who share the political views of party organizers are not convinced that organizers can succeed in their effort, the would-be followers will not be induced to pay a reasonable share of the costs of collective action.* In a sense, collective action is like a chicken-and-egg problem. If one could persuade all those who want a new political party to pay even a small share of the costs, organizing a political party would be easy. However, the would-be followers have an incentive to hang back and not make a contribution until after they are assured that the effort will be effective. The net result is that the collective action—organizing the party—is defeated.

Collective action in the form of party organizing is possible only when a handful of people have both the motivation and the means to sustain the costs of organizing by themselves. When this condition occurs, others will be persuaded to join the effort because they are persuaded that it has a sufficient likelihood of success to warrant their own participation and contributions. These organizers are most likely to be candidates who desire to be in office, and the new party may be the most likely vehicle for sustaining their effort. A candidate has a special incentive to support the effort to create a political party. The organization of the party then simply becomes a byproduct of the candidate's efforts to win office. So far, however, these new-party efforts around the United States have not proven very successful in recruiting viable candidates for office.

The situation of Governor Lowell P. Weicker, Jr. of Connecticut makes this case as well as any. The new state party in Connecticut, called A Connecticut Party, did not exist prior to the candidacy of Weicker. Weicker, who had served in the Senate as a Republican, was able, because of his stature in the state, to raise the funds to run as an Independent. He won, and out of his candidacy arose A Connecticut Party, which ran candidates for office unsuccessfully during the next election round. The point is simple. Weicker paid the costs of collective action through his candidacy, but he had access to the funds to do that because of his prior service in office. The permanent organization that constitutes the political party is an outgrowth of Weicker's campaign, and not the other way around. Moreover, A Connecticut Party has yet to win a single other race in the state outright, although some of Weicker's cross-endorsed candidates did win in 1992. He has been singularly successful in restoring fiscal responsibility to the state government in Connecticut, yet he has not challenged the status quo on many of the other issues that form the basis for a stronger new party. One of the key problems is that if he did so, he would alienate many of the state legislators on whom he depends in his role as governor.

As one of the two standing Independent governors, Weicker has been in a position to assert leadership over some of the efforts to start a new national party. His hesitancy is a reflection of the difficulty of attracting an established politician, even an existing Independent, into the risky task of organizing.

Probably the easiest, fastest, and perhaps the only way to organize a new political party is to find the candidates who want to run for office under the party label. These candidates, if they are people well known and well liked in their communities, will have a much easier time raising the funds to support the highly specific objective of their candidacy than the much less specific objective of creating a political party. A political party is, above all else, an organization for recruiting candidates to run for political office. A political party that does not focus on candidates isn't really a political party in the traditional sense of the term. A political party with candidates will find permanent organization emerging as a by-product of the campaign. If one looks at history, even back to the American Revolution, the major leaders of political party movements have been candidates. Men like Adams, Washington, Jefferson, Madison, Monroe, Hamilton, and others did not fight the Revolution to turn power over to others who sat on the sidelines. They sought office and then ran the government. Lincoln helped to propel the Republican Party to national prominence and to establish himself as a presidential candidate through his unsuccessful senatorial race against Democrat Stephen Douglas in Illinois. Unless efforts to create political parties today focus on the recruitment of candidates, they cannot be successful.

United We Stand, America

The effort of Ross Perot to create United We Stand, America (UWSA) represents a different approach to organizing. In February 1993, Perot launched an organizing effort to create a nationwide citizens' lobby. Between February and the end of June 1993, Perot spent millions of his own dollars to persuade Americans to join UWSA for $15 per person. His support of this effort included three half-hour television broadcasts on NBC-TV, broadcasts on several radio networks, a large-scale advertising effort on radio and television, and newspaper ads. In addition, he spent nearly every weekend making speeches to large audiences in various parts of the country. By September 1993, he had personally made over 70 speeches to crowds ranging from a thousand to more than ten thousand people.

UWSA is a tax-exempt, educational organization. Contributions to UWSA are not tax-deductible, but the organization is not required to pay taxes. This organization is not a political party, and could not be easily converted to a political party because of the tax codes. The functions that the organization can perform are primarily educational, but public education is clearly an important condition for successful reform and change in the United States. Although millions of dollars have been contributed to UWSA in the form of membership dues, Perot has held most of these funds in reserve and has financed his organizational effort with his own funds. The purpose of this is to avoid any contention that the donated funds are being used for partisan political purposes, which would be inconsistent with the tax status of the organization.

Although UWSA is clearly and explicitly *not* a political party, there are several reasons for discussing it here. First, Perot represents an entirely different strategy for organizing, with personal resources that far surpass anything available to those individuals organizing state and local parties. Also, Perot is both *willing* and *able* to pay all of the costs of organizing for political action. Because of this, he has instant credibility with potential supporters. They believe that he can be successful, if he wishes, and are therefore willing to climb on the bandwagon he creates, contributing what they can.

We have special knowledge of the potential size of Perot's organizations because we have conducted some polls for Perot in order to measure his support. The percentage of Americans who say they plan to join UWSA rose from 13 percent in February 1993, to 20 percent in March, and then to 24 percent in April. To put this in perspective, less than 5 percent of all Americans say they worked for a candidate or a political party in 1992, and less than 10 percent indicated that they gave financially to a candidate or a political party.

Questions about the "intentional future behavior" of individuals usually provide estimates that are quite high. Even if these figures are high by 50 percent or 100 percent, they still represent what has the potential to be one of the largest and most powerful movements in American political history. Various sources put UWSA membership somewhere between two and three million as of the end of May 1993, and more than five million by early November 1993. The active membership list of UWSA is an undeniably powerful potential force. These are people who have put money on the line to support what Perot is trying to accomplish. They are people to whom he can probably return later for more money and for actions aimed at influencing state legislatures or Congress. In the Texas special election to fill the seat held by Lloyd Bentsen (D), the UWSA state leaders sent a postcard to every UWSA voter in the state and allowed them to express their preference. More than 85 percent preferred Kay Hutchinson, the state's Republican treasurer, which was announced with great fanfare. This process allowed UWSA members to endorse Hutchinson prior to the election, while UWSA stayed neutral as is required by its tax status. The important point, however, is that these are the very same Americans who could easily take a short walk across the intellectual corridor that separates a citizen's lobby from a political party.

The voters in the three polls were asked whether Ross Perot should convert UWSA into a political party. As shown in Table 6, overall, among all voters, the percentage saying "yes" rose from 43 percent in February 1993 to 49 percent in April 1993. Nearly half of all American adults wish Perot would convert UWSA into a political party, running candidates for office. Among those who plan to join UWSA (clearly the most relevant group), the percentages are even more impressive, ranging between 60

Table 6   **United We Stand, America as a Political Party (Spring 1993)**

	Percent Responding "Yes"		
Responses	February	March	April
Yes, I plan to join United We Stand, America.	13	20	24
Yes, Perot should convert UWSA to a political party.	43	48	49
Yes, Perot should convert UWSA to a political party (UWSA joiners only).	60	65	63
Would UWSA be more effective:			
a. As a citizen's lobby?	—	46	48
b. As a political party?	—	32	31
c. Neither of the above	—	3	2
d. Both of the above	—	4	5
e. Not sure	—	15	14

Adapted from data collected in a Gordon Black Poll for Ross Perot.

percent and 65 percent saying they would have Perot make the conversion of UWSA to a political party. On the other hand, these same people think that UWSA would be more effective as a citizen's lobby than as a political party by a margin of 48 percent to 31 percent, according to the last poll we conducted for Perot in April 1993.

The level of approval for a political party among UWSA supporters rose in the April survey, when respondents were asked to approve or disapprove of a variety of things UWSA might do, as shown in Table 7. The approval for running candidates for Congress and governor was exceptionally high—over 90 percent. Of those who would join UWSA, 60 percent strongly support running candidates for governor, and 58 percent strongly support running candidates for Congress. Even among the full population, the voters would like to see UWSA run candidates with approval that exceeds 80 percent. Conversely, the weakest support is for endorsing candidates, as opposed to running them.

In a final show of support, the respondents overwhelmingly endorse the idea of voting for reform candidates under the UWSA banner. Faced with a UWSA candidate running against their Democratic or Republican incumbent, with both candidates equal in qualifications, they would vote for the UWSA candidates by a margin of 66 percent to 13 percent, with 21 percent undecided. Moreover, 75 percent of those who would join UWSA indicate that they are "very willing" to contribute financially to a UWSA candidate. Assuming again that this

Table 7   **Approval of Possible Activities of UWSA (April 1993)**

Question: Do you approve of the following possible activities of UWSA?	Percent of All Respondents		Percent of Potential UWSA Members	
	Approve[1]	Strongly Approve[2]	Approve	Strongly Approve
Promote write-in campaigns	90	59	94	70
Circulate petitions	83	41	95	67
Run candidates for state governor	81	39	90	60
Run candidates for Congress	83	39	93	58
Half-hour show, every 2–3 weeks	69	29	93	58
Elect local leadership	73	29	88	51
Promote members through commercials	75	26	87	46
Full page ads to promote membership	75	24	92	44
Endorse Democratic and Republican candidates	76	34	82	40

[1]Includes strong and moderate approval.
[2]Only strong approval.
Adapted from data collected in a Gordon Black Poll for Ross Perot.

overstates a willingness to contribute to campaigns, the conclusion is still remarkable. UWSA candidates could likely be financed entirely out of small contributions generated within their own congressional districts.

These findings should create a chill in the hearts of career members of Congress and the Senate. Imagine a contest between an incumbent whose campaigns have been financed for years by PAC money from outside the district, facing a challenger financed entirely with small contributions from within the district. Given the deep and intense dislike of PAC funding, the incumbent would have to bear the burden of explaining to voters how these PAC contributions really didn't influence his or her votes. It would be very difficult for most heavily PAC-financed incumbents to successfully stand against a well-funded reformer running with money raised entirely from within the district in small contributions.

We have shown that Ross Perot has already largely solved the organizational problem of recruiting members to his political effort. He is in the process of developing local leadership around the United States, and that local leadership is developing and gaining experience. Perot's effort could easily be converted into a political party simply by creating an organization parallel to UWSA, which would operate in the arena of selecting and running candidates. He is appealing to the same centrist voters who are the basis for a new political party of the center, and he has far greater access to those voters through his organizational efforts.

However, Ross Perot also has the potential to ruin the movement toward a third party if he does not make UWSA a democratic institution but uses the organization solely as a personal platform from which to propagate his personal views. If Ross Perot does not live up to his own expressed ideals, not only will he fail to have an impact, but he will increase people's disillusionment and their sense that they cannot change the country for the better. With the public burned again, the present officeholders would become more powerful than ever against the forces of reform. However, the evidence is that UWSA is systematically holding organizational elections in congressional districts and states across the country, and that internal democracy and intra-organizational accountability are characteristics that are emerging within UWSA.

The Issue of Leadership

A political party is composed of leaders, followers, and voters. We have documented repeatedly, and we hope persuasively, that there are enough followers and voters to sweep aside the control over American politics by the Republicans and the Democrats. What has been lacking are leaders, particularly the kind of leaders who will step forward and assume the responsibility for running and holding office. The two major parties have dried up their supply of followers and voters, but they have retained a cadre of people who want to run for and hold office. They have people who want to govern. We may not like those people very much, and we may hate the system that elects them so easily each year, but the Democrats and the Republicans can produce candidates.

The anger of the voters can't be depended upon to automatically produce a supply of candidates. Moreover, candidates who lack money actually serve to reinforce the dominance of the two major parties by convincing the would-be future challengers that such behavior is hopeless. A contested congressional race requires, at a minimum, $300,000 to $800,000 on the part of a challenger to make the race feasible. The average person cannot hope to raise this much money on his or her own from within a district without substantial organizational help.

In the past, many candidates in seemingly hopeless situations came from the ranks of people whose ideological zeal propelled their candidacy despite the odds. Those types of candidates are more common on the extreme left or right of American politics, however, and would not be attracted to a party of the center. The leadership of the Republican Party, for example, benefited enormously from the Abolitionist movement, the Free Soil Party, and disaffected candidates and officeholders from both the Whig and Democratic parties.

Ross Perot, of course, could provide some of the leadership. Like him or not, he has put his views on the line and has put his energy to the task. At the same time, why is Ross Perot so seemingly alone in his task? Nothing is stopping others from taking up his challenge. He is not telling other would-be leaders to stay away. On the contrary, he is inviting everyone to get involved, although some remain skeptical that he means it. There are even more Americans who could become involved in the same way in their state and local governments. Without leadership in addition to Ross Perot, the potential that now exists for reform and a centrist third party will remain unrealized. If the story about discontent in America remains focused solely on Ross Perot, with an absence of other prominent leaders, it will fail.

So we come to a key piece of the puzzle that makes creating a political party so difficult. A political party requires people who are willing to pay a large or disproportionate share of the organizational costs themselves, which considerably restricts the number who might be available. Most occupations make full-time political participation impossible. Thirty years ago, most state and local political positions were part-time positions that most citizens could easily hold. However, two trends have converted most offices into full-time positions. First, as government grew, the process of arriving at decisions became increasingly complex, creating pressure to increase the time spent in the legislature. Second, the politicians themselves have sought to further this process precisely because it justifies the comfortable salaries and retirement programs they have allocated for themselves. The more politicians try to make politics a full-time career, the fewer people can afford the risk of running for these offices. The intentional *professionalization of politics* is one of the ways incumbents have created a barrier for others who might challenge them. Finding candidates is the single hardest task of all political parties, but a new party will find it especially difficult.

Ross Perot could resolve this leadership problem more easily than most of the other existing party efforts. With his mailing list, he could probably raise much of the cash required to run full-scale candidacies by direct mail solicitation. If candidates did not have to raise hopelessly large amounts of money purely on their own, a great many more people would probably step forward to seek office. In most congressional districts, a mailing list of 15,000 people who are committed to a commonly held set of views and direction would be a veritable army.

Other third-party efforts, by contrast, have yet to prove that they can generate leaders—both for party tasks and to run for office. Without leadership in the opposition, and that means many more people than Ross Perot, the Democrats and Republicans have little to fear, despite the alienation of so many Americans.

While the barriers to creating a successful new party are formidable, they are not insurmountable. It is clear that a large portion of the electorate is ready to embrace new leadership. The question that remains is whether that leadership exists outside the efforts of Ross Perot. Perhaps what has been missing from the centrist movement is a clear sense of mission for the discontented. Anyone can talk of reform in the abstract, but no one has yet defined the issues around which a nationwide movement will form. We have established who a new party appeals to and why. The final question, therefore, is what should a new party do? That is this subject of the next chapter.

≈ 7 ≈

The Agenda for Reform

What is wrong with Washington, then, is what is wrong with the rest of us. It won't be cured until we have a rebirth of patriotism— or if the word embarrasses you, a willingness to put the welfare of the national community above our own.[1]

—Charles Peters

Reform as a Party-Building Strategy

There is an old Taoist proverb that states "the longest journey starts with just one step."[2] At this point in the book, we take a specific look at the issues a new party would most likely and most effectively form around. None of our problems can be dealt with merely by creating a new party to repeat the follies of its predecessors, and the mere creation of a new political force will not succeed without a strategic plan to guide it.

Throughout our analysis, we have established that there exists an unorganized mass of voters whose alienation and discontent has created a considerable opportunity to reform American politics. What is missing is a direction and politically viable focus for this displaced and underutilized frustration. For a new party to have a fighting chance in the electoral process, it would need to present a programmatic platform of reform that would be both credible and different from those of either of the two existing parties. It could then turn a chance into a substantial advantage. The third party would, at the very least, have the undeniable advantage of starting with a clean slate.

If the Perot candidacy proved anything, it was that many voters approach third-party candidacies with open minds. In most cases, independent candidates are innocent until proven guilty. Therefore, a new party that won elections based solely on the promise of reform would have an enormously powerful mandate to institute those reforms. Given this opportunity, a third party needs a plan—both as a strategic vehicle to attract supporters and as a program to enact once the voters respond positively. What's left is the task of trying to identify the building blocks of a third party.

The fundamental goal of a third party should be to pursue reforms that, for whatever reason, have not and will not be addressed in a political system dominated by the current two parties. Any platform should have two separate thrusts. First, there must be a series of reforms aimed at reducing incumbents' ability to hold office indefinitely. These reforms are basically process reforms, the goal being to reestablish the connection between the governed and the government, which has been seriously undermined with the dissolution of the local political parties and a truly competitive two-party system. There can be no greater contribution for a new party to make than to challenge the methods of modern politics.

On the other hand, there must be more to a third party than simply changing the rules of the political game. The second thrust should be aimed at entire policy arenas that have been ignored for the last three decades by the two major parties. Public opinion research indicates that wide support exists for many policy reforms that have not been pursued. In addition, a third party has the advantage of being able to advocate reform in some of these major policy areas, which would sound completely disingenuous coming from the major parties. These reforms are the untapped "motherlode" of electoral politics. A third party could make itself rich with votes pursuing these reforms, which we will discuss in the remainder of the chapter.

We are going to avoid discussing the policy implications of every reform we cover. Other people have already argued about these reforms extensively in much of the literature we refer to. We approach the issue from a different viewpoint. We will argue that at this time these reforms are logical for a third party to pursue in a strategic sense. We are interested in what voters want, whether our own individual opinions agree or not. For example, we know from our polling data that people want to be involved in their governance and have control over their legislators. As a result, voters respond positively to the initiative and recall, and they will overwhelmingly respond to a party that offers them as a part of a platform. We are not going to argue whether or not the initiative and recall are, in and of themselves, a good or a bad thing. That argument should take place within the structure of party debate.

With this in mind, what changes do large portions of Americans want, but stand little chance of ever having seriously addressed in the current two-party system? And, of equal importance, what issues will give a third party a competitive advantage in the political marketplace?

We will identify the appropriate reforms by showing their degree of support in the key parts of the electorate most likely to form the basis for a new party. Much of the data for the following section is taken from three different polls conducted at the following times: May 1992, March 1993, and April 1993. When it is possible, however, we use polling results from other organizations to expand on our data.

The items and purposes of the three polls varied a great deal, and we have extracted pertinent sections for our purposes here. The first poll was conducted as a marketing study to investigate the feasibility of a third party. One major purpose of that study was to identify the proportion of respondents in the analysis who would be likely to support the efforts of a third party. The second and third polls were both conducted for Ross Perot and United We Stand, America. These studies were designed to investigate the issues they found relevant, not our own issues. As a result, the measures we use to identify the third-party constituency vary, depending on which study we are referring to. The following groups are most likely to comprise the constituency of a third party.

- Core Loyalists: We identified these voters in May of 1992. In order to be considered a core loyalist, the respondent had to affirmatively answer four separate questions scattered throughout the poll indicating that they would support a third party given various assumptions. The respondents had to respond positively to all four questions. The questions themselves can be found in Chapter 6.[3]
- Have Joined or Will Join United We Stand, America: These voters were identified in the poll conducted in April of 1993. We asked voters whether or not they joined or planned to join UWSA. Their willingness to join indicated a cognitive predisposition to believe in the issues around which a third party would form, and they are much more likely to be angry and alienated from the current system. Of course, in this group there is probably a percentage of older voters who are tied to one of the major parties, but this should not affect the overall result too drastically.

By using these two groups to identify the appropriate issue basis of a third party, we get two slightly different but comparable looks at the constituency that will most likely form its basis. By isolating issues that appeal to the general public, and especially to third-party constituencies, a new party movement can put together a winning platform and have an agenda to enact if given the opportunity.

Process Reforms: The Initiative, Referendum, and Recall

As we illustrated in Chapter 3, for 30 years Americans have felt increasingly ignored by and alienated from the political process. Right or wrong, much of the polity feels powerless—voting doesn't matter, special interests run the show, and politicians lie and dissemble on a regular basis. The modern political parties basically substitute technology for voter involvement, so they are of little help in fostering the connection between the government and the governed. Not surprisingly, therefore, institutional reforms designed to increase the power of the voter receive overwhelming support in the populace.

The Washington establishment is fond of pointing out that the voter already has all the power he or she needs—the ballot. They would say that direct legislative involvement by the voters is both redundant and dangerous. To affect policy change, unhappy voters can simply vote for or against a legislator based on his policy positions. This argument is, of course, nonsense. As we have shown in Chapter 2, when there is no real choice in elections, there can be no expression of public sentiment on policy issues at all. Choice exists only at the presidential level and in some gubernatorial and contested Senate races. In House and state legislative races, the public has very little power to enact change because they have no choice. Therefore, any institutional reforms that provide voters with recourse *outside* of the direct election of officials will always be overwhelmingly approved by a frustrated populace. That is one reason why the support for term limits is so widespread.

The story is simple. The voters want the power to influence policy in the tradition of the Progressive reform movement earlier this century. Americans want to put the power in politics back in the hands of the populace, for better or for worse. They trust themselves far more than they trust the incumbents who control the system. Table 1 shows the results of a poll we conducted in May of 1992, which explored these issues as part of the poll described earlier on demand for a new party. The "core loyalists" in the table are those consistently in favor of a new party.

The responses to these queries, which find broad public support regardless of political affiliation, illustrate the lengths Americans are willing to go to reform their system. There is almost no meaningful variation in the amount of support for these reforms. Everyone wants them.

However, support for using the referendum as a tool of reform has not always been in the 90 percent range. In fact, the Gallup organiza-

Table 1   **Public Support for Increasing Voters' Direct Influence on Policy (May 1992)**

Question: The right of citizens to sign a petition to have a law placed on the ballot for a vote by everyone is called the initiative. In general, do you favor or oppose giving citizens the initiative in your state?

Response	% Republican	% Democrat	% Core Loyalist
Favor	91	90	96
Oppose	7	9	3
Not sure	2	2	1

Question: Would you favor or oppose giving citizens the right to petition the federal government to have a law placed on the ballot for national elections?

Response	% Republican	% Democrat	% Core Loyalist
Favor	84	84	90
Oppose	11	11	6
Not sure	5	4	4

Question: Some states permit citizens to sign petitions asking for a recall election for an elected public official. When enough signatures are obtained, a special election is held where the voters can vote a public official out of office. Would you favor or oppose giving citizens the right to have a recall election where they can vote an elected state or local official out of office?

Response	% Republican	% Democrat	% Core Loyalist
Favor	80	85	91
Oppose	19	14	8
Not sure	1	1	1

Adapted from data collected by a Gordon Black Poll.

tion asked two questions measuring attitudes regarding a proposal to create a national referendum in 1978 and 1981. Unfortunately, the questions were worded significantly differently and used a different methodology (personal interviewing), which reduces their comparability with our poll. Although the methodological differences make our assessment cautionary, the magnitude of the difference, 30 to 40 percentage points, indicates that support for nationwide referendum has increased considerably since the late 1970s and early 1980s. The Gallup questions find just over 50 percent in favor of a national referendum in 1978 and 1981 (see Table 2).

Imagine for a moment that there is an election in which one political party is running on a platform of fundamental reform through voter empowerment. It is organizing rallies and running television advertisements promising to put the voters back in politics by giving them the power of direct democracy. How could the establishment respond to such a strategy? It would be difficult for the existing political parties to persuade the public that suddenly they are "reformists" who want to increase the political power of the electorate. Never before in modern politics has there been a well-funded national effort to institute, at the national level, the direct democratic practices that already exist in many of the states. The data show that advocating these issues has no downside.

It is not difficult to predict how a campaign to increase voter empowerment through direct democracy would play out in the medium of television. Consider this hypothetical copy for a radio or television advertisement:

> We at the——Party, think the American people have the right to affect the major decisions that will guide America's destiny. The people of this country should rule, not the politicians in Washington. Our candidates pledge to support legislation that will give voters the opportunity to place major issues on the ballot nationally so that we all can decide what is best. Our future is too important to be left to the politicians.

Table 2 **Public Support for a National Referendum (1978 and 1981)**

Question: The U.S. Senate will consider a proposal that would require a national vote, that is, a referendum, on an issue when three percent of all voters who voted in the most recent presidential election sign petitions asking for such a nationwide vote. How do you feel about this plan—do you favor or oppose such a plan?

Response	1978	1981
Favor	57	52
Oppose	21	23
Not sure	22	25

Adapted from data collected by Gallup, January 9, 1978 and April 13, 1981.

A true national campaign, by a well-funded third party, could take the "anti-Washington" rhetoric that has put three of our last four presidents into office to heights never before imagined. If Bill Clinton, Ronald Reagan, and Jimmy Carter could all be elected running as outsiders, imagine the appeal of a true outside party running a bevy of outside candidates who want to increase the power of the voter. Even if the major parties tried to adopt direct democracy reforms, the third party would still be able to take credit for forcing them to do so.

Campaign Finance and Competition

In general, despite what politicians and pundits usually say, voters are not stupid or blind to what is happening around them. When voters see a rat, they know it's a rat and not a whale. And they know our campaign finance laws are rats and the product of rats. Voters know that a system of campaign financing that relies on PACs and special-interest groups will not be a fair or responsive one. Remember that in 1992, PAC money accounted for 42 percent of all the money raised by winning candidates in congressional elections, making it by far the largest source of funds for political campaigns.[4] The public anger at PACs and the influence of money in general is not new to American politics. For this generation, Watergate remains the ultimate example of all that is wrong with American politics. Watergate unraveled as Woodward and Bernstein followed the money, the huge sums of legal and illegal contributions. Of course, then the problem was "fat cat" contributors from large corporations or foreign governments. Unfortunately, the reforms that resulted from the anger over the corruption in the Nixon years have proved to be long on strong-sounding rules and regulations but short on results. Does knowing where the money comes from lessen the importance of that money? It should be no surprise that more and more often we are seeing challengers make a campaign issue out of PAC money, and with considerable success. The public hates the influence of PAC money, and very likely, these anti-interest-group campaigns will surely become more popular in the future.

As a result, the big money dominating American politics leaves voters frustrated, angry, and ready to take steps that were distinctly unpopular in the not-too-distant past. As a policy issue, public financing of elections has never been well received in America. To many people, publicly funding elections sounds too much like using tax money to line the politician's pockets or to ensure their permanence in office.

In addition, the vast majority of voters simply do not understand the intricacies of campaign finance, and they miss the connection between public financing and improving the quality of our democracy.

Voters do, however, understand what special interests mean to the political process, and they do not like them. Public opinion data shows that a large majority of voters will support policies that seek to limit the influence of interests. If public financing is promoted as a vehicle to limit the power of interest groups, the public will support it. The voters know that a political system that relies on vast amounts of private, interest-driven money is a bad one. The underlying sentiment, from which the opinion on campaign financing flows, is a simple one: the voters believe in and strive for democracy. This may sound corny to the cynics, but the voters want a system that is profoundly democratic.

A study conducted in December 1992 and sponsored by the Center for a New Democracy investigated numerous rationales for campaign financing. This survey, which covered the issue of public financing in detail, found that the most powerful argument in favor of public financing was that it would give challengers a chance in elections against entrenched incumbents. Americans believe in fairness, and they will react positively to solutions that promise fairness. Among other highlights, the study found that

- 72 percent of the voters support extending presidential campaign finance to Congress and the Senate if the proposed reform includes limiting campaign spending and reducing individual and PAC contributions and if the reforms would be funded with an increase in the voluntary checkoff and a new tax on lobbyists.
- 86 percent of the voters want to limit campaign spending, in general.
- 75 percent of voters want to lower the amount of money that PACs are allowed to contribute to $1,000 from the current limit of $5,000.
- 68 percent of voters support an increase to $5 in the voluntary checkoff on tax forms used to fund elections.
- 65 percent want to limit congressional franking privileges and use the money that would be saved to publicly finance political campaigns.[5]

The level of frustration with the current PAC-money-dominated campaign system, indicated by the numbers cited in the previous list, create a unique opportunity for a third party. A third party can, from the outset, make party endorsement dependent on a candidate's promise not to accept one cent of PAC contributions. If it did so, the third party would create enormous political pressure for other candidates to steer clear of PAC money just by its presence in the election. In addition, when the opposing candidates did accept PAC money, the third party candidate would have a natural competitive advantage that has proven to be a powerful motivator in campaigns. The question in Table 3, although a bit long-winded, presents a hypothetical race in which PAC money is the differentiating factor.

Funding from PACs rose 52 percent in the 1992 election cycle.[6] There is little doubt that PAC money will remain an issue in the future. It is entirely possible that an effective third party running viable candidates could create such a stigma regarding PAC funding that it would be difficult for PACs to give money away. This scenario is probably a bit too hopeful, however, because there is another side to this coin. A third

Table 3   **Hypothetical Election Focusing on the Use of PAC Money (April 1992)**

Question: I would like to tell you about two candidates running for Congress and have you tell me which candidate you would be more likely to vote for. . . . Congressman Smith receives almost half of his campaign contributions from political action committees. He argues that running for Congress is very expensive, and besides, these political action committees represent groups that he supports such as business, labor, environmental groups, and teachers' associations. . . . Mr. Jones feels that political action committees have far too much influence on Congress. He feels that you can't take money from political action committees and truly represent the people. For that reason he refuses to accept any contributions from these PACs.

Response	Percent
Much more likely to vote for Smith	6
A little more likely to vote for Smith	11
A little more likely to vote for Jones	24
Much more likely to vote for Jones	47
No difference	4
Don't know/Refused	8

Adapted from data collected by American Viewpoint, April 1, 1992.

party would increase the competitiveness of elections all across the country, which would enhance the need for funding in a larger portion of elections. Hundreds of potentially threatened incumbent legislators need considerably more money than the current 25 threatened legislators. If this is the case, then public financing of the campaign could be put forth as a guarantee of competitiveness in elections. The cost would be large, but restoring choice in elections is well worth it.

This is an issue that the Congress will try to address in some symbolic way before the next election. However, it is unlikely that any reform proposals will actually increase the ability of challengers to displace incumbents. Reforms by incumbents are usually to the advantage of the incumbents, although this may not always appear to be so. In campaign finance, more than in any other area of policy, the so-called reformers in Congress often have a deep and abiding interest in helping themselves.

Aside from an all-out blitz to fully finance congressional campaigns, there are more moderate reforms that could be pursued with relatively little trouble or risk. Table 4 illustrates the public's reaction to various reform proposals.

Table 4   **Public Support for Election Reforms (1990–1993)**

Proposed Reform	% Who Favor	Organization	Date
A ceiling cap on all political action committee contributions a candidate can accept.	82	Harris	May 1, 1990
Encouraging small contributors by reducing the taxes of small givers, dollar for dollar, for their contributions up to $100.	72	Analysis Group	Feb 15, 1990
Instead of giving campaigns money, provide them with a fixed amount of free T.V. time and reduced mailing rates to cut the cost of campaigns.	69	Analysis Group	Feb 15, 1990
Laws that would eliminate political action committees and their financial contributions to political campaigns.	69	Gordon Black	March 23, 1993
Prohibit campaign contributions from foreign governments, corporations, or individuals.	78	Gordon Black	May 21, 1992

Adapted from The Roper Center Poll Database.

There is a cautionary recommendation with regard to advocating public financing of campaigns. Public opinion regarding public financing, like many topics that are poorly understood, has not yet fully crystallized. As a result, measurement of public attitudes is highly dependent on the rationale provided for the public financing. If no rationale is given, public support is somewhat weak. In addition, the core loyalists of a third party, identified earlier in this chapter, are *not* much more likely to support public financing than other voters. Part of this trend is probably due to the extreme distrust third-party voters have of political candidates. Any proposal that might sound like it would assist politicians is bound to be viewed with suspicion. However, in addition to asking a neutral question about public financing, we also asked those respondents who initially didn't support public financing if they would support it if it encouraged quality candidates. With this rationale, support increases dramatically, from 49 percent to 84 percent among the core loyalists. Table 5 documents these responses.

Outright public financing, although it seems an obvious solution to many of the electoral problems elucidated in this book, has not yet been completely accepted by the public. Many voters are uncomfortable with the idea of using federal tax money to finance candidates. As an issue, public financing needs to be tied to a direct goal, like improving the quality of candidates or reducing the influence of special interests. However, public financing should not be the centerpiece of a new-party campaign. The rationale for public financing needs to be more widely understood before a third party uses it as a campaign issue.

Table 5   **Support for Public Financing of Campaigns (May 1992)**

Question	Percent Who Favor		
	Democrats	Republicans	Core Loyalists
Currently, the public pays the cost of the presidential campaigns of both major parties. The presidential candidates accept limits on spending in order to get the public funds. Would you favor or oppose a similar system of public funding for House and Senate candidates?	50	50	49
If public financing of campaigns would encourage more good people to run against incumbents, would you favor or oppose public funding of campaigns?	81	76	84

Adapted from data collected by a Gordon Black Poll.

Term Limits

There are few political issues as widely popular as term limits. The success of the 14 term-limit movements in 1992 illustrated that the only people who don't like term limits are politicians. The idea that individual politicians should not be allowed to dominate the political process is at the very core of Americans' political beliefs. Yet the public never had any real or effective avenue to express its distrust of accumulated power. In an absolute sense, it is true that the electorate can always vote their member of Congress out. But, as we have discussed earlier, with the electoral cards *always* dealt overwhelmingly in favor of the incumbent, the public is never systematically provided with adequate choices or information on which to base its decisions. As the cliché goes, "The devil we know is probably better than the devil we don't." Predictably, the elected officials are never going to enact limits themselves.

The tremendous success of the states' term-limits measures illustrates that voters will react positively to *institutional* guarantees of electoral choice and *institutional* roadblocks against accumulated power. By choosing to limit terms, the voters were allowed to satisfy two electoral "needs" simultaneously. First, they were not forced to vote against their incumbent, of whom they generally held a favorable opinion as a result of the various incumbency advantages discussed earlier. At the same time, they were able to vent their frustration with the institution as a whole.

A majority of voters in this country has supported term limits since at least the late 1960s. The individual movements to enact term limits formed with relative ease, and succeeded no matter what the state or region of the country. The national organizing force coordinating the movement was U.S. Term Limits, a group based in Washington, D.C., that served as the national coordinator and provided over $1 million to the state campaigns. However, the movement was not centered in Washington, D.C. For example, a grassroots organization in Washington State called LIMIT raised $385,000 for its campaign, which is more than most congressional challengers are able to raise to campaign against incumbents.[7]

In contrast, the movement to maintain the status quo and to protect the ability of incumbents to stay in office was mainly financed by corporations that depend on their access to legislators to gain special privileges. For example, in Michigan, the main group opposing term limits was called Citizens Against Term Limitations. Using the word citizens in the title, however, was a truly cynical campaign ploy. The bulk of the money was provided by General Motors and other Michigan Corporations.[8] These corporations reacted logically and strategically to what they accurately perceived as a threat to their institutionalized access and control of their federal legislators. In California, according to a report issued by the secretary of state, the campaign against term limits was funded by such corporate interests as the Chevron Corporation, Pacific Gas and Electric, Lockheed, Rockwell International, and by such political committees as the Congressman Waxman Campaign Committee, Berman for Congress Committee, and the Democratic State Central Committee. In fairness, the California campaign for term limits was financed mostly by U.S. Term Limits and by the Republican Party.[9] Yet there certainly is a disturbing amount of corporate involvement in the effort to protect the legislators.

Despite the overwhelming support term limits received, there are still serious questions about their constitutionality. If they are ruled unconstitutional, then the only way to institute them will be via a constitutional amendment. The only way a constitutional amendment could ever get passed would be through the election of third-party candidates dedicated to its passage.

The future of term limits now rests with the federal courts. Within hours after 77 percent of Florida voters voted for term limits in an electoral landslide, a legal suit was filed seeking to invalidate the expressed will of the citizens of that state. Eventually, all 14 states will have to fight the battle in courts before term limits are instituted. According to some experts, the issue will not work its way up to the Supreme Court before 1995, further delaying the actual implementation of the limits.[10] At the same time, the members of Congress and their allies in the state legislatures have placed themselves squarely in opposition to 21 million Americans who voted for limits.

The Demographic Stability of Term Limits

The most striking aspect of the entire term limits movement is the demographic breadth that characterizes term-limit voting. This is another issue that has no downside. There are few issues that engender such wide support from such a wide number of people. The support for limits is strikingly consistent across any number of demographic items—education, sex, income, age, and others. The cleavages in the voting patterns only show up slightly when looking directly at party affiliation and political ideology. In most cases, conservatives, Republicans, and Independents show slightly higher levels of support. Even a majority of liberals and Democrats voted for term limits. The tendency can be explained simply by realizing that the Democrats have the most to lose if term limits are passed. After all, they hold a majority of seats that they will be forced to open up to competition. From a position of rational voters pursuing their self-interest through the political system, the support for limits among Democratic partisans is all the more interesting because it is directly against their interest in maintaining their lock on the House of Representatives.

The term-limit movement has provided the first chance for the public to pass judgment on the institution of Congress as a whole. In a way, one could look at the results as more evidence of the lack of democratic choice in House elections. Many voters undoubtedly voted to re-elect their congressman *and* to limit his term, and this is perfectly understandable. The former is a vote for the nice guy who sends you lots of mail and, as far as you know, spends his long, hard days fighting all those "other" terrible politicians who were elected by all those "other" people. A vote for term limits is a vote against all those "other" people.

As the data presented in Table 6 on term-limit voting illustrates, voters' feelings run deep and are very consistent. The table illustrates the stability of term limit support among various demographic groups in 5 of the 14 states that voted for term limits in 1992. The data are from exit polls administered as voters were leaving the polling place on election day, conducted by Voter Research and Surveys, the research consortium of the four major news organizations. The main measure to note is the difference between the vote for term limits overall and the vote for term limits by the specified subgroup. In the last column (actual vote–subgroup vote), a positive number means that that group supported term limits at a higher rate than the general population.

The deviation in support of term limits among these demographic groups is quite small, as one can see by analyzing the far right column. This issue is not a class issue or a generational issue. *A majority of every demographic segment in each of these states wants term limits.* Most political issues are characterized by clear demographic cleavages among the population. Term limits, however, seem to appeal to everyone—young and old, male and female, rich and poor.

A new party should champion term limits. It is obviously an issue that is popular among its partisans. One ironic point is that the creation of a centrist new party would greatly increase electoral competition, decreasing the need for a legislative solution to rid the system of entrenched incumbents. Short of term limits, a centrist party is probably the best solution to the problem of lifetime legislators and could differentiate itself in a highly positive way by asking all its candidates to take a public pledge not to serve more than 12 years in any one office. Not only would this pledge help the individual candidates, but it would also illuminate a stark contrast between the new party and the Democrats and Republicans.

Table 6 **Demographic Patterns in Term-Limit Voting (1992)**

Demographic Group	State	% Overall Actual Vote	% Subgroup Vote	Actual Vote– Subgroup Vote
Ages: 18–29	MI	59	66	2
	OH	66	64	2
	CA	63	66	3
	AZ	74	76	2
Ages: 30–34	MI	59	59	0
	OH	66	66	0
	CA	63	64	1
	AZ	74	77	3
Ages: 44–59	MI	59	51	−8
	OH	66	63	−3
	CA	63	64	1
	AZ	74	76	2
Ages: 60+	MI	59	56	−3
	OH	66	69	3
	CA	63	64	1
	AZ	74	70	−4
Sex: Male	MI	59	57	−2
	OH	66	68	2
	CA	63	64	1
	AZ	74	74	0
Sex: Female	MI	59	60	1
	OH	66	64	−2
	CA	63	65	2
	AZ	74	76	2
Income: Less than $15,000	MI	59	56	−3
	OH	66	63	−3
	CA	63	66	3
	AZ	74	75	1

(continued)

Table 6   *Continued*

Demographic Group	State	% Overall Actual Vote	% Subgroup Vote	Actual Vote–Subgroup Vote
Income: $15,000–$30,000	MI	59	61	2
	OH	66	69	3
	CA	63	67	4
	AZ	74	78	4
Income: $30,000–$50,000	MI	59	59	0
	OH	66	64	−2
	CA	63	65	2
	AZ	74	75	1
Income: $50,000–$75,000	MI	59	56	−3
	OH	66	66	0
	CA	63	67	4
	AZ	74	71	−3
Income: Over $75,000	MI	59	59	0
	OH	66	65	−1
	CA	63	57	−6
	AZ	74	N/A	N/A

Adapted by data collected by VRS 1992 State Exit Polls.

Real Fiscal Responsibility

The vast majority of economists feel that continuing and chronic deficits will undermine our fiscal solvency. In Chapter 3, we discussed the necessity of restoring the moral imperative for our legislators to produce balanced budgets. Before the explosion of spending that occurred in the late 1960s, our legislators understood that one of their primary duties was to ensure the proper expenditures of public money. In contrast, the present Congress views deficit spending as standard operating procedure. Our deficit is structural and it will not be resolved without electing people who are determined to do so.

There are two approaches to solving Washington's spending hemorrhage—elect people to Congress who are committed to balancing the budget, or institute procedural reforms that make it more politically difficult for Congress to spend irresponsibly. The goal of a new party should be to do both.

There is a common misperception that the public is unwilling to take the harsh medicine that is needed to cure our spending problems. The pundits say that people want all the services that government provides, but they are unwilling to pay for them. This may or may not be true, but research shows that if people are given leadership on this issue, they are willing to take on both the tax increases and spending reductions necessary to balance the budget.

The public's desire to control spending has been growing as awareness of the dangers of the deficit has increased. In the past, the complexities of the budget process were too abstract to crystallize into politically actionable attitudes in the populace. Once the red ink started to flow in such quantities that even the core New Deal Democrats started to take notice, the dangers of this relatively abstract issue started to become apparent to large portions of the public. The relative importance of the deficit among Perot voters and, to some extent, traditional Republican presidential voters, is evidence that fear of the deficit is now a defining issue in American politics. When we say a defining issue, we mean that identifiable cleavages among voters' opinions on this issue can translate into electoral success. Large portions of the public are willing to inflict real political pain on their representatives, even in a system designed to protect the legislators.

Despite the emergence of the deficit as an issue, it is nonetheless discouraging that large portions of the public still do not understand the long-term economic danger of chronic overspending. The truth is that the budget deficit is still relatively young as an issue. When in 1990 the Gallup Organization asked the open-ended question, "Why do you feel it is important to reduce the federal budget deficit?" 67 percent of the people they asked did not even attempt to respond.[11] Although the percentage might be a bit more today, there still exists a serious knowledge gap on this issue. In contrast, people know that government programs for the needy and Medicare are good things, but they don't necessarily know that massive overspending is a very bad thing. Therefore, without a concrete sense of the danger of the deficit, many people choose continued spending on government programs rather than reducing the deficit. However, this dynamic is starting to change as education on the deficit increases. As a result, one key to successfully controlling governmental expenditures, while retaining the support of the populace, is to have effective leadership on the issue. A leader must be half-salesman and half-educator to increase awareness of the problem and the seriousness of the situation. The next question, of course, is who can lead?

Without effective, careful, and very determined leadership, the over-spending will never stop.

It is not unfair, or somehow psychotically partisan, to say that the Democratic Party has serious structural impediments that render it unable to reduce or, arguably, even control governmental expenditures. There are simply too many networks, both through established inter-est-group structures and voting blocs within the Democratic consti-tuency, which depend on federal funds for sustenance. The core of the Democratic Party will resist spending reductions and always fully sup-port tax increases, because many of their clients benefit from the resulting redistribution of wealth which occurs under the current fiscal policies. To expect most Democrats, whose main goal is reelection, to bite the hand that feeds them is highly unrealistic.

At the same time, although the Republicans are more fiscally con-servative, they are of little help. The tax and spend policies of Reagan and Bush failed miserably, and both proved ineffective at controlling congressional profligacy. Moreover, the Republicans have proven abso-lutely unable to translate their electoral success at the presidential level and their fund-raising success at the party level into electoral success at the congressional level, and they have not been able to win over the needed Democrats within Congress on spending cuts. In addition, the Republican idea that somehow the budget can be balanced in the short term without increasing governmental revenue is simply not viable. Balancing our budget will require a balanced approach.

The two major parties provide a series of false choices. We must choose between the Democratic plans—which eschew spending cuts and real entitlement program control for increased taxes and chronic underestimation of the cost of current programs, and the Republican plans—which use their antitax rhetoric to try to beat the Democrats into submission, but fail to offer the specific cuts that are needed.

As the current distribution of opinion exists, a third party dedi-cated to controlling expenditures will create considerable downward pressure against spending increases. The data on spending decreases is clear. We illustrated in Chapter 4 how important the issue of the deficit was with the Perot voters. This will be a primary concern for the new party as well. With expectations regarding spending policies clear, leg-islators elected under the banner of a new party would have little doubt about where their loyalties stand.

To motivate third-party voters, various institutional reforms need to be pursued. The only way to decrease spending and eventually balance the budget is to create a third faction within Congress that can vote with the Republicans on spending bills and with the Democrats on tax issues, thereby breaking the cycle of increasing taxation with no spending controls. However, there are certain institutional controls that will make it more difficult for our government to spend irresponsibly, and advocating these changes will be effective with voters inclined to vote for a third party. Table 7 illustrates how partisans and the most likely third-party voters react to using direct democracy and a constitutional amendment to control overspending and spiraling taxation. Predictably, the overall support for these ideas is very strong, and the support among "core loyalists" is higher than the major party partisans. This is no surprise.

One of the main goals of a third party should be to pass a balanced budget amendment. A strongly worded balanced budget amendment, which would allow for deficit spending only in time of war or economic depression, would greatly increase the ability of fiscally conservative legislators to control excess expenditures. At the very least, an amendment would increase the moral imperative to control spending that disappeared before the 1940s. Right now, the system rewards legislators who defer payments rather than forcing choices between cutting expenditures and raising taxes. A budget amendment would, at the very least, increase the downward pressure on spending.

We are not saying, given the present dynamic of the Congress, that a budget amendment is the answer to our problems. If we simply pass a budget amendment but do not change the composition of the House, the current legislators will simply find ways to get around the amendment. (After all, we have elected a bunch of lawyers to Congress. *Lawyers are trained to get around laws, not to abide by them!* What we need are accountants.)

A third party, in concert with the Republicans, should pursue a balanced budget amendment. Right now, 41 states require a balanced

Table 7   **Support for Greater Voter Control over Spending and Taxation (May 1992)**

Question	% Democrats	% Republicans	% Core Loyalists
In general, do you favor or oppose requiring a referendum on the annual budget deficit in your state?	80	78	85
Would you favor or oppose a constitutional amendment to require that any federal tax increase be voted on in a national referendum?	71	69	80
Would you favor or oppose a constitutional amendment that would require Congress and the president to provide a balanced budget each year?	81	85	91

Adapted from data collected by a Gordon Black Poll, May 21, 1992.

budget, and these states are generally functioning without major fiscal disasters. At the very worst, a balanced budget amendment would not cause an increase in spending, so it is certainly worth a try.

As a campaign issue, a balanced budget amendment will be very appealing to third-party voters and will also attract some partisan Republicans whose party has failed on this issue. The amendment is important not necessarily for what it will do, but for what it means. It equates the importance of a balanced budget with the freedom of speech and the separations of power. It makes controlling spending one of the pillars of government. This symbolic declaration of the importance of spending controls will force the issue to the forefront of American politics. With the issue at the center of debate, and a third party dedicated to controlling spending, we might then be able to make the tough choices that must be made.

Wasting Money

One of the major hurdles faced by both the major parties and any third party is the widespread distrust of governmental action. One of the ironies of public opinion polling is the responses to questions that ask whether or not the government "should do more" to address one social ill or another. A pollster will ask a question like, "Should the government do more to fix the problems in the inner cities?" Invariably, 60 to 70 percent of respondents will say "yes." The pollster's client will then take this earth-shattering data and immediately call for increased funding for a program such as HUD. Yet there is another dynamic of public opinion that is not addressed as often—the belief that government and governmental solutions are usually failures and are extremely inefficient. For example, in February 1993, the ABC News/*Washington Post* Poll asked, "Out of every dollar the federal government collects in taxes, how many cents do you think is wasted?" They found that, on average, the public thinks government wastes 46 cents of every dollar it receives.[12] Therefore, it is not difficult to understand why large segments of the public think that the government should do more to solve problems, but are highly resistant to paying for it. One reason people resist tax increases is because they think they won't do any good, and the actions of the last 12 years have only reinforced this. In general, people are willing to take the steps necessary to balance the budget, as long as those steps are fair and they stand a reasonable chance of success.

Spending Cuts and Tax Increases

There is no area where the potential of a three-party system can affect real positive change more than in the area of spending cuts. In the two-party system, both parties are held hostage by the need to carry 51 percent of the vote to get elected. Professor Theodore Lowi states the implications of this dynamic well:

> With three parties, only 35 percent of the vote would be needed to win, as opposed to 51 percent in a two-party system. When 51 percent is needed, a candidate or a party has to be all things to all people—going after 80 percent of the voters to get the required 51 percent.
>
> At the 35 percent level, however, all three parties would be able to take clear positions as parties without fear of being hurt or immobilized by wedge issues—issues that threaten to alienate a segment of voters no matter what position the candidate or party takes. Thus each party could be a genuine party.[13]

In the case of cutting governmental expenditures, the "51 percent problem" is most acute. One must be very careful about who is angered, and nothing angers specific groups more than cutting, reducing, or even talking about reducing direct government payments. No action will motivate groups to take direct political action against a public official faster than cutting their flow of money. Once governmental largess has been made available, it is extremely difficult to take it away. Remember, for example, what happened to Dan Rostenkowski (D-Ill.), the House Ways and Means Committee chairman, when the House passed the Medicare Catastrophic Coverage Act, which was to be paid for by middle- and high-income elderly beneficiaries:

> An elderly woman draped herself on the hood of Rostenkowski's car as he left a meeting with senior citizens. Dozens more seniors banged on the windows, beat his car with their protest placards, screamed "Liar!" "Impeach!" and "Recall!" at him and finally chased him out of the car. Rostenkowski sprinted down the street with the angry mob in pursuit and rendezvoused with his driver at a nearby gas station before speeding away.[14]

This example sheds light on the fundamental legislative catch-22 that dominates the politics of spending and budgeting. A legislator whose primary goal is reelection cannot be expected to enact spending cuts that will almost surely result in his defeat. Today, so many people have become the beneficiaries of government programs that the threat of reducing funding creates enormous incentives for direct political action to protect those benefits. At the same time, the costs of those benefits are dispersed throughout the population, minimizing the value of action to reduce the taxation. In a system where a legislator must get 50 percent of the vote, this dynamic can dominate the policy outcome. However, in a system where a legislator needs only 35 percent of the vote, the probability that he or she can cut spending to specific groups and still get reelected is dramatically increased. This enables the legislator to satisfy the goals of reelection and to enact prudent legislation.

Tax increases are always a sticky issue, and the same will be true for any third party that attempts to run candidates. Sad but true, the federal government has created a monster that spends money uncontrollably and without remorse. More taxation seems to encourage this. For 12 years, both parties have been telling people that they could have all the benefits of governmental action without paying for them. In general, however, third-party supporters are willing to raise taxes if there is a clear goal of reducing the federal deficit and a promise of spending controls. Table 8 breaks down the voters' willingness to accept increased taxes by party affiliation and willingness to join UWSA.

This table illustrates the new dynamic very clearly. It also shows how a new third force (assuming it would pay attention to its constituents), would align with the Democrats on taxes dedicated to reducing the budget deficit or the national debt, but would align with Republicans on legislation that would decrease government spending. Republicans are clearly more likely to be against tax increases regardless of the reason or goal. This is not the case with the voters who support UWSA. However, the data in the table show that UWSA supporters are far closer to Republicans on the issue of domestic spending. Here the differences between the Democrats and the other two parties are dramatic. There just doesn't seem to be any kind of spending that the Democrats don't like!

On the issue of the deficit itself, the supporters of UWSA rate it as more important than do either the Democrats or the Republicans. In fact, it may be considered one common thread that holds the diverse

Table 8   **Voters' Willingness to Accept Increased Taxation (April 1993)**

Question: For which of the following would you be willing to pay more taxes?	% Yes			
	All Voters	Democrats	Republicans	Have/Will Join UWSA
To reduce the annual budget deficit.	64	70	60	71
To reduce the accumulated national debt.	61	66	59	67
To increase spending on domestic programs.	46	65	30	38

Adapted from data collected by a Gordon Black Poll.

Table 9   **Voters' Estimation of the Importance of Reducing the Deficit (April 1993)**

	% Yes			
Question: How important to you is the issue of reducing the national debt?	All Voters	Democrats	Republicans	Have/Will join UWSA
Not important at all	2	2	1	2
Somewhat important	23	24	20	13
Very important	52	55	56	51
The most important issue of all	22	19	22	35

Adapted from data collected by a Gordon Black Poll.

set of interests and ideologies making up this centrist movement. Table 9 displays the self-ratings of the three groups on the issue of the deficit. Over a third of the respondents who planned to join UWSA felt that the federal budget deficit was their single most important issue.

What the data shows is that the tax issue can be handled in a straightforward way: If third-party supporters were confident that tax increases would not lead to increased spending, they would support the increases. Therefore, third-party candidates should concentrate on balancing federal expenditures by combining tax increases with substantial reductions in spending. To say that a balanced budget would result only from tax increases or only from spending reductions is simply a lie. We know that from experience. Still, Table 10 shows that given the choice between deficit reduction and preventing tax increases, people are beginning to make the responsible choice.

The bottom line is that three-party politics would enable public officials to tell the truth without fear that they will be automatically swept out of office. A third-party candidate can run successfully on a platform that includes tax increases if these increases are adequately coupled with spending control. Making that connection convincing to voters is the key. Furthermore, a third-party candidate can be strident about cutting spending without fear of alienating key voting blocs. Let those voters who rely on the largess of government go to the other parties; there will be plenty of taxpayers left behind.

Welfare Reform

Every four years the politicians expound on their hatred for the current welfare system and what grand plans they have to reform it. Yet year

Table 10   **Voters' Preferences Regarding Deficit Reduction and Prevention of Tax Increases (January 1992)**

Question: Which do you think is more important—reducing the budget deficit or making sure taxes aren't increased?

Response	Percent
Reducing deficit	58
Preventing tax increases	33
Both equal (v)	4
Not sure	5

Adapted from data collected by *Time*/CNN, January 14, 1992.

after year, these grand plans disappear until the next election. In fact, one would be hard-pressed to find any issue on which there has been less progress than welfare reform. The welfare issue, like many others, has become completely distorted by the Washington establishment. In the process, the views of an overwhelming majority of Americans have been dismissed and forgotten. The issue of welfare reform is symbolic of the failing of the two-party system—the legislators from both parties talk tough during campaigns, but the issue never comes to a vote.

On one side of the Washington debate are the liberal Democrats. For many of them, the current welfare system is a sacred cow. Often they see themselves as society's conscience and feel that welfare is owed to people who the government decides are poor. And the more poor people, the better. They largely equate the appropriation of tax revenue with solving the problem of poverty. They are often closely allied with the massive bureaucracy that is dependent on the flow of federal money for its existence. The importance of the millions employed by the welfare bureaucracy—and their unions—in the Democratic Party makes it very difficult to make fundamental changes without alienating key constituencies.

On the other side of the aisle are the conservative Republicans. They are equally out of touch with the will of the people because they are simply against welfare in general. For them, welfare is the policy devil, causing massive budget deficits while the recipients lounge around the pool and drink martinis. They want to cut the money spent on welfare and let the free market solve the problem of poor people. There are some exceptions, but the Republicans would rather use welfare to divide people and gain votes than work to solve the problems that the welfare system causes.

The Public Opinion on Welfare

Welfare is an issue on which an overwhelming majority of people are in agreement, and they are not inclined to get rid of welfare completely. On the one hand, the American people profoundly believe in giving outright financial assistance to people who, for whatever reason, cannot support themselves. In truth, people recognize that the capitalist system, which has created the wealth of self-made billionaires like Ross Perot or Bill Gates (founder of Microsoft), fails to provide for even the most basic needs of millions of Americans each day. Table 11 shows that only a very small percentage of people want to eliminate the federal safety net that provides people, mostly women and children, with some minimal level of support.

So it is agreed that Americans have no intention of throwing poor people out in the street. The question in Table 11 measured one aspect of the support for welfare—that there should at least be some governmental assistance programs. In Table 12, the issue is taken to another extreme. The question asked is whether or not the government should *be responsible for guaranteeing* a level of sustenance for its citizenry. This position takes welfare beyond mere goodwill, indicating the recognition of a moral imperative to welfare. A surprisingly large number of people hold this view. (It should be noted that there is probably a bias involved in this question's wording.[15])

While it is agreed that we need welfare, Tables 13 and 14 show that there is equally strong sentiment that the current system is not working and that, in fact, it encourages behavior antithetical to the goals of

Table 11   **Public Attitude Toward Eliminating All Welfare Programs (March 1992)**

Question: Here is a list of changes many people would like to make in the current welfare system. Please tell me whether you favor or oppose eliminating all welfare programs entirely.

Response	Percent
Favor	5
Oppose	94
Not sure	2

Adapted from data collected by *Time*/CNN, March 11, 1992.

Table 12   **Public Attitude Toward Guaranteed Food and Shelter (June 1992)**

Question: (Agree/Disagree) The government should guarantee every citizen enough to eat and a place to sleep.

Response	Percent
Completely agree	32
Mostly agree	33
Mostly disagree	22
Completely disagree	10

Adapted from data collected by Times Mirror, June 10, 1992.

the social welfare programs. This is the dynamic of the welfare issue that has been in need of attention for the past two decades.

What these marginals indicate is that there is wide support for radical changes in the way the system operates. The voters seem way out in front of the leaders on this issue. As demonstrated in Table 15, a large majority of the population doesn't simply want to change and modify welfare, they want to tear down the system and build it back up.

What underlies opinion on welfare is the fundamental desire for welfare to encourage behavior leading to productive lives. The work ethic in America still runs strong. Simply providing benefits at no cost to the recipients does little good, and since the current rules discourage independence, marriage, and the incentive to look for work, this generally leaves people wards of the state, hopelessly mired in poverty. Table 16 breaks down the relative levels of support for various reforms that have been proposed.

Table 13   **Public Belief That the Welfare System Encourages the Poor to Find Work (March 1992)**

Question: Do you think the current welfare system encourages poor people to find work or discourages them?

Response	Percent
Encourages	12
Discourages	77
Not sure	10

Adapted from data collected by *Time*/CNN, March 11, 1992.

Table 14   **Public Belief in the Overdependence of the Poor on Welfare (June 1992)**

Question: (Agree/Disagree) Poor people have become too dependent on government assistance programs.

Response	Percent
Completely agree	35
Mostly agree	44
Mostly disagree	14
Completely disagree	4

Adapted from data collected by Times Mirror, June 10, 1992.

Commonly, proponents of the current welfare system argue that changes in the welfare system that respond to public opinion would be Draconian, cruel, racist, or inhumane. Yet the public opinion data itself does not support this view. Table 17 lists some commonsense options that would be possible to implement. They are quite reasonable and receive wide support across the spectrum of voters. The Democrats would have us believe that somehow welfare reform is just another partisan issue. The fact is that if 80 percent of the population supports welfare reform, most Democrats must support it too. Welfare need not be a punishment, but it need not be a free ride either. As we noted earlier, no one wants simply to eliminate benefits to the poor, or even to decrease them very much.

As you can see, the more harsh, punitive approaches do not receive even a majority of support. Any third-party effort in this area should avoid these approaches to the welfare problem. The public resists harsh

Table 15   **Public Attitude Toward the Need to Change the Welfare System (June 1992)**

Question: Considering the welfare system, please tell me whether the current policy should be:

Response	Percent
Continued and improved	17
Changed substantially	24
Completely overhauled	59

Adapted from data collected by a Gordon Black Poll, June 2, 1992.

Table 16   **Reactions to Welfare Reform Proposals (1992)**

Response	% Who Favor	Organization	Date
Take money out of the paychecks and tax refunds of fathers who refuse to make child support payments that a court has ordered.	92	Yankelovich	March 12
Cut off welfare to able-bodied people after two years but provide government services to help them find work.	89	Gallup	Sept. 15
Require teenage mothers to stay in school in order to receive benefits.	86	Gordon Black	June 2
Require every able-bodied adult to work, but provide day care support for every welfare parent with children.	87	Gordon Black	June 2
Require all able-bodied adults on welfare, including women with small children, to work or learn a job skill.	87	Yankelovich	March 12
Increase spending on the Head Start program, so it will be available to every child who is eligible.	75	Hart/Teeter	March 5
Replace welfare with a system of guaranteed public jobs.	71	Yankelovich	March 12

Adapted from the Roper Center Poll Database.

Table 17   **Public Support for Proposed Welfare Reforms (March 1992)**
Question: Here is a list of changes many people would like to make in the current welfare system. For each idea, please tell me whether you favor or oppose that change . . .

Response	% Favor	% Oppose
Cut the amount of money given to all people on welfare.	16	76
Eliminate automatic cost-of-living increases to welfare recipients.	37	55
End increase in welfare payments to women who give birth to children while on welfare.	39	54
Require unmarried teenage mothers to live with their parents in order to receive welfare.	42	48
Require welfare mothers to accept contraceptive implants.	43	50

Adapted from data collected by Yankelovich, Clancy, Shulman, March 12, 1992.

Table 18   **Public Attitudes Toward Welfare versus Assistance to the Poor (May 1992)**

Question: We are faced with many problems in this country, none of which can be solved easily or inexpensively. I'm going to name some of these problems, and for each one I'd like you to tell me whether you think we're spending too much money, too little money, or the right amount.

Response	... On welfare? %	... On assistance to the poor? %
Too much	44	13
Too little	23	64
Right amount	27	16
Don't know	7	6

Adapted from data collected by CBS/NYT, May 8, 1992.

treatment of the poor. The problem and the solution to welfare policies are based on how we *help* the poor, not how we *punish* the poor.

Frustration with welfare and other social programs has reached the point where large numbers of people no longer equate welfare programs with assistance for the poor and needy. They see the issues separately. If pollsters ask about welfare, they get very negative responses. The responses dealing with *poverty* are quite different. This dynamic, shown in Table 18, was captured in a CBS News/*New York Times* Poll.

Welfare reform should be one of the major focuses of a third party. Like the process issues discussed earlier, advocating specific changes in the systems that receive widespread public support would be effective. Considering the lack of progress on this issue since the 1960s, it would be difficult for the other parties to counterattack. The platform should embody specific changes that encourage independence, yet don't punish people for being poor.

An Educated Citizenry

At the federal level, the politics of education reform are complicated. The vast majority of political power lies at the state and local level, ensuring that national reform efforts under the current system would face strong opposition. Teachers' organizations, like the National Education Association and the American Federation of Teachers, are extremely well organized and financed, providing $5,817,975 and $2,332,490 respectively in campaign funds to federal candidates in 1992.[16] They stand directly in the path of any reforms that might be proposed.

The public understands the notion that education and economic success are inexorably intertwined. Unfortunately, the two parties don't seem to understand this. Education, like welfare, seems to be an area of policy that receives considerable attention during campaigns but never gets addressed in any major way after the election. As a result, we have no national educational strategy, few national achievement standards, few standards to ensure quality teaching, limited incentives to encourage achievement in the fields needed for our country to prosper, only modest coordination of state educational efforts, and limited practical vocational training for those people who don't want to go to college. We are wasting the talent of our people, and we have no accepted plan to reverse it. The verdict is in: According to the polling data in Table 19, our educational system has failed.

Americans understand that our educational system is weak and in need of reform, and they will support fundamental reforms in education. Education is an issue that pollsters find very important to voters. Nevertheless, it is another issue, much like welfare, that is more a rhetorical tool than a concrete policy issue. Educational issues are talked about but never acted upon.

The public's concern about education is serious. It rates our educational system as weaker than that of our key economic competitors. It is precisely the connection between education and our economic future that makes education a potent political issue. Tables 20 and 21 indicate how far our educational system has fallen in the eyes of the populace.

In short, Americans understand that education is the engine that drives the economy. For 30 years, the Republicans and Democrats have failed to provide leadership in educational reform. A central tenet of a third party should be to provide national leadership and national goals in educational reform.

Table 19 **Public Attitude Toward the Educational System (June 1992)**

Question: In general, do you think the American system of public schools does a satisfactory job educating children, or do you think the system has failed?

Response	Percent
Satisfactory	23
Failed	67
Mixed (vol.)	7

Adapted from data collected by Gallup, June 8, 1992.

Table 20   **Public Assessment of the Need for Change in Public Education
(June 1992)**

Question: For each of the following areas of federal government policy, please tell me
whether you think current policy should be continued and improved upon, changed
substantially, or completely overhauled. . . . Here is one area: Public education.

Response	Percent
Continued and improved	38
Changed substantially	24
Completely overhauled	37

Adapted from data collected by a Gordon Black Poll, June 2, 1992.

What Should We Do?

Americans view education as a tool to promote economic competitiveness, and they understand that our future depends on our ability to produce a qualified workforce strong in science and mathematics. These are
the skills of the next century. In addition, they want to encourage the
education of all Americans, not just the rich. Most importantly, Americans believe in making our school systems tougher by raising standards
of achievement and emphasizing useful skills. Table 22 shows that Americans are willing to invest federal funds in pursuit of educational reforms
that encourage study in science, engineering, and mathematics. If there
are reforms, the public is willing to pay for improving education, even
if it means an increase in taxes, according to Table 23.

School Choice: Only Partial Support

The issue of school choice has divided both the political and economic
communities. The typical Republican response to educational reform

Table 21   **Public Assessment of American versus Japanese Schools
(February 1992)**

Question: I would like you to compare the United States and Japan in some ways.
Which country, the U.S. or Japan, would you say has . . . better educated citizens?

Response	Percent
United States	36
Japan	55
Equal	4

Adapted from data collected by ABC News/WP, February 9, 1992.

Table 22   **Responses to Proposed Policy Positions (1992 and 1993)**

Policy Position	% Who Approve or Favor	Polling Organization	Date
Put more emphasis on teaching tougher, more challenging basic courses such as reading, writing, math, and science.	96	Harris	Aug. 31, 1992
Teach more practical skills that can be used in the workforce.	92	Harris	Aug. 31, 1992
Provide anyone who wants to attend college with a federal loan that can be paid off at low interest or by taking a public service job.	88	Gallup	Sept. 15, 1992
Provide more financial support to universities for high-technology research.	86	Roper	Jan. 26, 1993
Raise requirements for passing courses and graduating.	81	Harris	Aug. 31, 1992
Create a large national science scholarship and fellowship fund that will pay for all of the educational costs of American students who will major in the sciences, engineering, mathematics, and statistics.	77	Gordon Black	June 2, 1992
Hire more teachers.	75	Gallup	April 5, 1992
Institute national standardized testing.	71	Gallup	April 5, 1992
Use federal and state funds to pay for keeping inner city schools open as recreation centers seven days a week, and until 10 P.M. every night for the high schools.	65	Gordon Black	June 2, 1992

Adapted from the Roper Center Poll Database.

Table 23   **Public Willingness to Accept Increased Taxation to Support Improved Education (March 1992)**

Question: Would you favor or oppose the government spending more money on . . . improving public school education, if it meant that your taxes had to be increased?

Response	Percent
Favor	77
Oppose	22
Not Sure	1

Adapted from data collected by Harris, March 17, 1992.

Table 24 **Popular Willingness to Favor Funding of Public Education**

Question: Which would you rather see—the government spend more money to improve public schools, or cut your taxes so that you can send your children to private schools?

Response	Percent
Spend more money	66
Cut taxes	26
Don't know	8

Adapted from data collected by EDK Assoc., January 1993.

is to let all students choose where they want to go and let the free-market system magically produce educated children. The public reaction to school choice is decidedly mixed. In general, people support school choice when it is limited to the public school system. However, there is considerable opposition to any support of private schools with public money. A third party should not support such reforms because the support for them is not broad enough and there is little evidence that they work. There is more support for a position advocating school choice—limited to public schools. However, despite some misgivings about the performance of our public schools, Tables 24 through 27 show that the public is willing to spend more money on these schools, rather than cut taxes.

The Bottom Line on Education

In short, the public wants a strategy. Voters will respond positively to a plan—a coordinated national development strategy. The approaches to

Table 25 **Popular Attitude Toward Vouchers for Private Schools (July 1992)**

Question: Some people think that parents should be given a voucher that they could use toward enrolling their child in a private school at public expense. Do you support or oppose that idea?

Response	Percent
Support	32
Oppose	62
Don't know	6

Adapted from data collected by the Writhlin Group.

Table 26   **Popular Attitude Toward Assistance for Those Attending Private Schools (August 1992)**

Question: Should the government spend money to assist families who want to send their children to private or religious school, or should government money only be spent on children who attend public schools?

Response	Percent
Assist private and religious schools	23
Spend only on public schools	64
Don't know	6

Adapted from data collected by *Time*/CNN, August 20, 1992.

reforming the educational system are not harsh or radical. No one wants to abandon the public school system. The time is long overdue for the creation of national standards, increased teacher accountability, and the federal support of incentives to encourage the development of the technical skills this country desperately needs. We can't allow 50 teacher unions, dominating state governments, to guide by themselves the educational future of the country. A third party ought to make educational reform a national political issue.

Table 27   **Responses to Various Types of School Choice Proposals (1992–1993)**

Policy position	% Who Agree or Favor	Organization	Date
Parents should have the right to send their children to any public school they want to.	85	ABC News	July 8, 1992
Children should be able to attend the public school of their choice with government money going to the school they wish to attend.	69	Harris	Aug. 31, 1992
Parents should be able to choose which public schools their child attends.	68	AP	Sept. 1, 1992
Give families a tax credit for each child attending a private or parochial school.	53	Gallup	Sept. 15, 1993
Offer parents vouchers to help pay the costs of private or parochial school.	42	Gallup	May 10, 1992

Adapted from the Roper Center Poll Database.

The Politics of Pragmatism

The analysis in this chapter has sought to establish the policy positions that would lead to the national success of a new party of the center. These opportunities exist as a testament to the failings of the two major parties, and they are tailored to the middle-class values and moderate ideological bent of those voters most discontented by the conduct of modern American politics. The public is ready to go beyond the disingenuous optimism of the Reagan era and look beyond the series of false choices presented by the hopeless clash of liberal and conservative ideologies.

The use of ideology in politics limits our ability to construct real solutions to the problems we face. The definition of the word "ideology" demonstrates the corrosive effects of ideological politics. According to *Webster's New World Dictionary,* ideology is "thinking or theorizing of an idealistic, abstract, or impractical nature; fanciful speculation." Policy guided by ideology is always limited by the inability to accept ideas that are not in agreement with its intellectual underpinnings. The point is this: The solutions to the problems we face as a nation are no longer to be found in strict adherence to either liberalism or conservatism.

What could be the ideology of a third party? There cannot be such a thing as a "moderate" ideology. Ideology, by definition, cannot be moderate. Instead, the moderate movement should establish a theme that captures the essence of what the movement is trying to accomplish. Themes convey the central meaning of the movement in simple ideas understandable to a wide audience. Reagan was a master at creating simple themes like "It's morning in America" and "The government is the problem." In contrast, the Democrats have no theme because one theme cannot reconcile the pure liberal wing with the more moderate Democratic Leadership Committee (DLC) wing of the party. Their intellectual underpinnings are simply too different.

It is time for the politics of pragmatism. Pragmatism is "a method or tendency in philosophy . . . which determines the meaning and truth of all concepts and tests their validity by their practical results."[17] The time has come to move politics beyond ideology. We must continually ask what works, not where the ideas came from. We must strive for approaches that are efficient without regard to whether they are conservative or liberal. We must establish objective and realistic goals that take advantage of the best policymakers have to offer, without regard to the cultural battle characterizing the tensions between the two major parties.

The implication of pragmatic politics is the disengagement from the moral and cultural battle that so often immobilizes government and policymaking. A third-party movement must recognize the danger that ideological politics poses. The American public must strive to mitigate the political effects of divisive issues that divide us on moral and cultural grounds. Modern politics fails to find solutions when choices are defined in terms based on morality and not practicality.[18] Once policy becomes radicalized by moral considerations, our political system ceases to operate. The examples abound—abortion, affirmative action, family values, free speech, obscenity, and religion. Because these issues are based on moral beliefs, they will never be entirely solved. It is precisely the moral and cultural battles that eliminate the possibility of cooperation between the major parties. The Democrats have embraced the liberal multiculturalism of Bill and Hillary Clinton and the liberal wing of the party, as illustrated by the issues surrounding gays in the military and the blatant emphasis on gender and race in the nomination process. Concurrently, the Republicans are becoming increasingly dependent on the religious right as Perot decimates the moderate wing of the party.

In this atmosphere a new party must avoid taking sides in the moral and cultural debate. The politics of pragmatism dictate that moral and cultural issues should not divide us in our quest to solve the far more pressing problems that face America: the economy, a broken educational system, decaying urban areas, the budget deficit, and our poor and needy. These issues are too important to be sidelined by the activist with a moral cause. A third party needs to understand that its reason for existence is not to solve every debate in American politics. Its strength will be its avoidance of moral stridency. It is on these issues that a party must agree to disagree in pursuit of more noble and worthwhile goals. This is the politics of pragmatism and this should be the politics of a centrist party of reform.

⇒ 8 ⇒

Making the Choice

It's a democracy, if you can keep it!

—*Benjamin Franklin*

Democracy is a fragile thing. Here in America, despite constitutional protections, we have had to fight regularly against those in our midst who would manipulate our democratic institutions to serve the will of some special interest or cause. Many Americans still remember vividly the hearings of Senator Joseph McCarthy and his abuse of democratic rights in his crusade against "communists." A few decades earlier, many of our cities were dominated by corrupt and often vicious political machines. America has had its full share of those who have been willing, if not eager, to subvert the interests of the common good in order to pursue their private ends—whites over blacks, ethnic machine bosses over whole communities, ideological demagogues over "enemies of the people" and merchant pirates over whole industries or markets. In the past, however, we have as a people somehow found both the will and the leadership to fight back to preserve our democratic rights and values, and the partisans for democracy have generally prevailed. This book is intended explicitly as a call to arms for the current partisans for democracy.

If our political process continues on its current course, we will bequeath to our children a political system where democracy has been crippled, where financial influence is the primary force determining the distribution of government resources, and where our economy is hobbled by the weight of an ever-increasing mountain of debt. The gravest danger the nation faces comes not from Japan, Germany, or the developing nations. The most threatening danger comes from within, and it must be conquered from within.

Of course, if we do not understand why our system is broken, we cannot fix it. If we as a nation misunderstand the underlying causes of the ills in our political system, we are likely to try to fix the wrong things, and we may make our circumstances worse, not better. The nation has had a poor track record in recent years at fixing things in our political and social systems, and too often we have watched supposed solutions turn into disasters. We have repeatedly been misled by well-meaning specialists who, with the best of intentions, have had either the naïveté or the arrogance to believe that they can design quick-fix solutions to complicated national problems. Often, as in the case of the welfare system, the supposed solution itself becomes the problem and makes our society in some ways worse as opposed to better. Once enacted into law, some "solutions" become impossible to fix because they are perverse instruments of political stalemate. In the case of welfare we seem to have created an economically dependent class of citizens and an entire bureaucracy and organizational complex that flexes its political muscles as much to defend its own power, positions, and jobs as to help welfare recipients get off the rolls.

Although both parties would have us believe that they have different and persuasive answers to our problems, the real, underlying difference between the two major parties is not one of alternative solutions but rather the difference in the mix of particular groups to whom they provide political payoffs. Incumbents of both parties consistently behave as though they value the furtherance of their careers more than good public policy, more than honesty and candor, and certainly more than the preservation of the citizens' right to choose new leadership.

Of course, members of Congress have become masters at telling the public that they are not individually responsible for the nation's ills. They claim they do the best they can in a bad system, that everyone else is at fault except them, and that they fought the good fight, but lost. They use taxpayers' money to advertise this insipid message, spending a small fortune on propaganda-style mailings to their constituents. The public, however, has come to understand that lying is lying, even when it is called "spin."

When considering whether or not we should call the behavior of Congress corrupt, we might ask the following question: Which is more ethical—an outright $100,000 bribe or a $100,000 campaign contribution that has the highly desirable consequence of helping an incumbent keep a $2 million retirement package? If asked this question, politicians would surely in some way defend the superior morality of the latter, but the public wouldn't likely be deceived. If the American voters could choose between 435 serious candidates, financed entirely by small contributions from inside their districts, and 435 incumbents, financed at least half by the PAC system, we contend that Congress would see more turnover than it has seen in 100 years. Very few members of Congress could survive a reputable challenger financed with adequate funds coming from individual supporters within the congressional district.

The central problem highlighted in this book is the deprivation of the American people of the right to choose. The loss of real democratic choice is at the very core of our larger problems, the underlying reason, for example, that the budgetary process is out of control. The budget is the accumulation and summation of the payoff system that rewards the powerful interests who provide the campaign funding and resources to the incumbents, who because of these funds become all but invulnerable. If history repeats itself in 1994, most of the elected officials who have condoned, if not actively promoted, this fiasco in Congress will face little or no competition once again. Without a serious choice in congressional elections, how does a voter register protest? Incumbents will travel back to Washington in 1995, secure in the knowledge that they have once again evaded the anger of the American people. The millions of Americans who have been energized by Ross Perot will find out just how little influence they can have if, despite their anger at incumbents and traditional challengers, they have no real alternative choices for leadership. The opponents of reform will exploit the absence of serious alternative leadership and continue to promote inactivity and acquiescence to the two-party system.

Spreading the Risk

The best way to counter incumbents' ability to derail reform efforts is to broaden the base of the committed, reputable alternative leadership. Ross Perot represents millions of people, and he is the only real national spokesperson for fundamental reform. He has also created an impressive organization. UWSA and the movement of which it is a part must be taken seriously. Perot, of course, would argue that what he is really doing is creating the opportunity for average citizens to voice their opinions and to make them felt—through petitions, call-in campaigns, and write-in campaigns. Perot would probably also argue that it takes time for a new leadership to evolve in communities all over the country. On both counts, he is undoubtedly correct. At the same time, if Perot were to falter today, for whatever reason, there is no one really in a position to step forward and assume leadership of UWSA and the movement.

A broadened leadership, whether grown internally or recruited from the outside, is the only way to spread the risk inherent in the dependence of UWSA and the broader public desire for reform on the ideas, efforts, and decisions of a single individual. A broadened leadership would have several positive effects. A leader is enhanced by the quality of his followers. John Kennedy, Franklin Roosevelt, and Abraham Lincoln were all known for their ability to surround themselves with first-class talent. The apparent absence of such talent around Perot at the present time makes the entire effort of UWSA suspect in many people's minds, sustaining the argument that UWSA is nothing more than a personal vehicle for Perot. The recruitment of additional leadership would strengthen the persuasiveness of Perot's position through the support for his arguments by other prominent Americans.

Paying Lip Service

Other vulnerabilities limit the potential of UWSA. Incumbents who face no serious challengers for their jobs need not do more than pay lip service to groups such as UWSA, even when they have tens of thousands of members in their districts. Moreover, the more issues about which UWSA is concerned, the less influence it will have on any one issue. The endorsement process is fraught with complexities that render it less useful than it might seem on the surface. First, UWSA is a centrist organization that aligns itself to the right on some issues and to the left on others. On economic and budgetary reform issues, for example, UWSA would be inclined to side with Republicans, emphasizing greater use of spending cuts and reserving increased taxation primarily for deficit reduction. On political reform issues, particularly campaign finance reform, UWSA is likely to find a more sympathetic ear from a minority of genuine reformers in either party. On most trade issues, Perot seems closer to the Democrats. On welfare reform issues, he seems closer to the Republicans, and so on. Therein lies a central problem of the endorsement process for a centrist political organization. UWSA is going to be forever selecting among candidates who give them half of what they want on many issues, precisely because the radical middle is not aligned in reality with either party. In the special Texas senate race in 1993, four of the candidates carried "bragging rights" that they were card-carrying members of UWSA. The candidate that won, Kay Hutchison, was the front runner all the way, and none of the national media stories attributed her success to the late endorsement by 85 percent of the members of UWSA.

Politicians are experts at telling groups what they want to hear. They are also experts at making it difficult to determine who has done what to whom after the fact, so that the voters will never know what really went on. In most of the state and congressional legislative races, only one party will put up a seriously financed candidate, and the endorsement process is generally likely to be a farce. Endorsements have become simply the standard fare of all of local politics; and there is little reason to believe that an endorsement by UWSA will carry any more weight than endorsements by the Chamber of Commerce, newspapers, or local labor unions.

UWSA stands a real risk of becoming the bride who, after spending a small fortune on a wedding dress, gets stood up at the alter. An endorsement by itself is insignificant in the face of a teachers' union that contributes $10,000 to a campaign and then provides a phone bank with 30 or 40 teachers to call most of the voters in the district. In general, the teachers' union decides fairly early which of the Democratic incumbents to support and provides the early support that is by far the most valued in a political campaign. By nature of its character, UWSA cannot provide all of the services of the teachers' union; and it will prove nearly impossible for UWSA to provide any of its support early in a campaign. UWSA is controlled by the need to follow internally democratic procedures, a fact that makes it substantially different from most of the PACs, which are generally run autocratically by a small elite. Democratic endorsement processes take time because they require fairness and the education of members, both of which cannot be conducted quickly. Because of this, UWSA will generally not be able to make the kind of early endorsements that have the most value and can create the momentum for a candidate.

These arguments are not intended to suggest that the citizen lobby and endorsement processes are worthless. On the contrary, Perot and UWSA are already having a profound impact on the nature of debate in Washington. The tax and spend budget is under attack nationally for its failure to address realistically the budget deficit problem. Reform is on the lips of national and state politicians alike, and even entrenched incumbents are now beginning to talk about term limits. The argument here is one of relative impact, and we believe the relative impact of a political party of the mobilized center can be a far more powerful force for democratic reform in American life.

Democracy Is Never Easy

We have already made the case for a political party in some detail, and we will not rehash those arguments here. A political party that can recruit and finance credible candidates will do more to restore democracy than all of the proposed rule changes and reforms put together. Democracy isn't easy, however. Democracy is and always has been a harder taskmaster on the average citizen than authoritarian regimes are. The hard fist of tyranny is not softened appreciably by the velvet glove that encases it. If we want our democracy back, we are going to have to take it. No one is going to give it back to us. On the contrary, the supporters of the Washington paradigm will work hard to discredit and derail serious attempts to threaten their stranglehold. They will do this with a smile, protesting all along their commitment to democracy, deficit reduction, and our future. Even major elements of the national media will feel threatened by a movement that might reshape the distribution of power in Washington, and neither Ross Perot nor a new political party is going to glide into power unscathed.

The proponents of the status quo use a variety of tired arguments to undermine the potential for change. There is, after all, little outrage among the elite in Washington. Their capacity for outrage, we would propose, is dulled in direct proportion to their ability to earn sumptuous livings at the table so lavishly set by the politics of business-as-usual. The lobbyists, consultants, think-tank experts, lawyers, and assorted bureaucrats all profit handsomely from the excesses the public has paid for so dearly. After listening to their pet excuses and blame throwing, the only appropriate conclusion is that they have lost the capacity to look beyond their own self-interest.

The reality, however, is that they have power and we do not. They control the offices and we do not. They have the access and we do not. They shape the policies and we do not. And yet, despite the offices, access, and power they control, they would have us believe that they themselves are not responsible for the ill of the system, that government is perhaps an act of God or nature, or most underhanded of all, that the failures are entirely the consequence of the views of the public. "We can't raise taxes because the voters wouldn't like it!" "We can't cut that program because the voters would get upset!" "The voters want to increase spending and cut taxes, and Congress just can't do it!" These are the refrains of our officeholders, who slavishly pander to special interests in order to raise all the money they need so they do not have to worry about actually doing what the voters want.

The ethical question of responsibility is, however, one that voters must ask themselves. American voters have slowly been leaving the playing field of politics over the past 30 years, and they have their own refrains of irresponsibility: "My vote doesn't matter, so why should I vote?" "The system isn't fair, or just, or right, so why should I spend my time working in it?" We are fast becoming "ethical emigrants" from our democracy, but before accepting culpability, we must ask where else we have to go.

And Where Are the Leaders?

Worse than the defection of voters, is the defection of the potential leaders who are required to make any change a reality. Is Ross Perot really the only person in this country of sufficient substance, stature, and moral persuasion who is prepared to launch a highly public and sustained challenge to the status quo? The thought that he *alone* would pick up the mantle of responsibility is perhaps the most distressing thought of all. Where are America's great entrepreneurs and business leaders, who have been long on criticism and short on commitment? Where are our learned academics, many of whom have been documenting the demise of our democratic processes and the stagnation of our economic system for years? Where are the political leaders that America needs so desperately—women and men, young and old, who share the common conviction that they accept responsibility for the larger community of which they are a part?

The lack of committed leaders is the most chilling commentary of all on the current state of American politics. In the 1850s, when the Republican Party formed, hundreds of local leaders around the country stepped forward as a matter of conscience. Officeholders in both the Democratic and Whig parties actually defected to join the Republicans, and many prominent business and professional leaders put themselves on the line in support of the movement. Today, America has Ross Perot, and he has shown that he is simply not enough. A country that can no longer generate real leaders in politics when it needs them is a country that must necessarily decline.

America is ready and waiting for a new political party that will provide a new beginning. Disaffected, dissatisfied voters are ready to put aside doubt, skepticism, and even cynicism and vote for the candidates of a new, centrist political party. Our research, conducted over four separate studies, has established that there is a constituency easily large enough to create this new party, if it is a party of the center. The obstacle yet to be overcome is not the understanding and willingness of the voters to follow. The key obstacle is the recruitment of men and women who are ready and willing to lead, both as active candidates and as the organizational and financial support for the party. Without such leadership, a political party of sufficient size and power will never successfully emerge. We are not talking about huge numbers of people. A handful of talented leaders can organize a congressional district, but the process will surely not happen by itself. Ross Perot is recruiting and training such local leaders for UWSA, but these are not necessarily people who themselves will want to run for office. If our aim is to confront and defeat incumbents, then we must have able candidates and the supporting leadership structure required to elect them.

The End of One Journey,
the Beginning of Others

All across the United States, in tiny hamlets and in large urban centers, Americans are awakening. The country entered the 1960s with faith, optimism, and a basic belief in the efficiency of our governmental institutions. We are moving into the 1990s bitter, skeptical, and with a deep disdain, both for our institutions and the people who currently control them. Post-war America inherited a healthy federal budget and a real growth rate of more than 3.5 percent. It is leaving the America of the next century $4.2 trillion of debt and a real growth rate that will be lucky to average more than one percent per year. Change cannot happen quickly enough.

Whether it is called the Independence Party, the Patriot Party, the New Party, or the New Alliance Party, a new party can make things happen if enough members of the public will not only say they support it but will actively do so. A political party is, after all, an organization built up out of smaller organizations in local communities. These smaller organizations are made up of friends and neighbors, of the people next door or on the next block. Building a political party begins by getting five people together in a living room; then reaching out to 25 people for a meeting at a church or community center; and eventually enlisting the support of several thousand people who are committed enough to contribute money to support candidates who will run for office. Most of all, a political party is built out of commitment.

The Central Issue Is Choice

We wrote this book to give readers a set of facts that would help them understand an enormously complex problem. Fifty years from now we will know whether enough of us stepped forward to change the downward spiral of American politics and the economy. For now, all we can do is to hope.

A healthy democracy is no guarantee of perfection in public policy, but the failure of our democracy is a virtual guarantee that policy will be insensitive, unrepresentative, self-serving, and expensive. If we will focus as a nation first on the restoration of our democracy and commit our best efforts to it, those efforts will in the long run enable us to regain control as a public over the government that is meant to serve us. This is a choice we will all have to make individually, but it is a choice we must make.

Notes

Chapter 1

1. Quoted in Mike Feinsilber, Associated Press, April 21, 1992.

2. All the data in this paragraph came from Beth Donovan with Ilyse J. Vernon, "Freshman Got to Washington with Help of PAC Funds," *Congressional Quarterly Weekly Report*, March 27, 1993, p. 724.

3. ABC News/*Washington Post* Poll, June 1992, cited in *The Public Perspective*, vol. 4, no. 1.

4. Federal Election Commission.

5. Clifforn Kraus, "Congressional Memo; Freshman Runs Foul of Status Quo," *The New York Times*, April 4, 1993, Section 1, p. 25.

6. Jerry Gray, "New Congressman Picks Old Congressman for Aide," *The New York Times*, January 6, 1993, Section B, p. 5.

7. Quoted in Kenneth J. Cooper, "Old and New Sound Much the Same," *The Washington Post*, November 10, 1992.

8. Kraus, p. 25.

9. Kraus, p. 25.

10. All data in this paragraph came from Gerald F. Seib, "Parties, President, and Taxpayers Are United by Stakes They Have in Deficit Bill Fight," *The Wall Street Journal*, Monday, July 12, 1993, p. A14. Calculations of contribution amounts were done by the Center for Responsive Politics.

11. For the best discussion of the way Americans personalize their hope in the presidency, see Theodore J. Lowi, *The Personal President: Power Invested, Promise Unfilled* (Ithaca, NY: Cornell University Press, 1985).

12. Morris P. Fiorina, *Congress: The Keystone of the Washington Establishment* (New Haven, CT: Yale University Press, 1977), pp. 12–13.

13. This is an estimate based on a detailed examination of four of the largest states—California, New York, Illinois, and Texas—and a summary examination of eight other states for 1992—Florida, Pennsylvania, Ohio, New Jersey, Georgia, Michigan, Washington, and Missouri. The races were classified as "noncompetitive" if one of the candidates received more than 57 percent of the vote or if the incumbent had an overwhelming advantage in financial resources. Incumbent reelection rates were routinely over 95 percent.

14. Illyse J. Vernon, "A History of Spending Limits," *Congressional Quarterly Weekly Report*, June 19, 1993, p. 1,538.

15. Beth Donovan, "Senate Passes Campaign Finance by Gutting Public Funding," *Congressional Quarterly Weekly Report*, June 19, 1993, pp. 1,539–1,540.

16. James Sundquist, "Strengthening the National Parties," *Election American Style*, A. James Reichley, ed. (Washington, D.C.: The Brookings Institution, 1987), p. 200.

17. Our arguments about creating a new party are somewhat related to some of the old "responsible party" literature. There has been a long-standing debate within the political science community about the proper role of American political parties. In 1950, the Committee on Political Parties of the American Political Science Association published a report called *Towards a More Responsible Two-Party System* (New York: Rinehart, 1950), which sought to strengthen the two-party system and give it more power to govern. Some of the relevant literature includes Austin Ranney, *The Doctrine of Responsible Party Government* (Urbana: University of Illinois Press, 1962), and E. E. Schattschneider, *Party Government* (New York: Rinehart, 1942). We are not advocating a strict "responsible party" view of government in the sense of British parties. Given the procedural impediments in the way strong, centralized parties operate (i.e., the direct primary and the separation of powers), it seems unlikely that America will ever have very strong, disciplined parties. However, we are arguing that by creating a political party based on a few central principles, we can achieve some of the benefits of strong parties, despite the institutional impediments that lead to a diffusion of their political power. By maximizing electoral competition, we can achieve some of the fundamental advantages of stronger parties without the radical constitutional or legislative overhaul that would be necessary to fundamentally alter the current parties.

18. A Gordon Black Poll of 1,000 delegates conducted in the two weeks prior to the Republican National Convention. The poll was released by NBC and *USA Today* during the convention in July, 1992.

19. A Gordon Black Poll of 1,000 delegates to the Democratic National Convention, conducted in the two weeks prior to the convention. Released by NBC and *USA Today* in August, 1992.

20. Roy C. Macridis and Bernard E. Brown, *The DeGaulle Republic: Quest for Unity* (Homewood, IL: The Dorsey Press, 1960), p. 2.

21. Ibid., p. 5.

22. K. L. Kamal, *Democratic Politics in India* (New Delhi: Wiley Eastern Limited, 1984), p. 85.

23. Kay Lawson, "How State Laws Undermine Parties," *Elections American Style*, ed. A. James Riechely, p. 242.

24. Steven J. Rosenstone, Roy L. Behr, and Edward H. Lazarus, *Third Parties in America: Citizen Response to Major Party Failure* (Princeton, NJ: Princeton University Press, 1984), p. 3.

25. Ibid., Appendix A.

26. Frank Sorauf, *Party Politics in America*, 3rd ed. (Boston: Little Brown and Co., 1976), pp. 40–41.

27. A. James Reichley, *The Life of the Parties* (New York: The Free Press, 1992), p. 354.

28. For a more complete discussion of this, see Gordon S. Black and Benjamin D. Black, "Perot Wins! The Election That Could Have Been," *The Public Perspective*, January/February 1993, vol. 4, no. 2, pp. 15–16, 18.

29. News conference, National Press Club, June 6, 1992.

30. For an excellent discussion on the limitations of presidential power, see Lowi, *The Personal President.*

Chapter 2

1. Closing lines from T. S. Eliot's "The Hollow Men."

2. Sandy Maisel, "The Incumbency Advantage," *Money, Elections, and Democracy*, Margaret Latus Nugent and John R. Johannes, eds. (Boulder, CO: Westview Press, 1990), p. 119.

3. The best exposition is found in the 10th and 51st Federalist Papers, written by James Madison. See *The Federalist Papers*, Clinton Rossiter, ed. (New York: New American Library, 1961).

4. Editorial, *Wall Street Journal*, Sept. 22, 1992, p. 36.

5. The campaign financing figures in this section all come from Michael Barone and Grant Ujifusa, *The Almanac of American Politics* (Washington, D.C.: The National Journal, 1992), p. 901.

6. Herbert E. Alexander and Monica Bauer, *Financing the 1988 Elections* (Boulder, CO: Westview Press, 1991), p. 54.

7. The data on Louise Slaughter can be found in the *Federal Election Commission Reports on Financial Activity and Disclosure Series.* The authors tabulated the results from the raw data. In doing so, we concentrated on the largest union contributors. Thus, the $200,000 figure is an underestimation of the true amount.

8. All the financial data on congressional candidates referred to in this paragraph can be found in the Federal Election Commission media release titled "1992 Congressional Election Spending Jumps 52% to $678 Million," March 4, 1993.

9. ABC News/*Washington Post* Poll result from June 1992. Result published in *The Public Perspective*, vol. 4, no. 1, p. 86.

10. "Undeserving Grandfathers," *New York Times*, January 18, 1992, Section 1, p. 10.

11. The quote and information cited in this paragraph are from Charles R. Babcock, "Hefty Pensions Ease Departure," *The Washington Post*, November 10, 1993, p. 15.

12. Data compiled by *Congressional Quarterly*, October 3, 1992, p. 3,093, and from election returns, *Congressional Quarterly*, November 7, 1992.

13. Maisel in *Money, Elections, and Democracy*, p. 119.

14. Sundquist in *Elections American Style*, p. 179.

15. ABC News/*Washington Post* Poll, June 1992.

16. Alexander and Bauer, p. 59.

17. U.S. Bureau of the Census, *The Statistical Abstract of the United States: 1992*, 112th ed. (Washington, D.C., 1992), p. xx.

18. Political/Media Research Poll cited in *The Public Perspective*, Jan.–Feb. 1993, p. 25.

19. Thomas Mann, "Is the House of Representatives Unresponsive to Political Change?" in *Elections American Style*. A. James Reichley, ed. (Washington, D.C.: Brookings Institution, 1987), p. 261.

20. Maisel in *Money, Elections, and Democracy*, p. 119.

21. Barry Keene, "Senate Leader Lists Sweeping Solutions to Government Gridlock," *Institute of Governmental Studies: Public Affairs Report*, vol. 34, no. 1, January 1993, p. 15.

22. Rhodes Cook, "House Republicans Scored a Quiet Victory in '92." *Congressional Quarterly Weekly Report*, April 17, 1993, p. 966.

23. Richard Fenno, Jr., *Home Style: House Members in Their Districts* (Boston: Little, Brown, 1978), pp. 31–50.

24. Ibid., p. 44.

25. The most complete discussion of this can be found in Cain, Ferejohn, and Fiorina, pp. 18–25.

26. John Pontius, "U.S. Congress Official Mail Costs, Fiscal Year 1972 to Present," (Washington, D.C.: Congressional Research Service, June 13, 1989), tables 3, 4.

27. "Court Curbs House on Non-District Mailings," *New York Times*, August 1, 1992, p. 7.

28. James T. Bennett and Thomas J. DiLorenzo, *Official Lies: How Washington Misleads Us* (Alexandria, VA: Groom Books, 1992), p. 41.

29. Federal Election Commission, "1992 Congressional Election Spending Jumps 52% to $678 Million," news release of March 4, 1993, p. 2.

30. *The Statistical Abstract: 1992*, p. 275, and the FEC release "1992 Congressional Election Spending Jumps 52% to $678 Million," March 4, 1993.

31. Federal Election Commission.

32. Alan Abramowitz, "Incumbency, Campaign Spending, and the Decline of Competition in U.S. House Elections," *Journal of Politics*, vol. 53, no. 1, February 1991, pp. 35–36.

33. Paul S. Herrnson, *Party Campaigning in the 1980s* (Cambridge, MA: Harvard University Press, 1988), p. 70.

34. Federal Election Commission.

35. Federal Election Commission.

36. Data from a study by the Center for Responsive Politics, quoted in "The 1992 Campaign: Companies Going beyond PACs, Study Finds," *The New York Times*, July 19, 1992, section 1, p. 19.

37. Data from a Common Cause report quoted in an editorial, "Political Reform," *The Washington Post*, November 10, 1993, page A16. Authors used data from this article to calculate the averages.

38. Figure from report was also cited in George Will, "What Voters Did for the System," *The Washington Post*, November 12, 1992, p. A21.

39. The data is from the Federal Election Commission. In the general election, the 213 Democratic incumbents received $61,543,784, the 137 Republican incumbents received $29,372,388, the 139 Democratic challengers raised $6,495,232, and the 210 Republican challengers raised $4,182,884.

40. Federal Election Commission, press release, December 30, 1992.

41. Larry J. Sabato, *PAC Power: Inside the World of Political Action Committees* (New York: W. W. Norton & Co., 1984), p. xiv.

42. Theodore Lowi has expressed this view and used this terminology in many of his writings. We owe him our apologies for borrowing it for this writing.

43. All the data in this paragraph came from Beth Donovan with Ilyse J. Vernon, "Freshman Got to Washington with Help of PAC Funds," *Congressional Quarterly Weekly Report*, March 27, 1993, p. 724.

44. Ibid., pp. 723–727.

45. This was not true, however, in Illinois or California. Both had the information available as provided free of charge.

46. All the data in this section is from the report "Illinois Money and Elections in 1990," issued by the Illinois State Board of Elections, January 1992.

47. David Mayhew, and later Morris Fiorina, used histograms to display data for congressional elections in the same manner we use here. We have borrowed their format. See David Mayhew, "Congressional Elections: The Case of the Vanishing Marginals," *Polity* 6 (1974), pp. 295–317.

48. The data for this paragraph came from a report issued by the California Secretary of State, "Late Contribution Report Summary: Received by Ballot Measure and Candidates, October 18, 1992 through November 3, 1992."

49. Figures cited in Sam Howe Verhovek, "The 1992 Campaign: Incumbent Legislators Face Few Primary Challenges," *The New York Times*, September 15, 1992, Section B, p. 6.

50. Election results in Sam Howe Verhovek, "The 1992 Elections: New York State—The New York Legislature Keeps Balance Intact," *The New York Times*, November 5, 1992, Section B, p. 20.

Chapter 3

1. Theodore J. Lowi, *The End of Liberalism: The Second Republic of the United States* (New York: W.W. Norton & Co., 1979), p. 297.

2. This is not intended to be a technical book, and we have treated a rather complex issue here more briefly and simply than we would for a more academic audience. When the public actually votes on a referendum, either on spending or on taxes, they are given at best a crude way to register a preference. The budget or tax proposal usually is a bundle of different elements, usually designed by lawmakers to try to ensure passage. The best example comes from education, where budgets are voted on in most areas of the country. The most the public gets to do is to determine the total amount of the budget, and not the parts. Right now, if the state and federal budgets were placed before Americans, they would vote those

budgets down with great regularity, just as they are increasingly voting down school budgets in large portions of the country. Therefore, we will grant that the concept of "over" or "under" spending is more complicated than we can develop here, but there is little doubt that the public is angry and frustrated with state and federal politicians for allowing the growth of spending at rates that far exceed what the public finds acceptable.

3. Jodie T. Allen, "Keep Your Fingers Crossed," *The Washington Post National Weekly Edition*, August 16–22, 1993, p. 23.

4. Nancy Gibbs, "The Low Road To Revolution," *Time*, August 16, 1993, p. 23.

5. Laura Michalis and Catalina Camia, "From Farm Aid to GI Bill: Working Out the Details," *Congressional Quarterly Weekly Report*, August 7, 1993, p. 2,139.

6. *Time*, August 16, 1993, p. 11.

7. George Hager and David S. Cloud, "Democrats Tie Their Fate to Clinton's Budget Bill," *Congressional Quarterly Weekly Report*, August 7, 1993, p. 2,139.

8. Allen Schick, *The Capacity to Budget* (Washington, D.C.: The Urban Institute Press, 1990), p. 7.

9. James L. Payne, *The Culture Of Spending: Why Congress Lives Beyond Our Means* (San Francisco: ICS Press, 1991), p. 61.

10. Harold W. Stanley, *Vital Statistics On American Politics: Third Edition* (Washington, D.C.: CQ Press, 1992), p. 327.

11. George M. von Furstenberg, "Taxes: A License to Spend or a Late Charge?" *The Great Fiscal Experiment*, Rudolph G. Penner, ed. (Washington, D.C.: The Urban Institute Press, 1990), p. 170.

12. Schick, p. 30.

13. Schick, p. 66.

14. Schick, p. 9.

15. John Ferejohn, *Pork Barrel Politics: Rivers and Harbors Legislation, 1947–1986* (Stanford, CA: Stanford University Press, 1974).

16. For a good discussion of how group benefit and costs play out in Congress, see R. Dougles Arnold, *The Logic of Congressional Action* (New Haven, CT: Yale University Press, 1990).

17. Payne, p. 3.

18. Ibid., p. 13.

19. Ibid., p. 2.

20. Ibid., p. 65.

21. James Q. Wilson, *The Politics of Regulation* (New York: Basic Books, 1980), chap. 2.

22. Jason DeParle, "Private Interests Are Said to Benefit from U.S. Plan for Needy," *The New York Times*, March 18, 1992, Section A, p. 16.

23. *Statistical Abstract: 1992*, p. 357.

24. *Statistical Abstract: 1992*, p. 458.

25. Bennett and DiLorenzo, p. 89.

26. Allison Harper, "With Health Overhaul on Stage, PACs Want a Front Row Seat," *Congressional Quarterly Weekly Report,* July 31, 1993, p. 2,048.

27. The financial figures were obtained from the 409 Committee Cross Index, Public Records Information Sheet provided by the Federal Election Commission.

28. *Statistical Abstract: 1992,* pp. 322, 330, 651.

29. The items are cited in a list from Harry Figgie, Jr., *Bankruptcy 1995: The Coming Collapse of America and How to Stop It* (Toronto: Little, Brown and Co., 1992), pp. 52–53.

30. Lawrence J. Haas, *Running On Empty* (Homewood, IL: BusinessOne Irwin, 1990), p. 12.

31. Ibid., p. 13.

32. *Statistical Abstract: 1992,* chart no. 496. "Federal Budget Outlays in Constant (1987) Dollars: 1940 to 1992," p. 320.

33. Schick, p. 41.

34. Rudolph G. Penner, "The Budget Deficit: Political Monster Born of Political Pets," *The Journal of Law & Politics,* vol. IX:137, 1992, p. 140.

35. Payne, p. 15.

36. Ibid.

37. Study cited in Alan Deutschman, "The Great Pension Robbery," *Fortune,* January 13, 1992, pp. 76–78.

38. Examples from Deutschman, pp. 76–77.

39. John Crawford, "Hidden Pacmen: Future Liabilities," *Congressional Quarterly Weekly Report,* February 3, 1990.

40. Schick, p. 186.

41. Brian Kelly, *Adventures in Porkland: How Washington Wastes Your Money and Why They Won't Stop* (New York: Villard Books, 1992), pp. 36–37.

42. Michael Barone and Grant Ujifusa, *The Almanac of American Politics* (Washington, D.C.: The National Journal, 1994).

43. Figures calculated by the author using data from the *Statistical Abstract: 1992.*

44. The analysis can be found in Janet Novack, "Antifreeze," *Forbes,* April 12, 1993.

Chapter 4

1. Stephen Earl Bennett, *Apathy in America 1960–1984: Causes and Consequences of Citizen Political Indifference* (Dobbs Ferry, NY: Transnational Publishers, 1986), p. 169.

2. Ruy A. Teixeira, *The Disappearing American Voter* (Washington, D.C.: The Brookings Institution, 1992), p. 75.

3. For a good discussion of the history of voter turnout see Walter Dean Burnham, *The Current Crisis in American Politics* (New York: Oxford University Press, 1982).

4. For a good discussion assessing some of the impact of the attitudinal changes see Teixeria, chap. 1.

5. Arthur H. Miller, "Political Issues and Trust in Government: 1964–1970," *The American Political Science Review*, vol. LXVII, no. 3, 1974, pp. 951–972.

6. The Harris Poll news release, January 1992.

7. Ibid.

8. Based on Gallup data published in *The Public Perspective*, vol. 4, no. 1, p. 86.

9. A complete list of presidential approval ratings can be found in *The Public Perspective*, vol. 4, no. 5, p. 82.

10. Data from the Roper Center Poll Database. The wording for the question is "How much of the time do you think that you can trust government to do what is right—just about always, most of the time, only some of the time, or never?" *The Washington Post* survey was conducted from February 25–28, 1993, (n=1216). The finding was consistent with other polls. CBS News/*NYT* polls found 76 percent indicated some of the time or never in Jan. 12–14, 1993 and 72 percent in December, 1992, and 76 percent in October 1992. Interestingly, an *LA Times* poll in March of 1992 found that by changing the last response category from "Never" to "Hardly ever," the percentage who choose it rises from low single digits to 25 percent.

11. Data from the Roper Center Poll Database. The Gallup/CNN/*USA Today* survey was conducted on April 20–22, (n=1273).

12. Survey by CBS News/*New York Times*, October 8–10, 1990.

13. All the data quoted in this paragraph is taken from Warren E. Miller and Santa A. Trauge, *American National Election Studies Data Sourcebook 1952–1986* (Cambridge, MA: Harvard University Press, 1989), pp. 263, 265.

14. CBS News/*New York Times*, April 20–23, 1992. Question: How much do you feel having elections makes the government pay attention to what the people think? Responses: A good deal (33 percent), Some (46 percent), and Not Much (20 percent). n = 1530.

15. All data from this paragraph is cited in Teixiera, p. 44.

16. Seymour Martin Lipset and William Schnieder, *The Confidence Gap: Business, Labor, Government, and the Public Mind* (Baltimore: John Hopkins University Press, 1983), chap. 1.

17. Ibid., p. 390.

18. For a good discussion of the various aspects and explanation, see Teixeira, chap. 1.

19. Walter Dean Burnham, *The Current Crisis in American Politics* (New York: Oxford University Press, 1982), p. 152.

20. Data published in Thomas Galvin, "Limits Score a Perfect 14-for-14, but Court Challenges Loom," *Congressional Quarterly Weekly Report*, November 7, 1992, p. 3,593.

21. *The Congressional Quarterly Researcher*, January 10, 1992, timeline found on p. 9.

22. The latter figure was found in an NBC News/*Wall Street Journal* Poll in April 1992.

23. The ideas from this paragraph can be found in Kenneth Jost, "Term Limits," *Congressional Quarterly Researcher*, January 10, 1992, p. 3.

24. The data was taken from the Roper Center Poll Database. The "Right track/Wrong track" questions were sometimes worded with slight variations, though we tried to keep this variation to a minimum. Some research organizations choose to allow for a third response to convey neutrality, like "some of both" or "mixed" and sometimes this middle response is provided as an alternative. We have excluded these responses from the analysis because they are not comparable to the two-part question and, while being methodologically more satisfying, are not asked with nearly the same frequency. The surveys that were used forced a two-part response. The date cited is the day when interviewing was completed.

25. The original and best discussion of this is found in Mancur Olson, Jr., *The Logic of Collective Action*, (New York: Schocken Books, 1965).

26. Survey by Peter Hart and Breglio Research Companies, for NBC News and the *Wall Street Journal*, May 15–19, (n=1118).

27. Survey by Peter Hart and Breglio Research Companies, for NBC News and the *Wall Street Journal*, April 11–14, (n=1001).

28. The CBS News/*New York Times* Poll was taken from October 2–4, (n=1258).

29. The CBS News/*New York Times* Poll was taken from October 29–30, (n=1221).

30. Ibid.

31. For a more complete analysis of this, see Gordon S. Black and Benjamin D. Black, "Perot Wins! The Election That Could Have Been," *The Public Perspective*, January/February 1993, vol. 4, no. 2, pp. 15–16, 18.

32. This number is quoted in *The Public Perspective*, January/February 1993, p. 17.

33. Survey by Lou Harris and Associates, October 30–November 1, 1992, (n=3197).

Chapter 5

1. James L. Sundquist, *Dynamics of the Party System* (Washington, D.C.: Brookings Institution, 1974), p. 8.

2. For complete data, refer to charts in Chapter 1.

3. Reichley, p. 18.

4. *Ballot Access News*, June 27, 1993, p. 5.

5. In 1974, one of the authors, Gordon S. Black, presented a paper at the San Francisco meeting of the American Political Sciences Association. The theme of the paper dealt with the fact that computers and direct mail solicitation would lead to a growth of centralized party organization at the national level. This was heatedly disputed by several members of the older school of thought, who believed that the political parties would always stay local and legislative in character. The debate was widely reported in the national press at the time.

6. James McGregor Burns, *The Deadlock of Democracy: Four Party Politics in America* (Englewood Cliffs, NJ: Prentice Hall, 1963).

7. The best expression of this ideal can be seen in the report of the Committee on Political Parties of the American Political Science Association in 1950. An explanation of the importance of this work can be found in William J. Crotty's "The Philosophies of Party Reform," *Party Renewal in America,* Gerald M. Pomper, ed. (New York: Praeger Publishers, 1980).

8. Charles H. Longley, "National Party Renewal," Ibid., p. 79.

9. The figures for 1976 can be found in Paul S. Herrnson, *Party Campaigning in the 1980s* (Cambridge, MA: Harvard University Press, 1988), p. 32. The recent figures can be found in the *Statistical Abstract: 1990.* The 1992 data comes from the Federal Elections Commission press release of March 11, 1993, titled "Democrats Narrow Financial Gap in 1991-2."

10. Staff estimates as of March 1993.

11. The data can be found in Herrnson, pp. 97–105.

12. The congressional candidates were asked to rate the importance of local parties, state parties, national committees, congressional committees, unions, PACs and interest groups on a scale of 1 to 5, 1 being not important and 5 being extremely important. In the areas of fund raising and issue development, Democratic candidates' mean rating for issue development and fund raising were less than the other groups mentioned. In addition, Republican candidates consistently rated their congressional committees higher than local parties, except in gauging public opinion and mobilizing volunteers.

13. Reichley, p. 368.

14. Larry Sabato, *The Party's Just Begun: Shaping Political Parties for America's Future* (Boston: Scott Foresman and Company, 1988), p. 42.

15. Reichley, pp. 366–7.

16. Voter Research and Surveys National Exit Poll, November 4, 1992. The question presented four options. Abortion should be "Legal In All Cases," (34%), "Legal In Most Cases" (29%), "Illegal In Most Cases" (23%), "Illegal in All Cases" (9%) (n=15323).

17. For a quick description of ideology in the parties see Nelson W. Polsby and Aaron Wildavsky, *Presidential Elections: Contemporary Strategies of American Electoral Politics* (New York: The Free Press, 1991), pp. 144–158.

18. A discussion of ideology in parties see Sorauf, pp. 393–404.

19. Chuck Alston, "Democrats Flex New Muscle with Trio of Election Bills," *Congressional Quarterly,* March 20, 1993, p. 645.

20. The Gordon Black Poll was conducted in the third week of May and was sponsored by B. Thomas Golisano. The sample of 1,604 registered voters has a margin of error of 2.5%.

21. Anthony Downs, *An Economic Theory of Democracy* (New York: Harper and Row, 1957).

22. Work on partisanship has been dealt with by a considerable number of academics starting with Warren Miller and the Michigan group in *The American Voter.* For a good discussion on partisanship see Martin P. Wattenberg, *The Decline of American Political Parties 1952–1988* (Cambridge, MA: Harvard University Press, 1990), pp. 7–23.

23. Sabato, p. 113.

24. Steven J. Rosenstone, Roy L. Behr, and Edward H. Lazarus, *Third Party Politics in America:* Citizen Response to Major Party Failure (Princeton, NJ: Princeton University Press, 1984), p. 176.

25. Wattenberg, p. 162.

26. Stanley and Niemi, *Vital Statistics on American Politics*, p. 147.

27. Wattenberg, p. 130.

28. Sabato, p. 133.

29. The Harris Poll 1992, #54, (n=1256).

30. The Harris Poll Press Release, "Large Majority Would Like to See the End of Two-Party System," September 13, 1992, p. 1.

31. Howard P. Nash, *Third Parties in American Politics* (Washington, D.C.: Public Affairs Press, 1959), p. vi. List provided in introduction by William B. Hesseltine.

32. Reichley, p. 72.

33. Joseph Lincoln Steffens, *The Shame of Our Cities* (New York: Sagamore Press, 1957).

34. Neimi and Stanley, pp. 23–24.

Chapter 6

1. E. E. Schattschneider, *Party Government*, (New York: Holt, Rinehart and Winston, 1942), p. 1.

2. The original source for this story is no longer available to us. It was included in Gordon Black's notes for his introductory course on American politics, but it undoubtedly came from a textbook or some other book on American politics.

3. The 30 million figure is based on approximately 20 percent of households who watched or listened to the programs, with an average of 1.77 people per household. The question captures both the television and the radio audiences, but it will provide an overestimate of the television audience based on standard ratings.

4. Perot's staff called the phone company that afternoon, receiving the estimate that the White House switchboard had received nearly one million calls by that morning.

5. Following each of the three broadcasts, we conducted a large-scale national survey of Americans, exploring both their reactions to the broadcasts and their feelings raised in regard to the issues covered in the presentations. With the exception of the first survey, the national media simply ignored our results, although the media were perfectly happy to cover survey results released by Democrats, Republicans, and each other.

6. William Riker is the best source for understanding this argument. See *The Theory of Political Coalitions* (New Haven, CT: Yale University Press, 1962).

7. Macridis and Brown, p. 292.

8. R. Douglas Arnold, *The Logic of Congressional Action* (New Haven, CT: Yale University Press, 1990), p. 128.

9. An earlier version of this presentation appeared in *The Public Perspective*, in November, 1992. *The Public Perspective* is a publication of the Roper Center, at the University of Connecticut at Storrs.

10. These core partisans are, therefore, people who say we need a new reform party, who believe that neither existing party is capable of moving the country in the right direction, who are angry at both parties and their candidates, and who would prefer to vote for reform candidates of the new party.

11. There are several other party efforts also underway, but these tend to share a perspective that is somewhat more to the left. One of these is the New Alliance Party, organized to support the presidential candidacy of Dr. Lenora Fulani and composed somewhat disproportionately of Blacks and other minorities. Another is the New Party, which is organized by people with ties to the labor movement, but which attracts voters and activists more to the left of the political spectrum. And finally, there is the Libertarian Party, which is composed of people who share policy perspectives that are supportive of "free economic markets" coupled with a philosophy of support for minimal governmental interference in the lives of people. There are other party efforts as well, but they tend to be restricted to a narrow political perspective either on the left or the right, or in support of some special issue such as outlawing abortion.

Chapter 7

1. From Charles Peters, editor-in-chief of the *Washington Monthly. How Washington Really Works* (New York: Addison-Wesley Publishing Co., 1992), p. 164.

2. Benjamin Hoff, *The Tao of Pooh* (New York: Dutton, 1982), p. 137.

3. The four party questions we used to identify the most likely third party supporters were worded as follows: (1) (Agree/Disagree) We need a new political party to reform American politics. (2) Some people are angry at both political parties and their candidates. Would you say that describes how you feel right now? (3) Some people are saying that neither the Democrats nor the Republicans are capable of getting this country going in the right direction and that we need a new national political party. (Strongly agree, moderately agree, moderately disagree, strongly disagree) (4) Suppose that a new reform-oriented political party is created to run candidates for Congress, the Senate, and even your state legislature. Assuming for a moment that this new party was supporting your positions on many of the issues you care about, would you be most likely to vote for the candidate of the new reform party or would you be most likely to continue to vote either for the Republican or the Democratic candidates? The fourth question is obviously biased to ascertain the lowest limit of absolute party affiliators—the people who would not vote outside of their party for any reason. In order for a person to be considered a core loyalist, they had to answer all four questions in the positive direction in support of a third party and angry at the two existing parties.

4. Federal Election Commission.

5. Data taken from a report titled "Money Talks," by Celinda Lake and Steve Cobble of Target, Inc., analyzing the results of a national poll of 805 likely voters, conducted in December of 1922. The study was sponsored by the Center for a New Democracy.

6. Federal Election Commission Press Release, March 4, 1993.

7. Galvin, p. 3,593.

8. Ibid.

9. California Secretary of State. "Late Contribution Report Summary: Received by Ballot Measure Committees and Candidates October 18, 1992 through November 3, 1992." The data can be found in the Ballot Measure Late Contribution Report, pp. 9–10.

10. Galvin, p. 3,594.

11. Poll conducted by the Gallup Organization. May 17–20, 1990. n=1255.

12. ABC News/*Washington Post*, Feb 25–8, 1993, (n=1216).

13. Theodore J. Lowi, *The Chronicle of Higher Education*, December 16, 1992, p. 38.

14. George Hager, "Entitlements: The Untouchable May Become Unavoidable," *Congressional Quarterly Weekly Report*, January 3, 1993, p. 22.

15. This question is probably not a fair one. It could be read that respondents are being asked to say that people should not have enough to eat and a place to sleep. Some people might feel pressured to take the more magnanimous position or they might appear fairly heartless to the interviewer. Recognizing the underlying concept of whether or not government is ultimately responsible for the welfare of its citizens is a fine distinction to make. Therefore, we are not entirely comfortable with the question as worded. However, it still taps a deep recognition of the plight of the underprivileged and the need for governmental action to alleviate their situation.

16. Federal Election Commission.

17. Both definitions were taken from *Webster's New World Dictionary of the American Language* (New York: Simon and Schuster, 1980).

18. Theodore Lowi has expressed this concept regularly.

Index